An Archaeology of the Iron Curtain
Material and Metaphor

An Archaeology of the Iron Curtain
Material and Metaphor

Anna McWilliams

Södertörns högskola

Södertörns högskola
SE-141 89 Huddinge

www.sh.se/publications

Cover Photo: Anna McWilliams
Cover Design: Jonathan Robson
Layout: Per Lindblom & Jonathan Robson

Printed by Elanders, Stockholm 2013

Södertörn Doctoral Dissertations 86
ISSN 1652-7399
ISBN 978-91-86069-78-0 (print)
ISBN 978-91-86069-79-7 (digital)

Södertörn Archaeological Studies 9
ISSN 1652-2559

Stockholm Studies in Archaeology 59
ISBN 978-91-7447-819-8

Abstract

Doctoral thesis written at the Department of Archaeology and Classical Studies at Stockholm University, Sweden, and as part of the Baltic and East European Graduate School at Södertörn University.

The Iron Curtain was seen as the divider between East and West in Cold War Europe. The term Iron Curtain is closely connected to the Cold War and expressions such as 'behind the Iron Curtain' or 'after the fall of the Iron Curtain' are common within historical discussions in the second half of the twentieth century. But what does it really mean? Was it a metaphor or a physical reality? Even if the term was used regularly as a metaphor there was also a material side to it with a series of highly militarised borders running throughout Europe. The metaphor and the material borders developed together and individually, sometimes intertwined and sometimes separate.

In my research I have carried out two fieldwork studies at sites that can be considered part of the former Iron Curtain. The first study area is located between Italy and Slovenia (part of the former Yugoslavia) in which the division between the two towns of Nova Gorica on the Slovenian side and Gorizia on the Italian side was investigated. The second study area is located on the border between Austria and Czech Republic (formerly Czechoslovakia) within two national parks: Podyji Park on the Czech side and Thayatal Park on the Austrian side. A smaller study was also carried out in Berlin as the Berlin Wall is considered of major importance in the context of the Iron Curtain. All fieldwork was carried out between 2008 and 2011. I have carried out field walking surveys, interviews, literature studies, archival studies and studies of other materials such as popular culture. This research has resulted in large quantities of sources and information and a constant need to re-evaluate the methods used within an archaeology of a more recent past.

This thesis falls within what is usually referred to as contemporary archaeology. This is a fairly young sub-discipline of archaeology. Few large research projects have so far been published, and methods have been described as still somewhat experimental. This thesis aims to test archaeological methods within a more recent context and to take the discussion of contemporary archaeology methodology further. I aspired to use methods that allowed me to follow the material and the sources in a flexible way. Through my fieldwork it has been possible to acknowledge and highlight the problems and opportunities within contemporary archaeology. Through my research it has become clear how the materials stretch both through time and place demonstrating the complex process of how the material that archaeologists investigate can be created. I have also wanted to explore this material of the Iron Curtain, a material which is well worth studying in its own right.

Keywords
Archaeology of the contemporary past, Iron Curtain, Cold War, material culture, memory, cultural heritage, Berlin Wall, Austria, Czechoslovakia, Czech Republic, Italy, Slovenia, Yugoslavia.

Contents

Acknowledgements   11

CHAPTER 1
Introduction   15
Standing on the shoreline   15
The materiality of the Iron Curtain   16
Studying the Iron Curtain   17
Recording the Iron Curtain   26
Case studies   28

CHAPTER 2
A physical metaphor   31
The changing rhetoric around a wall   35
"…love walks lonely by the Berlin wall…"   38
The image of the Berlin Wall today   42

CHAPTER 3
The materiality of the Berlin Wall   45
Methods and aims   45
Background   46
    On the edge of the western world   46
The material   50
    Berlin today   50
    The 'enemy facing' wall   56
    Crossing over   60
    Memorials and Museums   63
    Back to nothing   65

CHAPTER 4
Case study 1: The Italian/Slovenian border   67
Methods and aims   68
Background   69
    The town on the hill   69
    Between the wars   73
    WWII and new borders   73
    One city becomes two   76
    A border in constant change   78

The material	81
Remains of the former militarised border	81
In the company of saints and bunkers	82
Patrolling the city	90
The physical border	92
Signs	96
Crossing over	98
The border as an advertising point	104
Resisting the border	106
People and the border	111
Some concluding points	114
Reference plan and gazetteer of sites	119

CHAPTER 5

Case Study 2: The Czech/Austrian border	127
Methods and aims	128
Background	134
The castle on the rock	134
World Wars	135
A new political order	136
Militarised border in the study area	139
Guardians of the border	141
The material	144
A changing landscape	144
Fence line	145
Searching the landscape	154
Border guard stations	156
Archive studies	172
Voices from Austria	175
Some concluding points	177
Different sources – different stories	179
Reference plan and gazetteer of sites	182

CHAPTER 6

An archaeology of the Iron Curtain	187
Artefacts, text and everything else in between	187
Moving in memories	192
The experience of things	194
To go with the flow	199
The mundane war	205
An archaeology of a metaphor	209
The end of a journey	212

Sammanfattning (Summary in Swedish) 215

Bibliography 226

Acknowledgements

Writing a thesis is certainly like being on a long journey. Sometimes you travel on your own and at times you are accompanied by many lovely and helpful people. If I were to thank all those who have helped me in my work the acknowledgement would probably be longer than the thesis itself. But there are some people that do deserve particular thanks. Firstly my two tutors Mats Burström and Anders Andrén who have read, commented and guided me along the way. I am indebted for the numerous suggestions and comments you have so generously provided me with.

My home during these years has been at the archaeology department at Södertörn University and at the Baltic and East European Graduate School (BEEGS) at the same university. BEEGS provided a fantastic starting point where both the academic and administrative staff made the start of my journey not just an easier task, but also much more fun. Thanks to all my fellow doctoral students here for advice, comments on drafts and well deserved beers! Thank you also Jorid Palm at the School of Historical and Contemporary Studies at Södertörn for all her help and support during the final stages of my work.

At the archaeology department at Södertörn University I have had the opportunity to grow, learn and test ideas and doors have always been open for advice, so thanks to Kerstin Cassel, Johan Rönnby, Björn Nilsson, Hans Bolin, Niklas Eriksson and Oscar Törnqvist for their always enthusiastic support. This thesis would not exist without your help and encouragement!

At Södertörn University the 'open door policy' has also stretched across departments and I am very grateful to those of you that have helped me find my way in disciplines that have been somewhat new to me, especially Beate Feldman Eellend, Thomas Lundén and Anne Kaun. Thanks also to my cousin Charlotte Hagström at the Ethnology department in Lund who has provided useful advice.

Thank you Chris Beach for providing me with such great maps and illustrations which helped to lift my material in such a great way and to Jonathan Robson and Per Lindblom at Södertörn University Publications for their excellent work with the layout and graphics of this thesis. Thanks also to Rodrigo Trompiz for his always patient help and comments on my language and to Mirja Arnshav who made sure my Swedish was legible.

Always making me feel welcome during visits to Stockholm University were fellow doctoral students Jenny Nyberg, Cecilia Ljung, Ingrid Berg and Elin Engström. Thank you!

I must also thank everyone who helped me during my fieldwork to access areas, find information, get in contact with people or who shared their own stories and memories. Thank you Claudia Melisch and Jamie Sewell for being such lovely guides and friends during my visits to Berlin. A big thank you goes to the Swedish-Slovenian Friendship Association and in particular Lojze Hribar who has shown such interest in my work and helped me in all ways possible – even being my personal guide in Slovenia! Great help was also provided by the Nova Gorica Regional museum and the director Andrej Malnič during my fieldwork in Slovenia and by the Podyji Park administration during my fieldwork in the Czech Republic. The fieldwork in the Czech Republic was made possible through a grant from Albert and Maria Bergströms Stiftelse which I received in 2010.

I also want to thank family and friends who have always supported and put up with me through times of stress, confusion and great excitements. A big thank you to my former colleagues, and good friends, Andrea Bradley and Sefryn Penrose for always listening, reading, commenting and generally just being there. Thank you Lisa Söderbaum-Beach who is always on the other end of a phone, Anke Marsh with whom I have shared the adventures of archaeology ever since we first started as undergraduates, Kristin Ilves with whom I have shared the aches and pains of doctoral life as well as an office during part of my research, Anders Udd for helping me see my material in a less academic and a more colourful way and to Cecilia Minning who has been a good friend and neighbour always at the ready with a cup of coffee. Thank you all for your friendship and support!

Thank you to my mum and dad, Eva-Lena and Lennart Nilsson, and my sister Åsa Moberg for always showing an interest and for providing all that critical support with babysitting, dinners, wood chopping and other things that makes a stressed doctoral student's life so much easier. And last but by no means least thank you John and Tage: to my John for always understanding and providing all that ground service when I have had my head

ACKNOWLEDGEMENTS

stuck in a book or been locked in front of the computer for hours and days; to Tage who just gives me such joy and happiness. This is to you and to our new family member who is about to make an appearance in the very near future. Love always.

Stockholm, December 2013
Anna McWilliams

CHAPTER 1

Introduction

Standing on the shoreline

Growing up on the east coast of Sweden a walk on the beach was like a treasure hunt where washed up plastic bottles or cans with Russian writing were like messages from another world. I could not see this other world but I was told that it was very different from my own. I did not know what the Iron Curtain was back then but the Baltic Sea most certainly felt like a big barrier in which Russian submarines would occasionally take a 'wrong turn' and surface a bit too close for comfort, a big barrier that separated 'us' from 'them' and which was to colour my views of Eastern and Western Europe. Years later I was working as a Heritage Consultant in London. Following guidelines such as Institute for Archaeologists (IFA) guidelines and best practice documents from English Heritage, I worked on Desk Based Assessments, Conservation Plans and Environmental Impact Assessments. I directed fieldwork to mitigate the negative impacts of roadwork, new pipelines or other construction projects. Together with my colleagues we were looking out for the heritage of our past and making sure it was preserved for future generations, if not *in situ* then at least through records. There was, however, little discussion in how this heritage had come to be. What factors and processes are involved in making these sites that we investigate?

What has come to fascinate me more and more whilst carrying out the work on my thesis are the processes involved in creating the past that we see around us. Heritage does not just happen; it is created and recreated as part of our history writing. To an archaeologist it should probably not come as a surprise how important the material is to the way we view and write our history, but somehow it still did. In this thesis I look closer at how a material part of our history that we see around us today has come to be the way it is. By looking at how the material of the Iron Curtain has developed over time, how it looks today and how it is viewed by people around it I hope to demonstrate one example of the kind of processes in which a materiality can be formed in history writing and in creating, or not creating as the case may be, a heritage.

The materiality of the Iron Curtain

The aim of this thesis is to explore what knowledge about the Iron Curtain can be reached through the material traces it has left behind as well as the effects these remains have on people around them. The aim is also to contribute to the continuous discussion and methodological development of the archaeology of the contemporary past.

Why use the Iron Curtain as material? Whenever you deal with Cold War history the term Iron Curtain is never far away. Sentences such as "behind the Iron Curtain" or "after the fall of the Iron Curtain" are often used. But what was it really? When I had just started as a PhD student I explained to a friend of mine what my research was going to be about. He looked quite concerned and then said "But you know that the Iron Curtain never actually existed? It was a metaphor." This inconsistency, the paradox of the real and imagined Iron Curtain is what makes it such an interesting material study. On the one hand there was the metaphor of the Iron Curtain: an idea of a Europe divided by two political blocs. On the other there were a series of heavily militarised borders running through Central Europe physically dividing it. Do they tell the same story? If not, does one story take precedence when we write our Cold War history? How do the stories that emerge from the metaphor and the materials fit within the local and world history?

Another reason why this is such interesting material is that it is now in the process of becoming heritage. In some places it has already come a long way, in others it may never be seen as heritage at all. What are the processes involved in this 'becoming'?

But maybe most importantly, it is a very interesting material in itself which is well worth studying. Seeing that the term Iron Curtain is frequently used and well known to a lot of people in the western world, its physicality is little understood. Studies have been made in Germany of the materiality of the Inner German Border (Sheffer 2007 and 2008, Rottman 2008) but generally studies have mainly focussed on the social consequences inherent in a divided country. There have also been archaeological studies carried out of the materiality of the Inner German Border and the Berlin Wall (Klausmeier and Schmidt 2004, Schmidt and von Preuschen 2005, Faversham and Schmidt 2007, Rottman 2008, Klausmeier 2009). Elsewhere, however, there is little research to inform us of what the militarised borders looked like, how they functioned, how they affected the people around them and how the borders, and the remains thereof, have continued to affect people also after the events of 1989.

I have used Churchill's description of an Iron Curtain stretching from the Baltic to the Adriatic to limit myself geographically but this is of course just a limitation I have set as a necessary approach to what would otherwise be too vast a material. I have also limited myself to the time period between 1945, the end of World War II and 1989, the fall of many of the military borders in central Europe. The reader should be aware, however, that the Iron Curtain can be described in many different ways both metaphorically and geographically and can be seen to stretch throughout the world and across different time periods.

Studying the Iron Curtain

Discussions of methodology have been an important part of the work of my thesis from beginning to end. During a very early consultation with my tutor, before I was about to embark on my first fieldwork, we discussed recording methods. When I suggested that I would require some sort of GPS to record the coordinates of any finds that I made out in the terrain my tutor asked me why I needed to be so precise, why not just mark them on a map? The question threw me and I thought to myself: "but this is what we do". We identify, we measure, we record, we describe and we report and it all needs to be exact so that we can demonstrate that it has all been carried out to good scientific standards. Otherwise it is just not good archaeology. Or is it? In her doctoral thesis archaeologist Laura McAtackney (2008:8 and 16) discusses the role of traditional archaeological empirical methods such as excavation and building surveys as well as artefact recording and suggests that sometimes we carry out our investigations just because that is what we are supposed to do. But does it always bring something to our research? In an article about the role of contemporary archaeology or an archaeology of the present and following discussion in 'Surface assemblages: Towards an archaeology *in* and *of* the present' archaeologist Rodney Harrison (2011) suggests that the connection between archaeology and excavation has become too accepted and that we need to change our attitudes towards a stronger focus on archaeology through its surface assemblages. In a response to Harrison's article archaeologist Paul Graves-Brown write: "Indeed, one might argue that the site and the digging thereof are what we have needed, subconsciously, to legitimate our practice" (Graves-Brown 2011:169). Harrison's article can be seen as a way of rethinking the way we conduct archaeology and turn "interest towards an emerging present" (Harrison 2011:181). This shifts the emphasis of archaeology away from being a study of the past to be a study of the past in the present. A shift in perception of time is also present in the work of archaeologist Laurent Olivier who claims that we should view archaeology more in relation to memory as fragmented and constantly created and recreated instead of as fitting into a unilinear history writing (Olivier 2004:209–211). What happens when we apply these perspectives of time on the material that we study?

Methodologies for studies of contemporary archaeology sites are still somewhat experimental and unproven and as Harrison and archaeologist John Schofield (2010:88) write the productivity of the research techniques to be used in studies of a more recent material will only be demonstrated by further work. My research should therefore be seen as a part of this current discourse and a way to test and further the understanding of the study of sites from a contemporary past. I wanted to understand the materiality of the Iron Curtain and how this related to the popular idea of this iconic, Cold War divider between the East and West. The choice stood between concentrating on one site and studying several in order to compare. This comparison between sites along the former militarised borders throughout Europe offered the best possibility to understand the material and so I chose to include more than one case study in my research. Research into sites closer to our own time often provides a rich source material and it therefore becomes important to make decisions of how to approach what can be a vast assemblage of material evidence. Archaeologist Bjørnar Olsen, with his cry for a return to things within archaeology (2010, 2003), suggests that although materials are studied they are not seen as interesting in themselves but are always only used in order to reach something else: "The material is a source material, an incomplete representation of the past, traces of an absent presence – not part of the past (or society) itself" (Olsen 2003:90). It is by turning to the material and looking at the smaller pieces that we can begin to understand the bigger picture. Archaeologist Jonathan Westin writes: "…a single letter of [an] inscription is not accountable for the meaning of those words or sentences it helps form, political or religious as they may be… It is not a process where the primary movement is that of cultural values trickling down and affecting the parts, but a process where the greater movement is that of parts soaring upwards" (Westin 2012:39). It is not in the discourse about heritage that heritage itself is created, but it is in the movement and networks of the smaller interconnecting parts, whether objects, humans or customs on which the discourses about heritage rests. In light of this I want to start at the things themselves and by looking at how the materials have been used, and viewed, over time, including their situation today, to get a better understanding of how a heritage can be created, out of the things themselves on their journey to their appropriation today. The discourse should have its grounding in the material we study. If not, it is possible that the materials and the discussions we carry out end up being out of phase, estranged and lost from each other or that generalisations are made which are not based on a solid foundation. In my fieldwork I have found Actor Network Theory (ANT) a useful inspiration in that it is descriptive rather than explanatory and this helps to understand how relations between different actors assemble (Latour 2005). By turning to the materials themselves and in my fieldwork focussing on the networks at work within the sites themselves, in the past and in the present, I attempt to discuss how heritage has been created, or not created as the case may be, in the study areas. Apart from the materials themselves these networks are created out of the actions of many different actors who have created the sites as they appear today as well as the attitudes people have towards them. Although the material is my starting point other sources, such as memories and stories, both oral and written, have been weaved together with the material, inseparable as they are. I have looked to other disciplines such as anthropology, history, art history, ethnology and human geography to assist me in tackling a vast material. Often the line between the disciplines is blurry and many points overlap. Harrison and Schofield suggest that studying the recent past "is always going to be simultaneously archaeology *and* anthropology, because it involves an archaeological approach while also existing as a form of participant observation or ethnographic inquiry into contemporary life" (Harrison and Schofield 2010:91). My starting point, as well as my point of return has, however, been archaeological. It is in the materials that have been left behind that I have started my investigations. By using the materials as a starting point and seeing them as the smaller building blocks that are, again in the words of Westin, "parts soaring upwards" (Westin 2012:39) rather than saturated with the cultural values and heritage categories trickling down from the top I hope to get a better understanding of how the material of the past is created at these sites.

A large part of my fieldwork has been carried out in what can be called a walkover survey. Walkover survey is defined by English Heritage's National Monuments Records Thesaurus as "A planned programme of investigation conducted within a defined area aimed at identifying and surveying previously unrecorded sites and checking the condition of known sites" (NMR Website). Similarly to this definition my investigation was carried out to identify and record remains of the former militarised border and its infrastructure that still remain in the border landscapes today. These investigations can also be considered a kind of observation. As the walkover surveys worked as a way to investigate what the border areas look like today and also how these areas are used in the present my own observations became very important. The researcher's own influence on the material that is studied is, of course, nothing new. Whether we are conscious of it or not, we are always part of the results that we produce. Within archaeology there has been an increased focus on the reflexive since the 1990s, in particular through the work of archaeologist Ian Hodder who has written extensively on the subject and applied a more reflexive methodology at excavations at Çatalhöyük (Hodder 1997, 1999, 2000, 2003). Also involved in this research at Çatalhöyük as well as applying a reflexive methodology at the Citytunnel Project in Malmö, Sweden is archaeologist Åsa Berggren (2001, 2002, Berggren and Hodder 2000, 2003). Berggren points out that although reflexivity made a relatively late entrance on the archaeological scene it has been part of other fields such as sociology, anthropology and philosophy for longer (Berggren 2002:22). To put it simply one can say that reflexivity is about making the process of interpretation as clear as possible. To be reflexive means that we are aware that our thoughts and the choices that we make are affecting the results we get and that we as researchers have an impact on the material that we study. In this thesis I have tried to be as open as possible about the different stages I have gone through and about the development of the thought process in order to be as transparent as possible in the production of this text.

Everyone makes observations but there is a distinction in using observations in a research capacity. Ethnologists Gösta Arvastson and Billy Ehn make a distinction between the everyday observations that we make as humans, an action that they claim is essential to being part of society, and the scientific observations that are part of the ethnographic method. They claim that the difference mainly lies in the reflexive nature of the latter where the observer has the ability to scrutinise his or her own observations (Arvastson and Ehn 2009:20). Ehn writes that "ethnographic observations are not something one just does, but something that is created and used for a more or less conscious purpose. It is here the researcher's objectivity and fantasy meet" (Ehn 2009:54 [my translation]). But our interpretations are not created out of nothing. By being transparent about how a site affects us we can make the process of our interpretation more clear. We may interpret a site in different ways but it is still based on the material we have at hand. My way of writing can be seen as a less traditional archaeological approach as I place myself firmly in my texts. As archaeologist Joanna Brück points out, as we observe, we interpret and this means the author is always present (Brück 2005:56). I am not suggesting that the impressions that affect me would necessarily have affected others in the same way in the past and I am therefore not suggesting that people who were in the vicinity of the border areas during the Cold War period would have had the same thoughts as me. I do believe, however, that our impressions affect us whether we are aware of this bias or not. As researchers, the impressions of a site will affect our results and our conclusions.

It is, however, more difficult to describe the feeling of a place, or the way it affects us than to describe the physical features of it. The subjective has previously had little room in the reports that we produce even if it has always affected the way archaeologist work (Berggren 2002:24). The body's interaction with the material we interpret is something that has become more acknowledged in more recent years (see discussion in Harris and Sørensen 2010, Edgeworth et al. 2012). By referring to the writings of Heidegger, Merleau-Ponty and Latour, Olsen (2010) challenges us to rethink the ontology that our attitude towards things is based on and to emphasise the importance of the body in the world. He quotes Heidegger: "we are always-already in the world, the world is part of our being – not something external, 'out there' to eventually be embodied" (Heidegger 1982:137 quoted by Olsen 2010:96). In *Persistent Memories* Andreassen, Bjerck and Olsen write of their work at a former Soviet mining community in Svalbard, which closed in 1998: "Our fieldwork was preliminary and experimental, attempting to grasp and *sense* the place" (Andreassen, Bjerck and Olsen 2010:24, emphasis in original). Harrison and Schofield highlight the importance of experiencing a place and write that "an experimental approach can work, conveying a sense of what the place is like, in situations where detailed survey is just too vast an undertaking" (Harrison and

Schofield 2010:207). I would say that this is important in any level of survey, detailed or more overarching.

My walkover survey was carried out in two ways. During a systematic study of sections of the former militarised border, all remains relating to the border or border infrastructure were recorded on a map and notes were taken, and targeted surveys were carried out in particular places. The second type of walkover survey was more spontaneous in character. These surveys consisted of visits to sites, areas or buildings that had been raised as possible areas of interest, either through other kinds of research such as maps, documents, literature, or looking at satellite photos. They were also often based on tips that were given by people that I met during the time I spent in an area and where therefore often spontaneous and not researched beforehand.

This way of looking at an area or a material, has been called "bimbling", a concept first described by Anderson (2004), and which has been used by archaeologist John Schofield and Emily Morrissey during their research of Strait Street in Valetta, Malta. They describe the difficulty of approaching a material which is often only available during short moments when shown by a property owner or when pointed out by people passing by. They found that "bimbling" described as "interviews conducted in and through a place, to generate a collage of collaborative knowledge and give people the opportunity to re-experience their connections with landscape and to reminisce, prompting 'other life-course memories associated with that individual's relationship with place'" (Harrison and Schofield 2010:76) was the best way to approach the material. They write: "So we bimbled – walking up and down Strait Street, talking with those we met, making notes and using the digital video camera where it felt appropriate. We were told what bars were where, and we began to gain an impression of what many of these places were like" (Schofield and Morrissey 2007:93). In a similar way I used this more walkabout and flexible style of surveying to gain an understanding of the places along the former Iron Curtain and to be able to follow the connections which they provided.

Interviews were also important for my understanding of the material. Sometimes these were combined with the walkover surveys such as my walk with Maria and Antonio along the border near Trieste, visits to sites along the Slovenian-Italian border with Andrej, or the time I spent with the guide David in the Podyji National Park in the Czech Republic. In fact most of the people that I interviewed wanted to meet me at, or bring me to, a particular site that they felt had a connection with the border, the military or the former Iron Curtain. During my time in Slovenia, Anja brought me to the Solkan Bridge from where the border as well as the Slovenian road corridor through Italy can be seen, the group interview conducted in Sofije, Slovenia, included a visit to the former Morgan line (the Italian-Yugoslavian border between 1945–1954), and Maria and Antonio drove me to the border near Trieste, Italy, to show me an old sign that had survived in the landscape. During these visits the importance of the material as a mnemonic became obvious but these visits also helped to provide ample time for conversation to flow a bit more freely than during a more formal interview situation. There are several different methods and techniques for how to conduct interviews (see for example: Ehn and Löfgren 1996, O'Reilly 2005, Kaijser and Öhlander 2011). My interviews were carried out in what can be referred to as unstructured interviews (O'Reilly 2005:116, Fägerborg 2011:99) in which I used a general plan of the topics that I wanted to cover with a few specific questions but generally the conversations were allowed to flow freely in order not to be tied down. The aim of the interviews was not necessarily to gain answers to particular questions but rather to understand the ways different people viewed the border and the Iron Curtain and this was best reached through allowing the interviewees to speak freely about what they considered to be of importance. The interviews varied in how many people were present, usually just one or two, but there was also one group interview in which seven people participated. How interviews were conducted also varied somewhat depending on the people being interviewed. It was clear that an approach that worked with some people, such as those living near the border in Slovenia and Italy who talked rather freely about life in the area was not necessarily successful when interviewing others such as the former military officer of the Czechoslovakian border who preferred more specific questions. What was most important during interviews was therefore being flexible and reflexive in the way to proceed. As sociologist Karen O'Reilly writes "…qualitative research is as often art as science, it is not easy to set out what should be done and how in a given set of circumstances" (O'Reilly 2005:4) but she also points out that in order to be confident in making those choices the researcher has to be aware of the options available and be able to adjust according to the situation.

In this thesis I do not use the word informant which is often the chosen term within ethnographical studies. This is mostly due to the thesis' Cold War context where the word informant often brings to mind the word informer and as such has connotations and meanings connected with spying (Gerber 2011:28). Instead I use the word interviewee to try and steer away from any such connotations. It was my hope to reach across different age groups and include people from both sexes with the people that I interviewed. This proved more successful in my fieldwork in Italy/Slovenia where seven of the informants where women aged from their 30s to 80s and seven were men aged from their 40s to 80s. In the Czech Republic and Austria the interviewees were, however, almost exclusively male and their ages ranged between their 30s and 60s. This is mainly due to the fact that the people I reached and gained information from here were often those who had had a connection with the military sites along the border, something few women came in contact with. As the Berlin case is not as extensive as the other two studies I did not have the opportunity and time to interview many people here. The interviews in my two study areas were not meant as a full ethnographical study including large numbers of people but rather as an additional source, often deeply connected with the materials and sites that I visited.

How much researchers write about the interviewees tends to vary between different studies depending on how much is required as well as personal taste. I have used first names and have also provided information on gender as well as approximate age and ethnicity partly to help the reader obtain some background and for the simple fact that it actually reads better and makes it easier to follow. Although knowing the person's gender does not necessarily add anything it also does not take anything away from the study either. Ethnicity helps to understand what background the interviewee has which is important as ethnicity is often featured as an important factor in cultural identity in border areas such as those that I describe (for a discussion on ethnicity and borders see Lundén 2004, McWilliams 2011). The approximate age is added to understand the interviewees' historical background as life in the study areas changed throughout the Cold War period. Exact age, however, has not been mentioned in order to help to keep the anonymity of the people I have spoken to. This is also the reason why I have given them different names in the thesis even though many of them would have been happy for me to publish their actual names. This is an important factor that should always be considered in studies where interview material is used. Even though they may have given their consent to publish their words they do not have any control of the way that the researcher uses the interviews or in the conclusions he or she may draw from them. That responsibility lies solely on the researcher and therefore it is important to protect the anonymity of the interviewees. To respect the people that we interview and to make sure we do not leave them open to criticism from others is an important part of the research ethics that we must abide by and something that needs to be considered through all parts of our work from planning our interviews and conducting them through to the way we publish the words of others in our work (Pripp 2011:65). This is also something that is particularly important to stress within contemporary archaeology where people often do not have the same training in ethnographic fieldwork as for example an anthropologist or ethnologist. In this thesis I have made a distinction between those who have spoken to me in an official capacity as for example museum staff or historians, who are not anonymous, and those that have spoken to me about their private life who have been given other names. The distinction is not always clear as those in an official role have also told me personal stories but the distinction is still there and their official role is important to know to understand the context or to validate the information.

Archive research was carried out in the Czech Republic, Slovenia, Italy and the UK. These were not meant to be full archive studies but rather a way to get an idea of what kind of material is available about these sites. Anything more would have been too much of an undertaking within this project. Although language was sometimes a problem, these archive studies did help in providing background knowledge. Of particular use were maps and photos as these helped to provide an understanding of the kinds of physical material that had existed along the Iron Curtain and how the borders' different areas had looked in the past. Photos, often of a more personal nature, were also found on an online forum for former Czechoslovakian soldiers. Through this forum I also managed to get in contact with three former border guards who could tell me about their time as soldiers along the borders. Conversations between the soldiers themselves on the online forum were all written in Czech and therefore could only be understood in small parts (Army Forum Website).

Outside Germany there is little literature written about the former Iron Curtain or the guards who once protected the militarised borders. Instead literature was mostly used to provide historical background to the larger political events. In Germany, however, the situation is different and I was able to gain a good understanding of both the general history as well as the physicality of the Inner German Border and, in particular, the Berlin Wall through literature (Huyssen 1997, Faversham and Schmidt 1999 and 2007, Dolff-Bonekämper 2002, Klausmeier and Schmidt 2004, Harrison 2005, Schmidt and von Preuschen 2005, Taylor 2006, Sheffer 2007 and 2008, Rottman 2008, Klausmeier 2009, Hamberg 2009).

Recording the Iron Curtain

Conveying the information gained through these studies to the reader is a complicated process in itself in which materials, documents, photos and impressions are converted into text. Here there is an element of interpretation every step of the way. Ehn writes that the observations we make become history as soon as we verbalise and communicate them (Ehn 2009:56). In an attempt to write an objective description of the Docklands in London, Högdahl became aware of the difficulty in writing a description of something without letting one's personal assumptions and preconceptions interfere. She describes the process from the first observations, a selective process in itself where some things fall within our sphere of interest, others outside. We then use words to initially write down our observations and later we will process these words into a text using different analytical tools. She explains this process as a series of translations (Högdahl 2009:111). The texts we eventually produce are therefore a result of this long line of interpretations of which we may only be aware of some parts. Hodder has suggested that archaeological writing in the field has stayed largely unchanged due to a feeling of a kind of "guardianship" keeping records for the state and is often seen as separate to the process of making interpretations (Hodder 2003:57). As Hodder points out, despite this tradition of viewing the fieldwork as something objective, we in fact interpret every step of the way and we therefore need to be transparent about this process.

Photos have been important throughout my work. I have taken thousands of pictures throughout my fieldwork. They have worked both as a document for me to constantly go back to in my work as a way to help my memory or to discover new things that I have not previously seen. The photos have helped me discover and rediscover both physical objects and relationships at the sites that I have studied or helped to capture a feeling encountered. In the writing of this thesis they have become a way to portray how I interacted with the material as well as an attempt to demonstrate the relationship between objects or the feelings that the sites have evoked. Archaeologists Yannis Hamilakis and Aris Anagnostopoulos (2009) have discussed the role of photography within archaeology and suggest that photographs often falls within three categories: the official site photography and laboratory photography; the unofficial photographs taken by those who are excavating or by visitors (these two categories also stated in Bateman 2005); and the photographs that can be seen as positioned somewhere in between a visual ethnographic commentary and artwork (Hamilakis and Anagnostopoulos 2009:288–289). According to Hamilakis and Anagnostopoulos the problem with the way that photography has traditionally been viewed in archaeology is as a "faithful, disembodied representation of reality" (Hamilakis and Anagnostopoulos 2009: 283). Instead they suggest that photographs should be seen more as a material artefact and as a mnemonic, "[i]n other words they are memories, that is reworked renderings of the things they have witnessed. They do not represent but rather recall. They do not show, but rather evoke. As such, they are material mnemonics, and as all memory, they are reworkings of the past, not a faithful reproduction of it" (Hamilakis and Anagnostopoulos 2009:289). For me the photographs are an important part of my work not because of their differences to the text but rather their similarities to it. It is through the interaction with the material through site visits and again through the photographs that I have taken that this thesis has taken shape. It is also through the interaction of both text and photographs that these pages have been created.

Archaeologists Þora Pétursdottír and Bjørnar Olsen (forthcoming) have discussed the relationship between text and images and suggest that photographs are often seen as more biased than text. They mean that photographs are often considered a supplement and instead they argue that photographs should be seen as an engagement with the material. Discussing the aesthetic aspects of ruined photographs they describe the aesthetic experience as a prelinguistic condition which can be described as "an immediate reaction to confrontation with reality" (Olsen and Pétursdottír, forthcoming). Although I started photographing as documentation during my fieldwork it became so much more than this. It became an extension of the bodily engagement with the material that I came across. Some of the photos in this thesis are more of documentary character while others may seem more art-like. There has been a lot of criticism both within as well as outside the archaeological field of the more art-like aesthetic style photos (see Olsen and Pétursdottír, forthcoming) but this may also depends on who is taking the photographs. Photographer Angus Boulton's film and photographs of Forst Zinna (2007), a Soviet military base in former East Germany, has received a lot of positive feedback. Although speaking about moving images Harrison and Schofield discuss Boulton's film of the Forst Zinna site where they describe how he captures the feeling of the place and its abandonment, and although they suggest Boulton uses techniques that are not all that different from traditional archaeological and building recording methods he also manages to convey a feeling of having been there: "One feels as though one knows the site intimately – not so much its layout and plan-form, but the character of the place, its aura, and the ghosts of place that inhabit the decrepit rooms and open spaces" (Harrison and Schofield 2010:119). There are several examples of archaeological research using artists to provide an alternative perspective on the sites investigated (for examples see Cocroft and Wilson 2006, Talbot and Bradley 2006, Schofield *et al.* 2012) but the recording of these sites have still tended to be traditional archaeological with the artist brought in to provide the aesthetic.

Within the work for this thesis I have often found myself somewhere in between: between the archaeological, the ethnographical, the photographical, the literature, the emotional, the historical, the personal and the official. And maybe this is exactly what characterises the study of an archaeology of the contemporary, you are never quite at home but never completely lost, just somewhere in between. My hope is that I have been able to shed some light on this in-betweeness and how one can make this part of a functioning methodology.

The structure of the thesis follows much the same way I have come to experience this material in my work. I started with the term Iron Curtain and tried to understand where it came from, what it meant and how people had seen it throughout the twentieth century. An image of the Iron Curtain started to take form, something which is described in Chapter 2. Even though my first fieldwork was carried out in Italy/Slovenia, not Berlin, the Berlin Wall had become an important site early in my work as it was highly connected with the metaphor of the Iron Curtain, as discussed in Chapter 2. Two visits to Berlin were the result of this emerging connection and in Chapter 3 I discuss the materiality of the Berlin Wall as experienced during these two visits as well as through archaeological and literary sources. The fieldwork in Italy/Slovenia (Chapter 4) and Czech Republic/Austria (Chapter 5) provides the majority of the empirical material on which my discussions and conclusions are based. These conclusions are mainly presented in Chapter 6 although they are also present in Chapters 4 and 5.

Case studies

The area used for my first field research is located on the border between Italy and Slovenia around the two towns of Gorizia (in Italy) and Nova Gorica (in Slovenia) (Chapter 4). The border was re-drawn here following

World War II dividing the area between Italy and Yugoslavia. On either side of the border the two towns of Gorizia and Nova Gorica grew separately but still intertwined, affected by Cold War politics. The border between Italy and Slovenia has had a long and complex history and its relationship with the Iron Curtain is far from clear. Many would say this border, formerly between Yugoslavia and Italy, was never part of the Iron Curtain. This is why I chose this border for my first case study as it would help my discussions of what the Iron Curtain really was, or was not. Located in a valley south of the Alps and north of the Karst plateau this area consists of arable land which has been cultivated for centuries.

Apart from my fieldwork in the Gorizia/Nova Gorica area I also travelled along the western and northern borders of Slovenia. Starting from the town of Koper, on the Adriatic Coast, I headed north until reaching the border with Austria and following the Slovenian-Austrian border I tried to cross the border in as many places as possible until I reached the tripoint between Austria, Slovenia and Hungary. I wanted to get an idea of how the landscape changed throughout this border and what the actual border and its crossing points look like today.

My second field study was carried out on the border between the Czech Republic and Austria in the area around the Podyji Park located near the town of Znojmo in southern Czech area of South Moravia (Chapter 5). The park developed as part of the grounds of Vranov Castle in the 18th century and became part of a war landscape from the 1930s as it was drawn into World War II and subsequently the Cold War. The, then Czechoslovakian, border was heavily militarised from the 1950s until early 1990s. My studies here, in contrast to the study in Slovenia, dealt with the type of border that we traditionally connect with the Iron Curtain. The study here was mainly focussed on the Czech side of the border although some observations were also made of the landscape on the Austrian side.

I also conducted research into the situation along the Inner German Border and in particular Berlin (Chapter 3). Although I did not carry out fieldwork to the same extent as the two other studies I was able to get a good understanding of the history and the changing fabric also of this border. The Inner German Border, especially the Berlin Wall, is highly important for the understanding of what the Iron Curtain was, or still is, and the fact that I did not carry out a study to the same amount of detail here does not suggest I find it less important. In the study of the German-German border I was also able to rely on the fairly extensive research that has already been carried out here, including archaeological studies of the Berlin Wall. I also carried out two trips to Berlin to make observations of what the remains of this wall look like and how it is treated today.

The fact that many people consider the Berlin Wall to be *the* symbol of the Iron Curtain and Cold War division makes this an important site, however, by stepping out of this area it is also possible to get new perspectives and challenge some of the preconceptions that exist about the Iron Curtain. The fact that I did not start my research in Berlin was, I believe, important in challenging some of my own preconceptions of what the Iron Curtain was. The study areas that I have chosen for my research represent three very different sites with highly varying material but also with many similarities. Studying these and comparing the results from all three sites has given me the opportunity to gain a broad understanding of a highly complex monument, the Iron Curtain.

CHAPTER 2

A physical metaphor

Concrete and barbed wire. For many people in the West this is the typical picture of the Iron Curtain. The Iron Curtain has become synonymous with the Berlin Wall. When discussing the location of the former Iron Curtain, people often refer to the inner German border, continuing along the borders of former Czechoslovakia, Austria, Hungary, Yugoslavia and Italy: a long barrier between Eastern and Western Europe, a divider of ideologies that kept the communist in and the capitalist out, or was it the other way around? These ideas of what the Iron Curtain was are a fusion of the physical and the abstract, a metaphor with a physical face.

But what was the Iron Curtain? Where does this picture of concrete and barbed wire come from? Iron curtains first appeared as a very physical feature in the theatres of London during the 19th century to stop the fires that had become all too common. During the First World War, the term was used as an abstract visualisation of the barriers between the fighting sides, and during the interwar period, to make clear the growing differences between Europe and the Soviet Union. It was, however, Churchill's use of the expression in his speech at Westminster College in Fulton, Missouri, in 1946, where he referred to an Iron Curtain, stretching across the continent from the Baltic to the Adriatic (Wright 2007:43), that cemented the image of the Iron Curtain in the popular imagination. Churchill may not have been the first to use this metaphor but by using these particular words he was pointing to something highly solid and impenetrable, a physical iron curtain imperative to stop fires and not letting them get out of control, he created an image in people's minds which was to have a massive impact on how people viewed the division of post-war Europe even before any militarised borders had been fully raised. This image of an Iron Curtain as a barrier between two superpowers of different ideological convictions was therefore created through words before they were set in stone. Reactions to

Churchill's speech demonstrate how the matter was more complex than the then former Prime Minister was making it seem. *The Times* expressed concerns that portraying Western democracy and Soviet Communism as two opposing sides was unwise and that both types of governments could learn from each other (Wright 2007:46). In the days following Churchill's speech both Prime Minister Attlee and President Truman distanced themselves from Churchill's opinions and Stalin made it known that he took this as a 'call to war' (Wright 2007: 47, 56). As the Cold War advanced the use of the term Iron Curtain increased and was frequently used in speeches, papers and the media. In the West, Europe was portrayed as two polarised halves of East and West, with the Iron Curtain standing as a barrier between them keeping the captive population of the communist regimes from escaping to the west. In the German Democratic Republic (GDR) the border was referred to as the Antifaschistische Schutzwall (Anti-Fascist Protection Wall) protecting the population from the West.

Following the division of Germany into sectors tension soon arose between them, in particular on the border between the zones of what was seen as the Western allies, American, British and French and the East, i.e. the Soviet controlled sectors. In her research into the development of the Inner German Border, looking specifically at how the border developed between the two towns of Sonneberg and Neustadt bei Coburg, historian Edith Sheffer (2008) demonstrates how the confusion and turmoil following World War II helped to justify the development of the border, not only the physical fortifications but also the mental border. She claims: "This mental boundary evolved surprisingly quickly and proved surprisingly powerful, not just reflecting, but itself propelling the growth of the physical border" (Sheffer 2008:599). The chaos that existed in the border areas where illegal crossings, a thriving black market and violence often got out of hand, affecting life in these areas, caused many of the locals to crave stability and clear rules. This in turn was used to justify stricter regulations in the border areas, which were even welcomed. Her research of the border between the two towns of Neustadt, subsequently in Federal Republic of Germany (FDR), and Sonnenberg, in German Democratic Republic (GDR), shows that it was the Americans who first started to demarcate and fortify the border here in the late 1940s. These actions were soon followed by the Soviets erecting their own barriers, making sure they reached higher than the American 1.8 m posts, as well as adding fencing and barbed wire in some places (Sheffer 2008:91). By the time the 1,380 km fence was erected along the entire border between East and West Germany in 1952 the border had already been sufficiently established in people's minds that this did not cause as much controversy as the erection of the Berlin Wall in 1961. As this border, as well as the fortification of other borders throughout Europe, had helped to stifle post-war chaos and violence and subsequently developed step by step, sometimes even with the consent of the local population, the final closing of the Inner German Border in 1952 did not receive that much attention. The fences were already there in peoples' minds. In other places in Europe, borders between the countries that aligned themselves with the western and the eastern bloc became more and more militarised. The difference in other places, such as the borders between former Czechoslovakia and Hungary with Austria was that the majority of the border infrastructure was constructed well inside the eastern side of the actual borders, often away from the gaze of the western neighbours. The official goal here, as in East Germany, was to keep the enemy out but the majority of the structures were focussed on the threat from within, their own population. The main focus in these long sections of militarised border zones was to make sure that nobody could get across these areas and through to the West.

In contrast during the 1960s, when the Berlin Wall was constructed, the European division became acutely obvious to the world. Here the border, which had previously been much more open than the borders between other East and West zones in the divided Germany went through a homogenous society. The border left West Berlin a floating island within what increasingly felt like 'enemy territory'. In her article *The Berlin Wall – a Symbol of the Cold War Era?* historian Hope Harrison (2005) looks at how the Berlin Wall came to be and points out that the wall is often seen as a result of Soviet aggression. Her studies of Soviet and East German documents show, however, that the Soviet leaders refused to sanction the building of a militarised border through the city of Berlin as they felt there would be too many negative consequences of such an act. Documents show that GDR leader Walter Ulbricht had been pushing for a building of a wall since 1953 but only in 1961 did he manage to persuade Soviet leader Nikita Khruschev into agreeing to such a construction (Harrison 2005:19–23). When the Berlin Wall was built in August 1961 it was the first time people could really see the division clearly, even touch it. Before this the militarised borders that had developed across the European continent had generally been hidden from view through protected zones and with fencing constructions placed several kilometres inside the different countries' western borders. The fact that this border also came to divide a capital also became an important factor in the attention it was given. In a war that was present in all aspects of life, even stretching out into space, but in most cases never tangible as a physical war of the kind previous experienced, the wall was seen as a material manifestation of the political situation. The physicality of the wall was seen as an act of aggression and making, not only the division of Europe very real, but also the Cold War as a whole. Right in front of the eyes of the inhabitants of West Berlin as well as a large amount of press, the Berlin Wall went from barbed wire to high, concrete walls, the images of which were broadcast across the world. The Berlin Wall was a frequent backdrop to political speeches throughout its existence such as Ronald Reagan's speech at the Brandenburg Gate in June 1987 in which he declared "Mr. Gorbachev, tear down this wall" (cited in Bruner 1989:324) (Figure 1). Even though John F. Kennedy's speech held in June 1963 was held at the Berlin's City Hall and not at the wall itself, it was very much present in his words. He also visited the wall and the pictures of the U.S. president standing on a platform looking into the East were reported in the press throughout the Western World.

Figure 1: Ronald Reagan speaking in front of the Brandenburg Gate and the Berlin Wall on 12th June 1987. Photo: White House Photographic Office.

The changing rhetoric around a wall

The Berlin Wall was a frequent actor in rhetoric between the two blocs but how it was used changed somewhat over its existence. Maybe not too surprisingly the media in East Germany blamed the construction of the Berlin Wall on the actions of the West but during the early period after the wall had been constructed there was also debate in the Western press about whether the wall was a result of a western failure as not enough had been done to stop the construction (Bruner 1989:321). This attitude changed, however, and in his 1963 speech Kennedy claims "… we have never had to put a wall up to keep our people in, to prevent them from leaving us" (cited in Bruner 1989:324) suggesting that the wall was in fact proof of eastern failures. Also during Reagan's speech in Berlin in 1987 the wall is used as evidence of failure of the Soviet Union and victory of the West (Bruner 1989:325). During its later years the way the wall was instead portrayed more as an anachronism, emphasising the absurdity in its existence (Bruner 1989:325). In contrast in East Germany the fortified border with the capitalist West became the focal point during celebration ceremonies (Figure 2). Following its fall it instead became a symbol of freedom and the victory of the people on both sides. This meaning of freedom has also come to extend outside the Cold War context and images of the fall of the Berlin Wall has found its way into other settings such as for example during the 2003 invasion of Iraq where images of the fall of the Berlin Wall was used in news coverage to illustrate images of liberation (Manghani 2008:59).

The picture of the Berlin Wall has become a recurring image in the media and was constantly used to represent the ideological divisions in Berlin and in Europe. Critical theorist Sunil Manghani (2008) makes the point that the media images of the fall of the Berlin Wall were not used to critically investigate the exact goings on but rather they were used to maintain an already popular and dominant interpretation of the events (Manghani 2008:59). Although Manghani has studied images of the events of 1989 in Berlin rather than the erection of the wall in 1961 his discussions can also be extended to how previous images of the Berlin Wall were used. It demonstrates how powerful images can be and how prevailing the story they convey can become. Manghani also uses other examples to show how this type of reporting, and in effect also history writing, is constantly occurring in other places, such as the toppling of the Saddam Hussein statue in Baghdad's Firdos Square in the summer of 2003. This event was immediately broadcasted across the globe and even if the toppling of this statue was not of particular importance as such the fact that it happened right in front of media cameras made it a major event and instantly referred to as an historic event (Manghani 2008:60).

Figure 2: East German parade as part of the celebration of 25 years of the Antifaschistische Schutzwall in 1986. Photo: German Federal Archives (Reference: Bild 183-1986-0813-460).

There are some images that just reach us, that sneak under our skin and come to represent a whole event. These are what Benjamin Drechsel, specialist in political iconography, calls 'key visuals' as they have the ability to project a powerful narrative and become symbols of a particular event (Drechsel 2010:17). The image of a naked girl, Kim Phuc, running in the streets following a napalm bomb being dropped on her village, came to represent the whole Vietnam War. The image was published in the New York Times (1972) and was later awarded a Pulitzer Prize (The Kim Foundation website). Images like this come to affect the way we remember events but also the places where the events took place. Manghani refers to images as a sort of shorthand by media professionals (Manghani 2008:59). In the same way there are some images that have been particularly prevailing in the history of the Iron Curtain, of which most of them are connected to the Berlin Wall, such as the image of an East German soldier, Conrad Schumann, jumping over the barbed wire throwing his gun as he leaps over to freedom in the west. These images may have just presented a particular angle of the division of Cold War but to the Western world these images became the Berlin Wall, and the Iron Curtain. They were an important part of history writing, an act which is always flawed by subjectivity, and in this case, camera angles. Whenever media reports in papers or on television required an image to quickly remind people of the Cold, the Berlin Wall and images of its dramatic erection or, as the wall had become more established images of watch towers and patrolling border guards taken from West Berlin, became a frequently used tool. What other images could one use to demonstrate the complexity of a war with no clear visible battle fields?

Drechsel likens the Berlin Wall to a political media icon, and argues that from its construction to its fall it became a major media focus and a political instrument on both sides of the Cold War divide. Whilst portrayed in the Western media as a 'concentration camp wall' or a 'Wall of Shame', it was presented in the East German media as a protection towards the threat of its fascist neighbours (Drechsel 2010:17). By the use of what Drechsel calls transmedial images the Berlin Wall was made into a political icon, either bad or good depending from what side it was viewed from, given powerful symbolic significance (Drechsel 2010:17). He means that different types of media such as photography and film but also other types such as fragments of the border, exhibitions, leaflets and memorials has become part of this iconisation of the Berlin Wall and that this process still continues today.

The morning paper is staring back at me from the kitchen table. It is July 2012 and a new spy story from the former DDR has hit the media in Sweden. New information from the Stasi archives is still front page news, and so is the Berlin Wall. One of the pictures on the front page shows two East German soldiers behind a curtain of barbed wire (Breitner and Lagerwall 2012:1, 8–9). Through binoculars they stare back at me as I sip my morning coffee nearly 23 years after the wall disappeared. The image of the wall still speaks and provides an instant understanding for those who look at it. An image of the wall immediately makes people think of East Germany, communism and the Cold War and is therefore a useful and very powerful image.

> "...love walks lonely by the Berlin wall..."
>
> Goanna, 'Common Ground'.

The Berlin Wall has played an important part not only in politics but also in our imaginations. The period and its paranoia became popular themes in films, books and music and this has also helped to formulate the image of the Cold War, Iron Curtain and Berlin Wall that we are left with today. In the video to Elton John's song 'Nikita', produced in 1985, Elton is infatuated by a GDR border guard and barbed wire, watchtowers and concrete walls provided the setting, keeping him from the object of his affection. The Sex Pistols sang: "...*sensurround sound in a two inch wall. Well I was waiting for the communist call. I didn't ask for sunshine and I got a world war three. I'm looking over the wall and they're looking at me...*" in 'Holidays in the Sun' and in America the country and western singer Reba McEntire claimed: "...*we have no curtain, made of iron or stone, we are not divided by a wall*" in her song 'Let the Music Lift you up'. Many film posters and book covers, especially for the then increasingly popular spy novels, depict the Iron Curtain and often the Berlin Wall such as John Le Carré's *The spy who came in from the cold* in which the Berlin Wall is described:

> Before them was a strip of thirty yards. It followed the wall in both directions. Perhaps seventy yards to their right was a watch tower; the beam of its searchlight played along the strip. The thin rain hung in the air, so that the light from the arclamps was sallow and chalky, screening the world beyond. There was no one to be seen; not a sound. An empty stage. The watch tower's searchlight began feeling its way along the wall towards them, hesitant: each time it rested they could see the separate bricks and the careless lines of mortar hastily put on.
>
> (Le Carré 1963:227)

In the 1965 motion picture *The Looking Glass War*, also based on one of Le Carré's books, we see a spy, sent out by British Intelligence, getting into East Germany by cutting his way through reels and reels of barbed wire, crawl across the death strip, dismantling a mine before cutting his way through the final wall of barbed wire whilst patrolling guards and their dogs pass at close distance. The idea of the Iron Curtain as an impregnable barrier with a physical form of concrete and barbed wire soon became cemented in people's minds. Its harshness often became synonymous with the Eastern bloc's authoritarian governments.

As time has changed and as the physicality of the Berlin Wall and the Iron Curtain have disappeared the attitudes towards it has changed, also in how it is portrayed in books and films. In the 1999 Leander Haußmann comedy Sonnenallee ('Sun Alley') we meet 17 year old Micha and his friends living on Sonnenallee, a street that was crossed by the Berlin Wall. Their biggest interest is western pop music which is difficult to get hold of, especially under the scrutinising eyes of the border guards patrolling just outside their apartments. The film portrays an almost comical side of the wall and of life in East Germany in the 1970s when the film is set. This would have been impossible or at least highly inappropriate for a film produced during the wall's existence and this was criticised by, for example, the news magazine Der Spiegel, which was critical of the nostalgia for former East Germany presented in the film and also thought it was uncritical of the former GDR government (Wellershoff 1999). Despite this criticism the film became hugely popular. This is connected to what has become known to *ostalgi* which is often explained as nostalgia about the former East Germany, which developed during the 1990s. In her study of how former East Germans define East and West, Ethnologist Sofi Gerber (2011) suggests that *ostalgi* is not necessarily about nostalgia as it does not automatically refer to a longing to a 'better past'. In her interviews with former East Germans she has instead seen a sense of loss that the country they once lived in and nearly all physical objects related to this disappeared as many East German products and objects quickly became exchanged for West German ones after the unification. Many of the people interviewed found that they had lost a lot of the material objects that could have reminded them about their childhood, and in a way also reinforced their identity. This was not the same as a longing for East Germany as such (Gerber 2011:153). The film Sonnennallee was also mentioned by several of the people interviewed as a nice reminder of what life was like in the GDR. One of these interviewees claimed that the film reminded her of her childhood and that it made it possible to talk about it to others (Gerber 2011:152). Another example of such a film is 'Goodbye Lenin' produced in 2003. It is not my intention here to go into a discussion about the subject of *ostalgi* as such but rather to show how later views and perspectives, some highly personal, can have a major effect on how people look at their history and how they form and transmit this history, be it in meetings with others or through films or books. In Sonnenallee the Berlin Wall became the backdrop as well a reminder of the constant omnipresent 'all seeing eye', the East German authorities, but it also helped to provide the setting for and portray a life that no longer exists.

Historians Robert Rosenstone (2006) and Alun Munslow (2007) have argued that film production as a way of writing history has to be taken more seriously than it previously has been. They mean that film can "create experiential and emotional complexities way beyond the printed page" (Munslow 2007:522). Historian Vanessa R. Schwartz emphasises the importance of imagination when we try to understand the past, something which has, she suggests, been aided by the use of film (Schwartz 2013:10-11). She also suggests that although we are well aware of the way politics affect "the methods, questions and problems of the historian and produce a certain optic on the past, there has been almost no consideration of the influences of mass culture and its media such as film on historians, historicity and the development of historical representation over the course of the cinematic century" (Schwartz 2013:2). When dealing with remains in periods closer to our own time this also has to be addressed in archaeology. Just as Schwartz means historians need to adjust and add to their methods in order to "making sense of the profusion of images that are so essential to the record of modern life" (Schwartz 2013:5) so do archaeologists working with modern material in order to understand how this affect the past that we study. Historian Alejandro Baer has, for example, discussed how the past is represented through commercial audiovisual media using the example of the Holocaust. He suggests that in the history of the Holocaust traditional boundaries between imagined and factual history has become blurred and that, in particular the film *Schindler's List* has "created new spaces within which it has become possible to associate oneself to the past" (Baer 2001: 495) He even suggests, using studies of historian Loshitzky, that the film has demonstrated that it is possible that "culture industry is capable of preserving (or reintroducing) the events of the Holocaust in the collective memory and historical consciousness of globalized audiences" (Baer 2001:494).

Archaeologist Cornelius Holtorf has discussed the importance of a so called 'experience economy' in which it is the experience of something itself that is becoming increasingly important. He means the importance lies in "*engaging* people sensually, cognitively, socially, culturally and emotionally" (Holtorf 2007:6). The medium of film can therefore also be seen as an important part of this experience economy which helps people experience the past in a more cognitive way. How these films are constructed and the images they produce of an historical event, of an object or an era are then highly influential in the way people view it. Baer is clear on how this is not necessarily a bad thing as he suggests that it can help create a richer understanding of history (Baer 2001:499). Whether we see this as a negative or a positive, and surely it has an element of both, we need to understand the impact popular culture has on the material we study and foremost the ideas that people have of this material and the period it represents.

The images produced in media as well as in books and films affect us more than we might think. In the article *Views of the Wall - Allied Perspectives* archaeologist John Schofield, gives us some of his memories of being a child in West Berlin in the early 1970s as his father Group Captain Schofield was posted in the city as a Wing Commander for the Royal Air Force (RAF). Schofield describes a situation during a visit in East Berlin when he and his mother found themselves followed. He describes the men that followed him and writes: "I remember upturned collars but I'm not certain how far that this is memory or merely the influence of the spy films that I have subsequently seen" (Schofield and Schofield 2005:39). The images that we receive can therefore alter our own memories as well as our perception of a situation or place. The way people view the wall today is in a similar way dependent on a vast amount of images of it that has been projected over the years. As our own memories fade they are recreated through the images we receive from outside ourselves. Many peoples' view of the Iron Curtain and the Berlin Wall is solely built on second hand information never having seen the actual wall during its existence. People who were never in Berlin at the time or those too young to have seen the physical divisions throughout Europe can only build an image of what this is through information through others, through media, films, books and songs.

It is summer 2013 and I am walking through the Military Vehicle Museum in Strängnäs, Sweden. The vehicles are presented chronologically and on the walls along the exhibit there are information boards describing the different historical events to give some context to the objects that I see: First World War, World War II and then the Cold War. Here I stop and look as the exhibit has included a couple of structures. The first one is a replica of the 1960s Checkpoint Charlie hut and the other a reconstruction of a section of the Berlin Wall. So dominant have these objects become in connection with the Cold War that now, without any real discussion of why they were chosen in this exhibit, they can stand here as a representation the whole of the Cold War. If this was an advertising campaign someone would be very proud of the product marketing achieved.

The image of the Berlin Wall today

In an article about the Berlin Wall and the traces that remain in the landscape today, conservation architect Leo Schmidt explains how the remains of the Berlin Wall today often do not meet the tourists' expectations, "There are no situations left in Berlin today that resemble the old press photographs of the Wall and watchtower type, therefore the authentic remnants present a challenge to the tourists' ability to review their memory and the perception and to modify them by new insights" (Schmidt 2005:16). This demonstrates how the prevailing idea of what the Berlin Wall was and what it looked like is still heavily dependent on those pictures broadcasted during its existence. Schmidt is particularly critical to how the area around the former Friedrichstraße crossing, also known as Checkpoint Charlie, has been recreated after the fall of the wall and lost its authenticity. It is true that the area here looks completely different now to what it did when the wall first came down. Instead of the 1980s control hut a replica of the 1960s hut has been erected where students often take turn to 'stand guard' in American uniforms and pose together with tourists in their holiday snaps. A line of recreated wall was also introduced here, although now in a slightly different position a few metres away from its original position which led to a lot of discussions and arguments. Next to the former crossing area the museum 'Haus am Checkpoint Charlie' presents a history that also very much corresponds to this image or idea that many people in the West have about the Iron Curtain and the Berlin Wall. This is also highly successful and maybe the reason is, as Schmidt criticises, that it does not require people to modify their image of the Berlin Wall as it represents it in a way close to idea of the Iron Curtain which has been produced and reproduced in the West since World War II, a process that is still going on. It shows that some people come to Berlin to experience not just the Berlin Wall but an already existing idea of what this wall should look like. Schmidt is right in that a different history about the Berlin Wall can be found but for many people the idea they have is sufficient and getting this image reaffirmed through the material, albeit a reconstructed image built on non-authentic materiality is considered enough.

The image of the Iron Curtain and the Berlin Wall has changed throughout the twentieth and twenty-first centuries. In particular the idea of the Iron Curtain has become increasingly linked with that of the Berlin Wall. In some ways it corresponds with the physical borders that existed but it has also taken on a different life from its physical origin. This is the more popular idea of the Iron Curtain which was portrayed in the media, both intentionally and unintentionally. This image was also used in films and media which helped to 'stereotype' the image. This idea of the Iron Curtain has also, to a much greater extent than the physical borders, changed as a result of political and historical developments and is still developing and changing today. The physicality behind this idea is being more and more forgotten and the image has taken on some sort of afterlife that is in one way stereotyped and the use of it and the attitude towards it is changing (for example it has changed in regards to *ostalgi* etc.) The Iron Curtain was first 'created' in words by Churchill, then physically created and then again changed and recreated through words.

CHAPTER 3

The materiality of the Berlin Wall

Methods and aims

As we have seen in Chapter 2, the Berlin Wall was very important to the way we view the Iron Curtain. In many ways the two became synonymous in people's minds and this has affected how people think of the Iron Curtain and the Cold War. I did not start my research here just for this reason, because I wanted to get away from my own preconceived ideas of what the Iron Curtain was, or still is. But the Berlin Wall was still present even when I visited other places. People that I interviewed in my study areas, particularly in Italy/Slovenia, would refer back to the Berlin Wall as a sort of case of reference of what the Iron Curtain 'should' look like. The reason this study is located ahead of my other studies within the thesis is to help the reader get a clear background before embarking on my other two case studies.

The aim of this study was to get a better understanding of the material side of the Berlin Wall as Chapter 2 mainly focussed on the idea of the Iron Curtain and the Berlin Wall and to get an understanding of what it used to look like as well as what it looks like today. This was not a case study as such and the fieldwork for this study was therefore not as detailed as for my two other case studies but here I was able to use the report of an archaeological study carried out by the Department of Architectural Conservation at the Brandenburgh University of Technology, Cottbus, Germany. In combination with this study I made observations of my own during two visits to Berlin in 2009 and 2010 during which the section of the former wall from Friedrichstrasse train station to Kreuzberg was covered. This was not a complete recording of all remains that endure from the former wall but rather a way of getting an understanding of what the wall looks like today and to help me understand what it may have looked like in the past. I also visited other sites along the route such as the Documentation Centre and the 'reinstated' wall at Bernauerstrasse, Haus am Checkpoint Charlie and other sections of the former wall such as by Kieler Eck, where a former command post is still located.

As the Inner German Border and in particular the Berlin Wall has been written about extensively I was able to draw on a large amount of literature in building the background information. My main means of recording was through photography and notes on which this chapter is based.

Background

On the edge of the western world

The fabric of the wall may have mostly gone but its ghost still haunts the Berlin townscape. The areas of nothingness where the wall once stood echo a past that many are trying to forget. Development projects are slowly erasing the traces, filling the voids and gradually eating away, piece by piece, the empty spaces. In other areas the memory of the wall is actively remembered: the tacky souvenir shops; the preserved wall sections and guard towers or as black and white photos in the small corner restaurant where I eat my lunch, previously located right on the edge of the Western world at Axel-Springer Straße.

On the morning of 13 of August 1961 Berliners woke up to a new landscape, a speedily assembled wall brutally cutting off the city's western section from its surrounding areas, making it a stranded island within communist German Democratic Republic (GDR). The border between East and West Germany had already been closed since 1952 but the GDR leaders saw the still open borders between East and West Berlin as a bleeding wound making this a too obvious escape route through to the West. Tension between the Western and Eastern blocs had been building for some time and failed attempts to solve the 'Berlin Issue' between US president Kennedy and Soviet leader Krushchev in June 1961 are likely to have affected the decision to erect the Berlin Wall (Rottman 2008). Studies of previously secret documents have demonstrated that between 1953–1961 the Soviets resisted repeated requests from East German leader Walter Ulbricht to close the Berlin border claiming that it would be too disruptive to Berliners as well as the peace keepers in the city (USA, England, France and the Soviet Union) and would "place in doubt the sincerity of the policy of the Soviet government and the GDR government, which are actively and consistently Germany" (Harrison 2005:20).

Figure 3: East German Soldiers marking the line of the Berlin Wall on the 13 August 1961 to protect the border while border fortifications were being erected. Photo: Steffen Rehm.

Krushchev, however, finally approved the plan, originally given the code name 'Rose', a few weeks after his meeting with Kennedy. The north, west and south sides of West Berlin had been closed since 1952 and it was now time to close the border to the east, the section of the inner city of Berlin. At 2 a.m. troops moved into position to guard the eastern border and the construction work. Traffic was stopped, as were over- and underground trains that crossed the border. When the Wall was up and serving its purpose, it was to cut through 192 streets and crossing could now only take place through 14 official crossing points (Rottman 2008). The U-Bahn trains were completely severed between the two parts of the town whilst the S-Bahn still functioned but highly controlled to avoid illegal crossing. By 4 a.m. trucks had arrived with prefabricated concrete blocks and the first sections of the wall were laid across Ackerstraße near Bernauerstraße. Other materials were also used during this early building phase and the labour was often poorly executed as speed was more important than thorough construction. Soon other structures were added such as watchtowers, anti-vehicle obstacles and searchlights. As time went on the Berlin Wall was upgraded and updated, particularly in 1975 when a major reinforcement operation was carried out. By 1989 it had become an almost impenetrable barrier consisting of prefabricated L-shaped reinforced concrete slabs, reaching 3,6 m high with sewage pipes cemented to its top, making climbing almost impossible. It was accompanied by anti-vehicle obstacles and ditches, control strips, patrol roads, trip flares, dog runs, signal fences and an inner, 3–4 m high, wall (Rottman 2008) (Figure 4).

Figure 4: Berlin Wall at the Potsdamer Platz 1975. Photo: Edward Valachovic.

The days and weeks following the Socialist Party official Schabowski's announcement of the opening of the border on the 9th of November 1989 saw the start of spontaneous demolition of the wall. Pictures of people out in force, chipping away at the Berlin Wall were broadcast over the world. We connect these pictures with happiness, freedom and democracy. Few times in history have people so clearly demonstrated their hatred towards a structure and such a clear wish of its removal. The official demolition was then started in June 1990 (Klausmeier 2009:97). At this point the goal was to remove the wall in its entirety. After the wall came down and Germany unified major discussions were started of how Berlin should be developed in the future (see discussion in Huyssen 1997). A surge of redevelopment took off, eradicating the scars left in the landscape from 20th century conflict. What we see in Berlin today is what Huyssen calls the 'desired identity' (Huyssen 1997:68), the result of many conscious decisions of how Berlin should look and how the past should be portrayed. The townscape was still scarred by the destruction of World War II and how to handle the redevelopment of these scars was far from clear. Discussions were also generated

3: THE MATERIALITY OF THE BERLIN WALL

around the materiality of the Berlin Wall. What was to become of this iconic but much hated monument? Most people just wanted it gone, but a few voices of caution were raised, both from professionals and concerned Berliners. A proposal to preserve sections of the wall was suggested by the Berlin State Office for the Preservation of Historical Monuments and following investigations seven sections were put forward for preservation. Strong feelings against its preservation by the general public and from politicians, however, led to demolition (Klausmeier 2009:97). Since the late 1990s there has been an increased interest in the remains of the Berlin Wall more than as a commodity and studies and research have been carried out on the material that remains (Feversham and Schmidt 1999 and 2007, Dolff-Bonekämper 2002, Klausmeier and Schmidt 2004, Harrison 2005, Schmidt and von Preuschen 2005, Taylor 2006, Sheffer 2007 and 2008, Rottman 2008 Klausmeier 2009,). These studies show that although great efforts went into the demolition of the actual wall structures there are other remains related to the wall still *in situ*. Although more and more of these traces are disappearing several of them can still be seen in the landscape today. A major archaeological study of what remained of the Berlin Wall was carried out between 2001–2003 by the Department of Architectural Conservation at the Brandenburg University of Technology, Cottbus, Germany on behalf of the Berlin State Authorities. The aim of the study was to record any remaining features of the former border structure. The results were presented in Alex Klausmeier and Leo Schmidt's book "Wall Remnants – Wall Traces". Presented in the format of a guidebook this archaeological survey covers the full length of the inner city wall through Berlin (Klausmeier and Schmidt 2004:13). This study together with two visits to Berlin, both in 2009, forms the base for my discussions about the materiality of the Berlin Wall.

The Berlin Wall is closely related to the idea of the Iron Curtain as they have developed together and often becomes synonymous. The Berlin Wall is not one of my study areas but it is highly important, especially for the idea of the Iron Curtain and for many people as a manifestation of the Cold War. In the introduction to their book "Wall Remnants – Wall Traces", Klausmeier and Schmidt write that the Berlin Wall "was not an inevitable product of the Cold War" (Klausmeier and Schmidt 2004:10). It is true that the Soviet Union only gave in to the demands of the leaders of the German Democratic Republic (GDR) for a barrier to stop the exodus of refugees from East to West Berlin (Harrison 2005:19). However, as discussed in Chapter 2, it is clear that the Berlin Wall became one of the most visible and tangible example of an East/West divide. The wall became a manifestation of the Cold War division rather than a result of it. As many of the other militarised borders across Europe at the time this was clearly visible to the Western world and it caught the attention of the media which helped to spread the image of the Berlin Wall across the globe.

The material

Berlin today

I turn a corner and a large open space suddenly opens up, a vast nothingness stretching out to my left and right. At this former death strip site grass and bushes have done their best to reclaim their hegemony, only interrupted by a few occasional paths that cross the space. I follow the cobbled line along the ground and as I walk along it I notice that all the buildings around me look very new, many not yet finished. I walk on, and after turning into Axel-Springerstraβe a series of art installations, colourful sections of the Berlin Wall, greet me from the parking lot in front of an office building. I keep following the cobbles, and am occasionally reassured by signage that I am following the route of the former Berlin Wall. Although I am close to the centre there are few people around. This soon changes as I reach Zimmerstrasse and the site of former Checkpoint Charlie. A bus pulls into the curb outside the Museum, Haus am Checkpoint Charlie, releasing a hoard of American teenagers. A couple of giggling girls break away from the rest of the group and walk over to have their picture taken with the handsome 'American soldier' stationed by a replica of the 1960s border checkpoint.

This large monument of the Cold War is still very much present in Berlin today. Although most of what is generally seen as *the Wall*, i.e. the concrete wall facing West Berlin, has been removed, much of the former border infrastructure can still be seen throughout Berlin. Major work was carried out in 1990–1991 to remove the wall but today many other features that were part of the wall infrastructure are still visible. Although what was most visible from the West was the final concrete wall this was only the final part in a series of obstacles constructed to stop any attempts to escape to West Berlin. When approaching from the East there would first be warning signs informing of the restrictions of access ahead. These would be red and white painted concrete pillars or low railings, also in red and white, delimiting the restricted areas where only those with authorisation was allowed to enter. There were also signs in German, English, French and Russian stating "Frontier area – Passage not allowed" (Klausmeier and Schmidt 2004:22). Although no signs were recorded in the archaeological survey many of the pillars and railings were found still scattered along the border landscape. Some of these have been reused, for example incorporated into fencing to adjoining properties (Klausmeier and Schmidt 2004:229).

The so called 'perimeter defences' were located in connection with and to reinforce the hinterland wall. This was the most eastern facing wall, constructed with prefabricated concrete sections with a white oblong surrounded by a grey frame. The side of the hinterland wall facing westward was painted white to make it easier to spot any unauthorised persons within this restricted border strip. In some places already existing walls or sides of buildings were incorporated into the hinterland wall. The perimeter defences were located to reinforce the hinterland wall where the topography was particularly difficult and consisted of extra walls, fences and various obstacles such as the so-called flower bowl barricades, large concrete flower pots placed so that it would be impossible to drive into the wall with a heavy vehicle. There were also metal grids on windows located near the hinterland wall and anti-climb features such as spiky objects.

Much of what remains of the wall in the townscape today is related to either the perimeter defences or the hinterland wall. Large sections of hinterland wall can be seen in several places (for examples see Klausmeier and Schmidt 2004:62 and 91). As this wall was not of interest to the so called *Wallpeckers*, who with their pneumatic hammers chipped away at the border following its fall in 1989, many sections or remains have survived. Although they may be harder to spot there are also many of the perimeter defences still located throughout the former route of the border. As these were much less obvious they also became less important to remove during the clean-up operations in the early 1990s. These remains such as the steel arrows located on top of a gate near the border defences by Ostbahnhof Station in the area Mitte (Klausmeier and Schmidt 2004:188) or the metal rods barring the windows at a power station at Kopenhagener Strasse in Pankow (Klausmeier and Schmidt 2004:55) are important to show the extent and the variety of the border fortifications.

The signalling fence was the next hurdle to get over after the hinterland wall for anyone trying to escape this route. The signalling fence was more elastic than other fences making it harder to climb (Klausmeier and Schmidt 2004:22). These fences have been reused as garden fences and they are still referred to by the garden owners as *Staatsdraht*, or government wire (Klausmeier and Schmidt 2004:35). Some traces of the electricity that was required at the border strip have survived in Berlin (for examples see Klausmeier and Schmidt 2004:62, 173, 230, 267). The electricity was particularly important to keep the many floodlights in the border area going. They made sure the border strip was always illuminated. Some of these lights are still used today whilst others remain in the landscape without a purpose (Figure 5).

Figure 5: Floodlight still present near the Bernauer Straße Berlin Wall Memorial no longer connected or used. Photo: Anna McWilliams

Between the light strip and the hinterland wall were the control paths and the dog runs. The long paths were often constructed in macadam or, more commonly, asphalt. Many sections of these paths survive today and some are reused for other purposes for example cycle paths (Klausmeier and Schmidt 2004:60). These paths stretched along the border to facilitate patrolling but also functioned as access roads to bring troops to and from their posts as well as bringing provisions to the watch towers and command posts. The watch towers are often part of the western view of what *the Wall* looked like as they were clearly visible from the West. They were located next to the patrol paths and as a clear, physical reminder of the wall great care was taken to remove these as well when the wall was demolished in the early 1990s. Therefore there are only two of the command post style buildings still *in situ*. These were box shaped and constructed of pre-fabricated concrete sections. They consisted of four levels with the command post on the second floor where large windows provided extensive views. On the first floor there was a common room with bunk beds, the ground floor housed prison cells whilst the basement held all the electronic devices required (Klausmeier and Schmidt 2004:135). The Kieler Eck command post located in the Mitte area has been given monument protection status. The tower itself therefore remain as it was when it functioned as part of the border infrastructure but its surroundings have completely changed with a new suburban area having grown up around it (Figure 6). The formerly tall-looking tower is now dwarfed by surrounding high rise blocks of flats, left as a curious feature in the otherwise residential courtyard. The second command post to remain is located at Schlesischer Busch in the area of Treptow (Figure 7). Here a large area of what used to be the border strip has been turned into a park, the tower located at its south-eastern edge. This tower is of the same type as the Kieler Eck tower, an observation and command station (Rottman 2008:27). There is none of the other type of watchtowers, BT-11 (Beobachtungtrum 11-metre), still in *in situ* although one is located near its original position near Potsdamer Platz (Figure 8). These more slender types of towers had much less room inside them and were used strictly for border guards to monitor the border fortifications and the control strip.

Figure 6: New residential buildings have grown up around the command post at Kieler Eck formerly located within the death strip. The tower has been given protection status and has therefore been left in its original place. Photo: Anna McWilliams.

Figure 7: Command post at Schlesischer Busch. In the background is the former death strip which has been converted into a park. Photo: Anna McWilliams.

Figure 8: Watch tower located near Potsdamer Platz having been moved from its original position to give way for new construction. Photo: Anna McWilliams.

The control strip, also known as the death strip, consisted of a large strip of sand that was raked so that any footprints or other marks would clearly show if an intruder had walked across it. This was important not only to try and stop the intruder crossing over the final hurdle which was the wall facing West Berlin, the so-called 'enemy facing wall', but also to show where there were weaknesses in the system and also, if the person had managed to cross unnoticed, to punish the guard that missed the breach.

There are many other types of features visible in the townscape today that were once connected to the former border fortifications, such as areas for maintenance, iron bars in the canals and traces of demolished buildings once considered too close to the border. All these features demonstrate how the construction of the wall had to adapt to the changing topography. Other remains demonstrate how the city around the wall had to change to adapt to the division such as turning loops where the bus route were cut off by the wall and closed down railway stations.

The 'enemy facing' wall

The wall facing West Berlin, the so called 'enemy facing wall' is often what people refer to when they speak about *the Wall*. As large parts of this wall were removed during 1990–1991 there is little left to indicate exactly where the wall was located although some traces have been recorded (Klausmeier and Schmidt 2004:122) and in places only the foundations remain (Klausmeier and Schmidt 2004:127). In some sections it has therefore been recreated such as within the centre of Berlin where a cobble stone line on the ground indicates its route in a way that does not obstruct or limit movement around it. I follow it through town, letting it be my guide. Some of the new buildings constructed on the site of the former wall have also incorporated the line in their interior. At the end of a day walking along the former wall as I am resting my feet in a restaurant near Potsdamer Platz I suddenly realise that I am sitting on the wall as the Berlin Wall line is running straight under my table (Figure 9).

3: THE MATERIALITY OF THE BERLIN WALL

Figure 9: The course of the former wall is today marked through much of central Berlin, even in this restaurant near Potsdamer Platz. Photo: Anna McWilliams.

This wall changed appearances several times in what is often referred to as 'four generations' of the wall. The first wall was hastily assembled in August 1961 and consisted of large square breeze blocks normally used for residential architecture. Tall Y-shaped iron rods were holding barbed wire in place on top of the wall. After some attempts at ramming the wall with heavy vehicles the breeze block wall was replaced in some areas with heavy concrete slabs. This is referred to as the second generation wall. From 1965 onwards the wall was replaced with a third generation wall of inserted concrete slabs into an H-shaped post structure of reinforced concrete. Sewage pipes were placed at the top of the wall to make it harder to climb. In the mid-1970s the co called 'Border Wall 75' was built. The result of several studies and tests, this wall was put together from prefabricated concrete sections, the L-shaped element UL12.41 (Klausmeier and Schmidt 2004:15–16). This is the wall that has received the most attention and that corresponds with most peoples' idea of what the Berlin Wall looked like. It is this wall we are used to seeing in media footage, the wall that Reagan demanded Gorbachev to move as well as the wall that hordes of tourists have had their photograph taken with since it's erection in 1975. It is also the wall that eventually came down, the wall that we have seen images of being hacked down by crowds (Figure 10).

Figure 10: Detail of 'Border Wall 75' showing iron rods clad in concrete. Photo: Anna McWilliams.

3: THE MATERIALITY OF THE BERLIN WALL

Figure 11: East Side Gallery. A section of hinterland wall built in 'Border Wall 75' style. This became an open air art exhibition in 1990. Photo: Anna McWilliams.

The materiality of the Berlin Wall is not limited to the city of Berlin itself but actually stretches across the whole world. Many sections were moved soon after the fall of the wall and scattered across the globe to be placed in office buildings, at universities and especially popular, as part of memorials. Sections of wall are today a commodity and in larger sections well-priced collector's items. Some people saw the potential in the materiality of the Berlin Wall already as it was coming down and collected large amounts of the concrete walls to sell on. Larger pieces are sold for considerable sums of money to collectors all over the world. In 2008 an auction house in Berlin reported to have sold one section of perimeter wall for 7,800 euros (BBC News 2008). Smaller pieces of the wall are sold in souvenir shops or on the internet and are often accompanied with a certificate to authenticate them. As the smaller pieces are easily moved and there are no restrictions on taking them out of the country they have contributed to the wall being distributed all over the world.

The long section of wall, 1.3 km, which after an international spray and paint event in 1990 became known as the East Side Gallery was actually a hinterland wall even though the same material was used as for the 'enemy facing wall', Border Wall 75. This was one of the only places where the eastern side of the border defences were visible to any state visitors as well as others who travelled on Mühlenstrasse which was the main route to Schönefeld Airport. It was therefore made to look the same as the wall seen from the West in order to play down the severity of the border fortifications (Klausmeier and Schmidt 2004:194). This wall is now one long, open air art gallery with a large number of visitors every year (Figure 11).

Crossing over

As the wall blocked the majority of the routes between East and West Berlin any traffic between the two had to be channelled through the official crossing points. There were 14 crossings from West Berlin to the GDR of which eight were located within the city centre. There were strict rules as to who was allowed to cross at the different crossings and the infrastructure put in place helped to control the flow of pedestrians or vehicles. The lanes used to route traffic through the crossing were still visible when the archaeological survey was carried out in 2001–2003 (Klausmeier and Schmidt 2004:82 and 126).

The most famous crossing was the so-called Checkpoint Charlie located at the corner of Friedrichstraße and Zimmerstraße. Only foreign nationals and members of the allied forces were allowed to cross the border here (Klausmeier and Schmidt 2004:163). In October 1961 the crossing was the site of a near confrontation between the Americans and the Soviets and tanks were facing each other across the border (Taylor 2006: 412). Today the site is a hot spot for Berlin Wall tourism. Although the wall and the crossing infrastructure was removed here in 1990 a reconstruction of the 1960s US Army control hut has been located just inside what used to be the American Zone complete with an American flag and bags of sand stacked to create protection from enemy fire. A US army sign is also located near the control hut stating *"You are entering the American sector. Carrying weapons off duty forbidden. Obey traffic rules"* in English, Russian, French and German. There is also a stall offering visa stamps. Two large photos have also been placed on either side of the former border, a picture of an American soldier looking into former East Berlin and an East German border guard looking back from the other side. The line of the border, as in most part of the inner city, is marked along the ground with a cobbled line. Located here is also the Museum Haus am Checkpoint Charlie, something I will return to later in this chapter.

I'm standing outside Friedrichstraße Station. People are rushing past, all with a purpose and a place to be. During the division of Berlin, Friedrichstraße station acted as a railway crossing between East and West. A complex system of corridors, steps and platforms kept separated to make sure people did not sneak across, a labyrinth of control. A structure that was closely connected to the Berlin Wall during the Cold War period, at least for those who used to cross it was the Tränenpalast, or Palace of Tears, a large hall at the Friedrichstraße Station. This was one of the main crossings between East and West Berlin both for Germans and people from other nationalities. The name refers to the many tearful goodbyes that were said inside the hall before those who were crossing over to West Berlin went through passport control here. There were several different windows for passport control, one for visitors, one for 'Inhabitants of capitalist states', one for inhabitants of West Berlin and a separate window for diplomats. After going through the controls in the hall travellers were routed through a series of corridors underneath the station to get to the train to West Berlin (Klausmeier and Schmidt 2004:146). The trains that ran in East Berlin were made completely separate from the train system in West Berlin. The train and underground system, which before 1961 had been one for the whole city of Berlin, was severed and separated in two parts so successfully that by the fall of the wall in 1989 they functioned as two completely different systems. By keeping the different areas separate and positioning passport control posts along the way it was almost impossible to get on a train to West Berlin without permission. The station has now been completely refurbished and looks like any other station with no visible traces of its former segregated layout. The Palace of Tears was used as a concert hall until 2006 and has since 2011 housed the exhibition '*Border Experiences – Everyday life in divided Germany*' by the Stiftung Haus der Geschichte der Bundesrepublik Deutschland. This exhibition aims to provide "a vivid insight into life in the shadow of division and the border" (Stiftung Haus der Geschichte der Bundesrepublik Deutschland website 2012).

When I interview Nina in London, where she now lives, some of her clearest memories of the wall relates to the Friedrichstraße Station and the Palace of Tears. This was the place where she used to help people escape over from East to West Berlin. She was a student in Berlin during in the early 1960s and through the university she got involved in helping people cross the border. "I was given some passports that I needed to smuggle over to East Berlin and then give them to those who were trying to escape", she tells me. Often they met in a flat where she handed the passports over and explained how the crossing worked. The passports were of different nationalities such as West German, English and Swedish. "I remember one time I turned up and the person looked nothing like the passport photo that was meant to be used. The girl in the photo had blond hair while the East German girl who was going to use the passport had really dark hair. We had little time so we had to improvise and covered her hair in flour to make it lighter. Amazingly it worked." She laughs at the story now but remember it being frightening at the time. The last time she went over to help someone across she soon discovered that she was being followed. Zigzagging through the streets around Friedrichstraße Station she managed to lose the man following her in order to get through the Friedrichstraße passport control and onto the train to West Berlin as soon as possible without being caught. That was her last passport trip over to East Berlin (Nina 2008, pers. comm.). Today the station looks just like any other station. Apart from the Palace of Tears, which is actually located just next to the main station building, there are no traces of the division. I try to figure out what platforms may have belonged to what trains, east- or westbound and what corridors that were out of bounds from those in the East but it is difficult. Not even the passage between the station building and the Palace of Tears seems to remain. As I walk away from the station building I wonder if this was the street Nina rushed through to shake off her stalker and get to the station.

Memorials and Museums

There are also several memorials and museums in Berlin dedicated to the Berlin Wall, serving a myriad of functions and purposes. They vary from large structures and monuments to small installations or plaques. There are different aims behind many of the sites dedicated to the Wall in Berlin today. Many are aimed to accommodate the remembrance of the Wall itself as well as the period and the people that were affected by its presence. In the Documentation Centre by Bernauer Straße I find the names of the confirmed 70 people that were killed trying to cross the border area, at Strelizer Straße I find plaques commemorating the tunnel that was built in 1962 bringing 59 people over whilst 1 was killed and by Tempelhof Airport I encounter the Berlin airlift monument. Near the Reichstag building the memorial Weisse Kreuze, White Crosses, has been installed to commemorate some of the people that died trying to cross the border. Other sites are have more of an art character such as the Parlament der Bäume, Parliament of Trees, and these often reuse the material of the wall itself as part of its fabric.

Figure 12: A reconstructed section of the Berlin Wall at Bernauer Strasse Memorial at the Documentation Centre. Photo: Anna McWilliams.

Many sites also aim to inform visitors and the younger generation that never experienced the wall themselves about the period, the political circumstances and the border itself. There are two main museums: the Documentation Centre at Bernauer Straβe which is Berlin's official museum of the Berlin Wall and the Haus am Checkpoint Charlie, which is a private museum. The stories told in the different places range between factual information about the wall itself and personal stories of people affected by the wall. The Documentation Centre, where research is also carried out, has a more academic background whilst the Haus am Checkpoint Charlie is based more on commercial grounds. Although some of the stories told at the different museums are based on the same facts the different approaches makes for two very different museums. At the Documentation Centre we find an exhibition where the visitors are allowed a lot of their own space and thoughts in order to process the information provided through information boards, photos and films. The reconstructed sections of Berlin Wall in their original place also help make the wall seem more real here (Figure 12). The site appeals to both people who have personal memories of the wall as well as visitors. "Sometimes I go to Bernauerstrasse just to remind myself of how it really was" I was told by one woman from the former GDR at the site. But others are critical to the reconstruction here. Axel Klausmeier, the director of the Documentation Centre, explains how people have such different experiences of the wall that it is difficult to create a memorial that will please everyone. He also says that for many people in East Berlin the wall was so inaccessible to people during its time as a divider that memorials connected to the wall itself does not really hold much importance to them (Klausmeier, 2009, pers. comm. 16th February). At the Haus am Checkpoint Charlie the emphasis lies on the experience of your visit (Figure 13). The stories here may be sold to you in a more sensationalistic way but the impressions you get here stay with you. This aim of providing an "experience" of the Berlin Wall may not always consider complete authenticity, especially in the exhibited material, but is more aimed at selling the stories to the visitors. As I walk through the Haus am Checkpoint Charlie I suddenly find myself amongst a group of American teenagers, probably around 14–15 years old. They move through the museum at a quicker pace than me and I decide to tag along, curious of their conversations as they experience the wall history. They are preoccupied with the exhibition and take no notice of me, in fact it is quite interesting to see how much the exhibition catches their interest. As they move along they pick up information from the different boards but in particular they look at the large scales photos of people escaping, or failing to do so, across the Berlin Wall. As we go along, with me now studying both the exhibit and the effect it has on these teenagers, their jolly chitter-chatter quietens down and they start looking around more as individuals than a group. At the exit they stop for a moment, make sure they are all there. "You know we've read all about this stuff but now I can really feel it!" says one of the boys in the group to his friend.

Figure 13: Checkpoint Charlie in 2009 with Haus am Checkpoint Charlie and a replica of the 1960s border checkpoint in the background and an image of an American soldier staring into former East Berlin in the foreground. Photo: Anna McWilliams.

Back to nothing

After days spent in the city centre where memorials and recreated wall heritage have informed me almost every step of the way I find myself back in the nothingness, the voids where the wall has been ripped out of the ground but yet not been replaced. This is the situation in several areas outside the centre. In many areas, even close to the centre of town, large areas of the death strip have not yet been developed but run like a wilderness straight through the townscape. During the Cold War these areas were kept under total control, as was the vegetation within it. This has kept larger vegetation such as trees at bay but the complete lack of attention here since 1989 has since created 'green corridors' where greenery has now established itself. These corridors through central Berlin are now slowly being developed and will soon be eradicated as a material reminder of the Wall. When the wall came down the area between Brandenburger Tor and Potzdamer Platz was largely open space due to the bombings during World War II and the building of the Wall. Huyssen described this area of Berlin as a "prairie of history [...] a void filled with history and memory, all of which will be erased" (Huyssen 1997:75). Today this area has been developed but the line of the Berlin Wall is still visible in the cobbled line along the streets and through collective memory. Although redeveloped after 1989 the wall is still apparent at the Brandenburg Gate. The Berlin Wall brutally cut off this historical monument from West Berlin and the wall in front of the gate became one of the most common images in the West of the division. The city continues to develop but the absence of the wall is still apparent, still making this an important place for the memory of the wall and to people who come to remember it (Figure 14).

The wall that kept the two parts of Berlin may have gone but in some ways it is more present than ever. The many different sites of border remains, memorials, information points, museums and voids left behind are all reminders of a divided Berlin, a piece of history kept alive through the materiality it has left behind.

Figure 14: Space on Alte Jacobstraße left open after the border infrastructure was removed and still undeveloped in 2009. Photo: Anna McWilliams.

CHAPTER 4

Case study 1
The Italian/Slovenian border

I started my research in what might appear an unexpected place, the border between former Yugoslavia and Italy. What does this have to do with the Iron Curtain, many people have asked me. I would say that it is as relevant as the Berlin Wall. It opens the question for what the Iron Curtain actually was, or what it is today. During my research, whilst discussing this border with people from Italy, former Yugoslavia and from other parts of Europe as well as the US several criteria have arisen as to what people consider the Iron Curtain to be, often unintentionally. For example I have heard comments like: "It was the Iron Curtain because they were communist on that side whilst we were capitalist on this side" (Maria and Antonio, 2008, pers. comm. 5th September) or "It was not part of the Iron Curtain because it was not impossible to cross" (Group interview Škofije 2008, 6th September). All these criteria that are expressed about the border between Italy and Yugoslavia being or not being part of the Iron Curtain show very clearly what people consider it to be. In this sense, studying a border that many people think was never even part of the Iron Curtain has therefore been vital to understanding what people think it is.

Apart from general research along the former Yugoslav border with Austria and Italy I have carried out a more detailed study in the area in and around the two cities of Gorizia (in Italy) and Nova Gorica (now in Slovenia), located directly on the border approximately 45 km north of Trieste. I first became aware of the two towns when a colleague asked me if I had heard about the "Berlin of the south", a city that, like Berlin, became divided by national borders after World War II. I had not heard about it and set out to investigate. As it turned out it was not exactly one city that had been divided into two as such, rather one city, Gorizia in Italian and Gorica in Slovenian, which after the new border was drawn following

World War II ended up on the Italian side with a large part of its hinterland falling within the Yugoslavian territory. A new city, Nova Gorica, was built on the Yugoslavian side to provide a new centre for the surrounding areas. The two towns developed side by side, divided by an international border and the effects of local and global politics (Figure 15).

Methods and aims

The aim of the research of the Italian-Slovenian border was to study the border between Italy and Slovenia to understand what this border looked like during the Cold War period as well as what it looks like today. The information gained during the research was then to be used in a discussion of this border's role within the Cold War division of Europe as well as people's attitude towards it today.

Two fieldwork trips were carried out, the first in September 2008 which consisted of a survey of the Italian-Slovenian and the Austrian-Slovenian borders. The second fieldwork, carried out in August 2011, focussed on the area in and around the towns of Gorizia and Nova Gorica. The length of the border from Šempeter to Solkan was subjected to a walkover survey, as was the southernmost section of Mount Sabotino/Sabotin. Archival research was carried out at the Goriški Musej Archive, Solkan, Slovenia, the Archivio storico – Biblioteca provinciale in Gorizia, Italy and the National Archives, Kew, UK. These studies were not meant as a full archival and documentary study but rather the documents obtained were a way to help understand the material discovered during the fieldwork. Of particular use were maps and photos as these helped to provide an understanding of the kinds of material that had existed along the Iron Curtain and how the border's different areas had looked in the past.

Recording was carried out through photographing and taking notes. Drawings were also produced wherever necessary to clarify certain features. Maps were studied both in advance and during the research in order to help direct further investigations. Remains in the landscape were recorded on maps to document their location and to help understand their distribution. Interviews were carried out both with people working with the area's history (museum personnel, historians) as well as citizens living in the area, either currently or in the past. Some of these interviews were taped whilst others were recorded through taking notes. I interviewed 14 people during my fieldwork in the area of which seven were women ranging in age from their 30s to their 80s and seven men ranging in age from their 40s to their 80s (see discussion in Chapter 1). I got in contact with most of the people before and during my trip by contacting museums or organisations that may be of help (such as the Swedish-Slovenian Friendship Association in Stockholm) and these in turn referred me on to other contacts. The interviewees were from different backgrounds both ethnically and socially and consisted of people who were working in the heritage and museums industry as well as people living, or having previously lived, in the area.

One distinctive feature of the study area, as with many other border areas, is the duality in language which is reflected also in place names as often both the Italian and Slovenian names are used. Where this is the case I will refer to these places first in Italian and then Slovenian. For the town of Gorizia/Gorica I am using both until the Second World War as after that the situation changed and the one town became two.

Background

The borders between Italy, Slovenia and Austria have had a turbulent history and the borders of the changing regimes have shifted dramatically over the last centuries.

The town on the hill

Gorizia/Gorica was first mentioned in 1001 together with the village of Solkan (Vecchiet 2008). The word is believed to derive from the Slavic word for hill (Jacob Marušič, 2008, pers. comm. 2nd September). The original town also centred on the hilltop castle from which it expanded. The town and surrounding areas have a fortunate position benefiting from the surrounding areas' different types of terrains such as the Alps, the karst plateaus and alluvial plains, all with very different types of economy. As a central point the town therefore became the meeting point and an important market between these different economies which led to a development of road networks and later also railways (Moodie 1950:89). The Habsburg Empire saw the significance of the location of Gorizia/Gorica, or Görz in German, and in the early 16th century, when they took control of the area, established administrative and military functions here (Moodie, 1950:89). When the Transalpine Railway was constructed at the turn of the 20th century Gorizia's position as part of a network was strengthened as it was now located on the route that connected Vienna with Trieste, the Habsburg imperial port. The station, which was opened in 1906, was built at the north-eastern outskirts of town which caused the town to expand in this direction. Postcards of the newly opened railway station shows how it was located in an area that mainly consisted of farmland (Figure 16). The town therefore developed to provide for the high society who enjoyed the town, much due to its clement climate, and several hotels were also built to provide for travellers stopping on their way to the coast (Edizioni Della Laguna 2006:7). Gorizia's older railway station, located at the southern part of the town, provided an access point to cities further east and a tramline between the two stations was built in order to provide transfers for travellers.

Darker times were to come when Gorizia became part of the frontline during the First World War. The border with Italy had previously run approximately 11 km west of Gorizia/Gorica near the town of Cormons. As the Italian army advanced the frontline moved further east and a series of particularly fierce battles, called the Twelve Battles of Isonzo, was fought in the Isonzo/Soča valley between 1915–1917. During two years the Italian and Austrian forces fought each other in a frontline stretching from the Alps down to the Adriatic, a fight eventually won by the Italians but at a high cost with 1,100,000 Italians dead or wounded at the end of the war. The Austrians, whose army was made up of people from all over the Habsburg Empire, lost 650,000 soldiers (Schindler 2001:xii). During the 'Secret Treaty of London' in 1915 Britain had offered large areas, including Trentino, Trieste, Gorizia, Istria as well as the Dodecanese and African colonies, to Italy after the war if they fought on their side (Sluga 2001:26).

Figure 15: The towns of Gorizia and Nova Gorica after World War II. Map: Chris Beach

Figure 16: Postcard of the newly opened Transalpine railway and station after it was built in 1906. The fields to the right of the station mark the location of the current town of Nova Gorica with the line of trees following the road now called Erjavčeva ulica. Property of Goriški Muzej, Nova Gorica, Slovenia.

4: CASE STUDY 1: THE ITALIAN/SLOVENIAN BORDER

Between the wars

After the First World War and the fall of the Habsburg Empire the southern part of the empire declared itself independent: the Kingdom of Serbs, Croats and Slovenes, later named the Kingdom of Yugoslavia. The border towards Austria was settled through a referendum in 1920 when Austria gained the northern sections of Carinthia. The border with Italy was settled in the Rapallo Treaty in 1920 (Medved 1993:136). In this treaty Italy acquired 8768 km² of territory extending east and south-east, including the ports of Trieste and Fiume (now Rijeka) which were the two main ports of the Habsburg Empire in the Adriatic, becoming the new province of Venezia Giulia (Moodie 1950:84–87). The population in these areas were a mixture of Italian, Slovene, Croatian and German. As fascism and its progressively heavy emphasis on nationalism grew stronger in Italy times became increasingly difficult for non-Italian groups within its territory. Even if the official line, expressed by Prime Minister Nitti in 1919, was to treat people of minorities with justice and sympathy, reality showed that treatment of minorities were highly inconsistent and depended on the attitudes of the local authorities (Sluga 2001:42). After 1922 the Fascist government started a more active policy of Italianising Venezia Giulia. As part of the nation-building process a renaming operation was carried out where street names, monuments and persons were given a new Italian identity through new Italian names, this was not an uncommon tactic used as part of nation building both in Italy and in other parts of Europe (Sluga 2001:47).

WWII and new borders

Yugoslavia was occupied by Nazi Germany in 1941 and in 1943 when the Italians capitulated the Germans also took the area around Trieste and the study area, which became included in the so called Operational Zone of the Adriatic Littoral. In Trieste a concentration camp was established, the Risiera di San Sabba, on the outskirts of town in a previous rice husking plant. The camp had a purpose-built cremation oven which was blown up by the Germans late April 1945 to hide the evidence of their crimes when it became clear that the Yugoslavian partisans were about to take over the area. It has been reported that as many as 25,000 Jews and Yugoslavian partisans may have been interrogated and tortured here and 3,000–5,000 people are believed to have been killed at the camp (Aktion Reinhard Camps 2011).

As the Germans were governing the Adriatic Littoral it was subjected to bombing by the allied forces although Gorizia/Gorica survived relatively unscathed. Several resistance groups worked in the area during this period, such as the Yugoslavian Partisans, a communist and antifascist group led by Marshal Tito. It was suggested by the British foreign minister, Anthony Eden, at the Yalta conference in February 1945 that the military responsibility for Gorizia/Gorica and Trieste should fall to the Americans and British and that Yugoslavian Prime Minister Joseph Tito's forces were given the responsibility to the east of these areas. On the 1st of May 1945, however, the Yugoslav army took over the majority of Trieste, soon followed by New Zealand troops. Trieste was held under Yugoslav control until the 12th of June, something called the "Forty days of Trieste" in Italian history (Sluga 2001:83–85). During this period there were many reports of partisans seeking out former fascists and any kind of nationalist manifestation was banned (Sluga 2001:89). Arrests and deportation of Germans and Italian fascists were carried out but there were also reports of executions by the Yugoslav army with some sources claiming that 6,000 people had been arrested in Gorizia/ Gorica and Trieste of which 4,150 were released, 1,850 were deported and 1,150 went missing. Later studies of these claims have suggested that the number of missing people was much lower but it is very difficult to know exactly what happened during the first chaotic days following the area's liberation (Sluga 2001:91).

During negotiations in May and June 1945 it was decided that the area around Trieste would be divided into two sections Zone A, which included the city of Trieste, which would be run by the Allies, and Zone B, including the Istrian coast, excluding Pula, would be under Yugoslavian government. The border between Italy and Yugoslavia that was agreed upon was to be known as the 'Morgan Line', proposed by British General William Duthie Morgan and this was the international border between Italy and Yugoslavia from 1945 to 1947 (Bufon and Minghi 2000:122). Establishing the location of the southern section of the Slovenian/Italian border, especially around Trieste, was highly complex and this remained an unsettled area for several decades. The location of the Italian-Yugoslavian border was established at a high political level by the allies. The idea was that this section of the border was to be established following ethnic distribution and ethnicity was mainly decided through language. In many areas, such as around Gorizia/Gorica, the border was therefore established between Romance (Italian) and Slavic (Slovenian and Croatian) speaking population (Bufon and Minghi 2000: 120, for a discussion on how this division was portrayed in the media at the

4: CASE STUDY 1: THE ITALIAN/SLOVENIAN BORDER

time see Mihelj 2012). At the Paris Peace Treaties of 1947 it was decided that Trieste would remain a free port, called the Free Territory of Trieste, which would continue to be run as two zones: Zone A under Anglo-American military administration and Zone B under Yugoslavian as a temporary solution (Sluga 2001:141) (Figure 17). After several years of tension between Italian, Slovene and Croatian groups, a permanent solution was reached in 1954 where the border was adjusted in some areas. Zone A that had so far been governed by the allies was assigned to Italy and the allied troops that had been a part of everyday life in the zone left in 1955. It was, however, not until 1975 that the border was officially accepted by both Italy and Yugoslavia through the Treaty of Osimo (Bufon and Minghi 2000:120).

Following the change of borders after World War II large, previously Italian, areas fell within Yugoslavian territory and around 100,000 people who considered themselves Italian emigrated to Italy from Istria (Ballinger 2003:89). Many ended up in Trieste and refugee camps were established here to house people coming over the border.

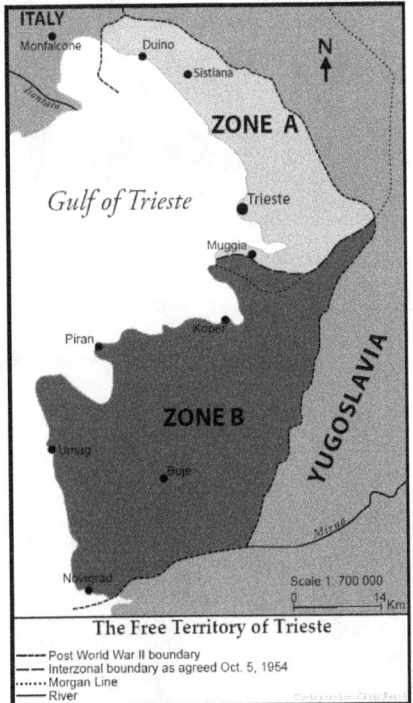

Figure 17: The Free Territory of Trieste.

Map: Chris Beach.

One city becomes two

After the location of the border had been established a commission was given the task of physically marking the new borderline on the ground. This was done by painting a line or through staking out poles (Figure 18-19). Although some consideration was shown to keep villages and cities together this did not always work in practice and villages and sometimes even single farms were cut through by the new border. In the study area many local stories tell of how landowners would go out during the first few nights after the border was marked and move the border markers in one direction or other so that their property would fall within one country. Soon, however, both Yugoslavian and Italian military arrived to patrol the borders making further changes impossible. Further border structures, fencing and even mines in places were soon installed to make crossing more difficult (Veluščk and Medved 2002).

Figure 18: Poles marking the new border line are erected by a group of workers in front of Nova Gorica railway station, 1947. Property of Musei provinciali di Gorizia, Italy.

Figure 19: The new border line between Italy and Yugoslavia is being painted by an American Soldier near in the village of Šempeter, 1947. Property of Musei provinciali di Gorizia, Italy.

4: CASE STUDY 1: THE ITALIAN/SLOVENIAN BORDER

When Gorizia/Gorica fell within Italian territory a large section of its hinterland, now within Yugoslavian territory, was suddenly without a centre. Apart from Solkan and Šempeter, which were only small villages, the majority of the land within the now Yugoslavian territory consisted of farmland (Figure 20). The railway station, the northern of Gorizia/Gorica's two stations, was the only infrastructure that had been given to Yugoslavia. A new Gorizia or Nova Gorica as it was called in Slovenian was to be built. Youth groups were brought from all over Yugoslavia to help with the building of this town. Many of the local people also took part in the work. According to the information and reports presented in the papers about the project at the time the workers were helping out as volunteers due to their conviction and belief in the socialist system. Historian Drago Sedmak, who works at the Goriški Musej Archive, explains however that for many it was more of an opportunity to work as food and three meals per day were provided (Drago Sedmak, 2011, pers. comm. 1st August). Pictures from the time show how the open fields were drained and how streets, streetlights and buildings etc. developed into what was to become Nova Gorica. In the period after the new border had been established times were difficult also in Gorizia as many of its producers of goods or customers no longer could get here. Over time new networks were developed on both sides of the border which came to separate the two towns more and more until they operated almost independently of each other.

Today a walk through the towns of Gorizia and Nova Gorica demonstrate their very different development. Gorizia with its windy, cobbled roads and sometimes highly narrow alleys demonstrates the slow, organic development the town has had. Old maps of the town show how the city started on the fortified hill above the current town and slowly spread downwards and outwards. Nova Gorica, on the other hand, shows all the signs of a planned town with its straight and broad streets crossing each other at straight angles. Nova Gorica is laid out in a grid with roads running in straight lines from north to south and from east to west. The exception is Ejavčeva Ulica which stretches from the San Gabriele crossing and Gorizia into the heart of Nova Gorica in a southwest–northeast direction. This was the original road heading out of Gorizia/Gorica eastwards and out to what used to be the town's former cemetery. This older road stands in contrast to the rest of Nova Gorica's planned and organised layout. The roads in Nova Gorica are not narrow and windy as in Gorizia but straight and wide. Over the decades since it was established the town has stretched out in all directions, the different building phases visible within its fabric: the municipal building, the first to be built, together with its immediately surroundings by the road Kidričeva Ulica; the first high rise blocks built in the 1960s to the south of the original cluster; and the recent suburbs expanding along the edges of the city all represent parts of the towns short history. I do not get lost in Nova Gorica but in Gorizia I lose my way all the time, taking a shortcut that leads somewhere completely different. The different stories of these two towns are apparent in their composition and their differences are the consequence of the border imposed on the area in 1947.

Figure 20: Picture of the area soon to become Nova Gorica photographed in 1947. The crossing in the picture is today the corner between the streets of Erjavčeva ulica and Škabrijelova ulica. Property of Goriški Muzej, Nova Gorica, Slovenia

A border in constant change
"A soldier is a soldier, fear is fear and life is life"
(Veluščdek and Medved 2002)

Between 1946 and 1948 security was at its highest with Yugoslavian authorities establishing a 5 km security zone along the border. The border was patrolled and soldiers had orders to shoot at anyone trying to cross. Mines and signals were placed by the border in the evenings and were removed in the mornings. Often both the people trying to cross illegally and the guards patrolling the border were armed which created a major insecurity on both parties and a risk of being shot or shooting someone yourself. Often just the insecurity itself led to shootings. It was not unusual for gunfire to be heard near the border, particularly at night and in the mornings bodies were removed by the guards (Velušček and Medved 2002). The borders were heavily guarded on both sides and even if particular passes and visas were given to people who lived near the border these crossings were heavily regulated. People from other parts of Yugoslavia or from further east in Europe were often denied visas to cross. In 1948 Yugoslavia was expelled from Cominform, the organisation of communist parties dominated by the Soviet Union, following a resolution in Bucharest on the 28th June (Benson 2004:94). After the break with the Soviet Union in 1948 there was some relaxing of the border security, however, during the 1950s the border was still intensely patrolled and those people within the area who were considered suspicious were often brought in for questioning. This could include people working in the area who had to be able to identify themselves when asked. Many people used the border to Italy as an escape route from the Eastern bloc. During the 1960s and onwards the security at the border was slowly toned down. This coincided with the economic upswing seen in Yugoslavia during the 1960s which led to more open borders and increased trade and exchange with Western Europe.

The Osimo Treaty that signed on 10 November 1975 in order to finally settle the border between Italy and Yugoslavia and deal with several problematic areas where tension had been rising along the border established in 1954. Although the border had been recognised and established at the Memorandum of London, in which Zone A, previously under allied government, was handed over to Italy there had been many disputes regarding the validity of the border. Its problematic route through mixed ethnic areas made it subject to constant challenge from both Italian and Yugoslavian sides (Ballinger 2003:92). Through the Osimo Treaty Italy and Yugoslavia agreed to a few adjustments to the border line to solve particular problems caused by the border. Examples of two of these changes can be seen in the study area. The first was of more practical nature along the border by Nova Gorica railway station where the border was moved a few metres eastwards in order to create more space on the Italian side. This was to make the streets here more accessible to larger vehicles, such as emergency services. The second change was seen on the top of Mount Sabotino/Sabotin where the border was again moved eastwards in one section so that it ran along the top of the mountain. This was a trade in order for Yugoslavia to be granted the rights to build a road corridor through a small section of Italian territory. This road was to be called Strada di Osimo in Italian and Osimska cesta in Slovenian and was opened in 1985. Apart from a better view to the east of the mountain, there were no great advantages to Italy gaining the extra land, however, Mount Sabotino/Sabotin has been of great symbolic importance to Italy since the First World War when their troops fought here. The change in border position was therefore not of great strategic importance here but had more of a symbolic value (Drago Sedmak, 2011, pers. comm. 1st August).

Even though conditions changed throughout the 20th century and security was subsequently scaled down this border remained more guarded and controlled than most of the borders in Western Europe until the 1990s. The security along these borders therefore changed gradually throughout the latter part of the 20th century. The fall of the Berlin Wall and the opening of the former Iron Curtain in many other parts of former Eastern Europe in 1989 meant that Yugoslavia's position as "straddling the fault line between east and west" became even more clear (Benson 2004:155). While other newly formed states in former Eastern Europe experienced a peaceful transition to independence, the so called Velvet Revolution, the Yugoslavian path to independence was reached through conflict and war two years later. 1989 was a defining year which brought major changes to borders between Eastern and Western Europe and therefore had very little effect on the border between Italy and Yugoslavia. Although Slovenia gained independence in 1991, the border's character did not change much at this point, instead the largest changes were seen in 2004 and 2007 when Slovenia joined the European Union and the Schengen Convention respectively.

On the 14th of February 2004 BBC News reported on the Cold War fence being removed between Italy and Slovenia which referred to the removal of fences between Nova Gorica and Gorizia two days earlier. Large crowds on both sides of the border watched as the mayors of both towns dismantled what BBC referred to as "One of Europe's last symbols of Cold War-era division" (BBC News 2004). The border was removed under major festivities. Gorizia's mayor stated "Today we are tearing down a real wall, but our hope is that a mental barrier will also be knocked down" (BBC News 2004). When Slovenia joined Schengen on the 21st of December 2007 the mayors of the two towns met yet again on the border to celebrate the abolishment of barriers between the two countries. Although checks had been carried out on people crossing the border right up until midnight, as the clocks turned twelve the mayors lifted the barrier at the Casa Rossa/ Rožna Dolina crossing, removing a barrier that had divided the town for 60 years. For the first time since WWII it now became possible to cross this line without showing any documents (Figure 21).

4: CASE STUDY 1: THE ITALIAN/SLOVENIAN BORDER

Figure 21: People at the international border crossing in Rožna Dolina on the night between 20th and 21st of December 2007 celebrating the end of border controls as Slovenia entered Schengen. The boy holds up an obituary of the border stating: After being a way of life this border, ours and yours (Italian and Slovenian) has, seized to exist 1947 – 2007. We say goodbye on Thursday, 12.22. at 00:00. Left mourning are: smugglers, refugees, border guards. Property of Goriški Muzej, Nova Gorica, Slovenia.

The material

Remains of the former militarised border

I travel along the border of Italy and Slovenia. I drive along it, at times I walk along it. I cross it, both by car and on foot. I photograph it, I draw it and sometimes I sit down and just look at it. Nobody takes any notice of me and I am never stopped in my work by any representatives of any official body. Generally I do not see any people around the border at all unless someone is in the process of crossing it themselves. There is a sense of quietness and calm resting over the border areas; nothing is really going on here. They are places of very little interest to people. This is an interesting contrast to the previous high levels of interest in these borderland areas, especially when they were created after World War II, and the surveillance they and any people moving near them were subjected to. In the study area the border passes through both the valley created by the Isonzo/Soča river and Mount Sabotino/Sabotin that rises to a height of 609 m above sea level just north of Solkan, once a village and now a suburb to Nova Gorica. The border runs through urban areas, in and around the two towns of Gorizia and Nova Gorica, and rural areas. The border passes through industrial areas, agricultural areas, woodlands and steep cliffs. The character of the landscape changes but the white border stones persist along the route. Although the white border stones have stayed consistent since the border was established after World War II the character of the border areas has changed considerably. These areas, at least on the Yugoslavian side, used to be under high surveillance. In some areas, such as urban areas, fences and barriers were used to help guard the border. As time went on and requirements changed, so did the materiality of the border. So are there any traces of these changing landscapes visible to us today?

In the company of saints and bunkers

The road to the top of Mount Sabotino/Sabotin twists and turns up a steep incline like a serpent, climbing higher with every bend. Thick woodlands cover large areas but at times the landscape opens up to reveal some extensive views before the road becomes enclosed by woodland again. Small villages surrounded by farmed terraces are dotted along the road. To get from the town of Nova Gorica to these hill settlements you have to cross Italian territory. A road corridor was built here in 1985 to aid access before which people had to go around the other side of the mountain making the road substantially longer. A section of the Slovenian hinterland was cut off after World War II by a barrier of Italian territory making it highly remote. Only after the Treaty of Osimo was signed in 1975 could negotiations of a road corridor through Italian territory start. Although it took several years for these negotiations to be finalised, ironing out issues such as how to deal with accidents or breakdowns within the road corridor, it was finally opened to traffic in 1985 (Figure 22). Still today this road is completely cut off from the surrounding landscape by high concrete walls on both sides making it impossible to divert at any point until inside Slovenian territory. The purpose of this corridor is to get people from one side to the other with no distractions. The high walls on the side allows no views into the surrounding landscape but channels sight as well as movement straight ahead through the corridor to Slovenian territory on the other side. No stopping is allowed. This whole section of road is, in fact, completely designed to move people along and only once inside Slovenian territory does the landscape open up, again allowing for views and free movement.

4: CASE STUDY 1: THE ITALIAN/SLOVENIAN BORDER

During the Cold War the section of the mountain closest to the border was a closed military area both on the Yugoslavian and the Italian side. Soon after the village of Gonjače a road leads up to the top of the mountain and large concrete roadblocks that were once part of a barrier system here to control movement of vehicles in and out of this closed area are now placed on the side of a car park to make sure nobody drives too close to the steep mountain edge.

At the end of this road, near the ridge of the mountain, former Yugoslavian barracks are located 266 m from the border with Italy. No information about these barracks are available in local archives and as most of the guards who were stationed here came from other parts of Yugoslavia not much is known of the place by people living locally. On the side of the entrance to the barracks I find a gate barrier discarded on the ground. It is blue, white and red with a faded red star on the square weight (Figure 23). In its original place there is now an iron gate, stopping any approaching vehicles.

Just on the other side of the gate there is a small guard hut, now without direct purpose. The compound is not very large and consists only of two buildings, 12x16 m and 9x15 m, and a large platform, 80x25 m at the widest point, out front where several commemorative stones to the First World War are located. The former Yugoslavian military barracks near the border are not big enough to have housed a large group of border guards but facilitated a constant, small scale border control force. Facilities to entertain the guards can be seen in the basketball court still painted on the forecourt to the barracks suggesting they spent time here when they were not in service (Figure 24). The basketball nets have been removed but their position is still clear in the ground where the metal poles have been cut off and are now rusting into the tarmac. On the side of the basketball pitch seats for viewers have been built into the slope behind it. A small museum is held in one of the buildings with some objects relating to the First World War history in the area but it was closed during my visits, both in 2008 and in 2011, and therefore not possible to gain access to.

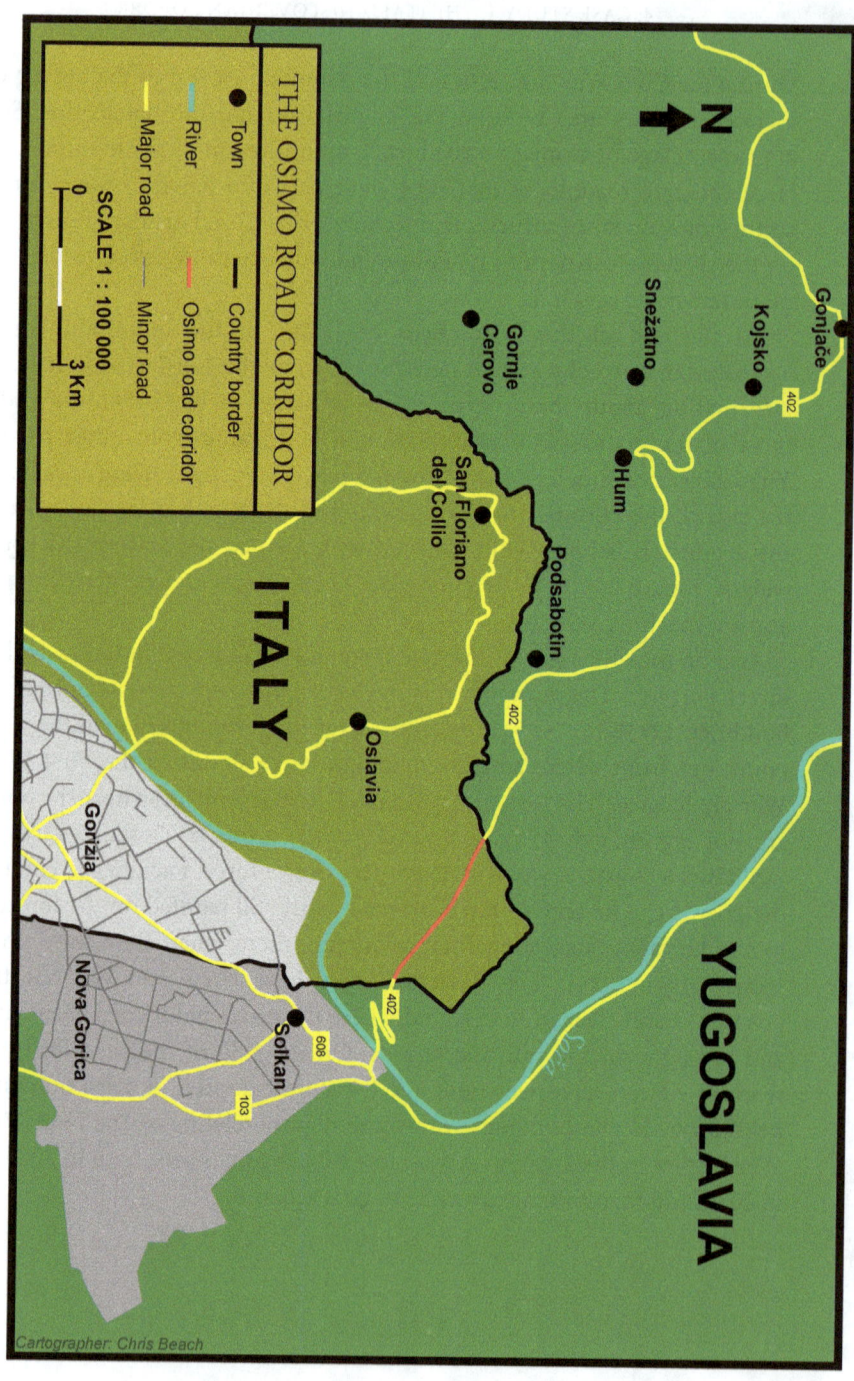

Figure 22: Map of Osimo corridor. Map: Chris Beach.

Figure 23 a and b: Discarded road barrier and close-up of red star painted on its weight by the former Yugoslavian border guard station on top of Mount Sabotino/Sabotin. Photos: Anna McWilliams 2008.

Figure 24: Former Yugoslavian border guard station with basketball court in the foreground and buildings in the background. First World War memorial stones can be seen at the back by the flagpoles. Photo: Anna McWilliams 2011.

Directly north of the compound, where the ground slopes downwards in a steep decline large systems of trenches from the First World War are located. To the south there are several paths leading up towards the top of the mountain and the border. The border is marked by white border stones which in part follows the ridge of the mountain following the 1975 Osimo Treaty when the border was moved here. They are located at a close distance from each other, sometimes as close as 10 m as the direction of the border, and the ridge of the mountain, constantly changes. Two tracks run here, one on each side of the boundary, created by Italian and Yugoslavian border guards patrolling their side of the border, not allowed to cross the border even by a step (Figure 25). The duality of the paths are still visible but are soon disappearing as the tracks now have a different purpose, allowing ramblers to climb the mountain with no restrictions of what side of the border to walk on. These tracks, created by the actions of people demonstrate that high fences do not always have to be present in order for a clear boundary line to exist. It is intriguing to imagine how patrols were carried out as the guards would have to walk so very close to each other. It was important to keep the sides at peace and not risk any confrontations of the border guards whilst working in such proximity. It was therefore, at least during the latter part of the Cold War period, a well worked out schedule, agreed by both sides, of when the different patrols were carried out. That way run-ins could be avoided (Drago Sedmak, 2011, pers. comm. 1st August).

Mount Sabotino/Sabotin shows the layers of different eras like nowhere else in the study area. On its southern most point, on what is called Saint Valentine's Peak, I find the ruins of a 14th century pilgrimage church run by Franciscan monks. This church was used for worship until 1782 when it closed down. After this the church was abandoned and left to ruin. Many of the walls of the complex were, however, still standing at the start of the First World War but the fierce battles here accelerated its ruination and little remained of the pilgrimage church after the troops left. In 1999–2000 excavations were carried out on the site and parts of the former church have been restored to better demonstrate what it used to look like (Andrej Malnič, 2011, pers. comm. 5th August). The border runs through the church complex leaving the church buildings in Slovenian territory whilst the monks' residential premises are located in Italy.

Mount Sabotino/Sabotin was a strategic point during the First World War as it was part of the Isonzo front, a natural obstacle reinforced by the Austrians to stop the Italians from reaching the river directly to its east. The Isonzo/Soča river has its starting point further up in the Alps and runs at the bottom of the Mount Sabotino/Sabotin before it heads south through the Italian countryside and eventually finds its way out into the Adriatic sea near the town of Monfalcone. During the twelve battles of the Isonzo the Italian army slowly took the mountain into possession. The armies used natural cave formations in the mountain but also built extensive trench systems along its ridges, many of these are still visible today. Also the remains of the pilgrim church was used which can be seen in a cave just underneath the church which has a reinforced entrance of concrete. Most of the bunkers located on the mountain date from this period even though a few of them have been improved for use much later. The Habsburg army's defences were often more substantial in their construction, often reinforced with concrete. This is not surprising as they had more time to construct their defences in contrast to the Italian army which advanced forward into enemy territory. The Austrian defences and trenches were, however, often used by the Italian troops as they had taken over an area. When advancing the Italian army used many of the trenches and defences that had previously belonged to their enemy.

Many of these constructions, especially some of the reinforced caves, bunkers and lookout posts were later used by the Italian and Yugoslavian border guards as they patrolled the border on the mountain. Messages from these guards can still be seen in the many of the structures today in the names and number of days of service remaining that are scratched into the walls and ceilings of the bunkers or even painted in red paint inside one of the reinforced caves (Figure 26).

Figure 25 (left): Dual paths on Mount Sabotino/Sabotin. Photo: Anna McWilliams 2008.

Figure 26 (right): Graffiti painted and scratched into the sides of a reinforced entrance to a natural cave underneath the remains of a 14th century pilgrimage church, Mount Sabotino/Sabotin. 2011. Photo: Anna McWilliams 2011.

Four bunkers were recorded during the survey on the mountain. One bunker, located inside Slovenian territory, is square in shape, approximately 2.5 by 3.5 m in size, constructed from red bricks with a cement bonding. The outside is plastered with white cement whilst the inside is grey. The ceiling is made out of a coarse pebble mortar. The door to this lookout post faces north. Two of the bunkers, one located on Slovenian and one on Italian territory are hexagonal in shape, also constructed out of red bricks with a grey coarse cement cladding on the outside and painted white on the inside. All three bunkers have rectangular windows at the top part of the structure with the remnants of a wooden frame still present. The window frames have traces of hinges still attached to them suggesting some kind of window or shutter was once present. These have subsequently been removed. One bunker is more recent than the others and has had electricity installed, something not available in the others (Figure 27). This bunker dates to the Cold War period. It is round in shape and has three windows facing north, east and south whilst the bunker is entered from a west-facing door. On the concrete steps the year 1977 has been scratched whilst the concrete was still supple enough for such treatment. Although this date cannot be completely trusted as it could have been added later other facts do point to this being a likely time for its construction. The bunker's location is of major importance as this section of the mountain belonged to Yugoslavia until 1975 when it was handed over to Italy as part of the Treaty of Osimo. This structure was likely to have been built to provide shelter for the soldiers closer to the border and as a lookout point closer to the new outline of the border, however, being so visible to the Yugoslavians would also suggest that it was a way of marking their new territory.

Figure 27: Italian bunker located on Mount Sabotino/Sabotin dating to the cold war period.

Photo: Anna McWilliams 2008.

150 m down the mountain from this newer Italian bunker was the Italian military headquarters on the mountain. It was not possible to access this site and therefore it had to be viewed from a distance. Being smaller than the Yugoslavian headquarters it could only have hosted a small number of border guards. This complex was much easier to reach from the town than the Yugoslavian barracks, which until the road corridor was built through Italian territory had to use the longer road on the eastern side of Mount Sabotino/Sabotin. Therefore the Italian border guards would have been able

to reach their barracks much faster from the town than the Yugoslavian guards, making less of a necessity to house any more than a small number of soldiers here.

Patrolling the city

Evidence of military and border police surveillance is also visible in the urban areas of the study area. The absence of structures near the border also demonstrates surveillance infrastructure. This is apparent on the former Yugoslavian side of the border in the town of Nova Gorica where a strip of land, directly east of the border to Italy, has been kept open within this urban area. Some of these strips followed former roads as well as a disused railway track of the former Transalpine Railway. Keeping an area open directly by the border by preventing any construction here made illegal crossing more difficult and helped to facilitate the patrolling of the border. These long, former patrolling tracks have now been made into cycle paths stretching almost the entire length of the town (Figure 28).

Figure 28: Cycle path along the border between Gorizia and Nova Gorica. Borderline runs along the brick wall to the left of the path.

Photo: Anna McWilliams 2008.

4: CASE STUDY 1: THE ITALIAN/SLOVENIAN BORDER

If you follow these former patrol paths south from Nova Gorica, past Šempeter you reach a watchtower approximately 10 m high, constructed of red bricks and cement (Figure 29). It stands 115 m back from the border surrounded by fields. The landscape around here is very flat. The director of the Goriški Musej, Andrej Malnič, and two local historians, Ingela Brezigar and Jacob Marušič, explain that they do not know the date of when the watchtower was built as this was classified information and they still have not been able to find any official records about it. It is believed it was built during the 1950s. The watchtower has now been made into a museum about the border. A spiral staircase has been added for the safety of visitors but the original steps, sticking out from the wall, still remain. Pictures of American soldiers marking out the border line, border guards patrolling the border or of signs and barbed wire now cover the inside of the walls in the tower as part of the museum display. The viewing platform has been left largely as found. Also in this place graffiti has been left by Yugoslavian soldiers, counting down the days left of their one year service. Watchtowers can be found along the border although they are not a common feature. Within the study area there is only this one structure purposely built as a watchtower remaining. Lookout points housed in already existing buildings and structures were common, many of which may still be standing but as no official documents are available and the buildings take on new functions the knowledge of them is disappearing. Natural heights, such as the surrounding hills were also used as lookout points (Figure 30).

Figure 29a (left) and 29b (right): Watchtower south of Nova Gorica with graffiti left by soldiers still visible.

Photos: Anna McWilliams 2008.

Other military functions and facilities were housed in already existing buildings. On the transalpine square where the border went right across the square in front of what is now the Nova Gorica train station, the Italian border police installed a head quarter in what was previously a residential building. Photos from the late 1940s when the building was used as headquarters show that no major changes were made to this building, at least on the outside (Figure 31). The building has since been converted back to a residential building and today it does not show any traces of its military history within its fabric.

Figure 30: A Yugoslavian border guard of the partisan of the Border Units of the Yugoslav national army, on guard duty on Kostanjevica hill. Property of Goriški Muzej, Nova Gorica, Slovenia.

Figure 31: Headquarters of the Italian Customs Service at the corner of the streets of Caprin and Percoto towards at the end of the 1940s. Two guards and a piece of the barbed wire at the State border between the Federative People's Republic of Yugoslavia and the Republic of Italy can be seen to the far right. Property of Musei provinciali di Gorizia, Italy.

The physical border

When you move around in the borderland terrain it is generally fairly easy to see where the border is with the boundary itself still clearly marked in the terrain through white painted, concrete blocks, as in fact along many borders across Europe. Many of these stones show signs of modification as the name of the country has been changed to adjust to new political conditions (Figure 32).

Figure 32: Border stone where the name of the country has been modified using cement following the independence of Slovenia.

Photo: Anna McWilliams 2008.

Maps dating to the 1950s which have the stones' number and location on them show that the stones have not changed position. In some places they are more frequent, like on Mount Sabotino/Sabotin near Nova Gorica, where the stones are located about 10 m from each other (Figure 33). This can be compared to the border near Trieste where the border stones are much less regular. This is due to the fact that the border stones are located where the border changes direction. The border stones are markers to demonstrate where the limit of one country's territory stops and another starts. In contrast to the signs often placed along borders, to inform a person that they are about to step into another states territory or possibly a prohibition of doing so, the border stones are intended just as a marker. The border stones are the physical manifestation of land agreements reached in negotiations when new boundaries are established. They mark these borders in the terrain to make sure there is no ambiguity of where one country's territory ends and another begins. As the border areas in the study area, especially on the Yugoslavian side, were restricted areas for most people, it was mostly the border guards that would see the border stones. In some places, such as on ridge of Mount Sabotino/Sabotin where space was limited on either side of the border, the stones could guide the guards, making sure they did not step over the border. In areas that were not restricted they helped people to make sure not to cross the border by mistake.

Figure 33: Border stones along the ridge of Mount Sabotino/Sabotin. Photo: Anna McWilliams 2008.

When the border was first established it was marked by barbed wire which was kept until 1955 when the border became more permanent. It was later replaced by metal mesh fencing between the towns of Gorizia and Nova Gorica. In some places the border followed already existing walls of houses or land boundaries. These were occasionally reinforced by metal or barbed wiring where the border was considered weak, such as near the Rafut/Pristava crossing where remains of wire fencing on top of an approximately 1.5 m stone wall are still visible. There is also metal fencing topped with, now decaying with rust, barbed wire along the border between the Rafut/Pristava and the San Gabrielle/Erjavčeva ulica crossing (Figure 35). The barbed wire still continued to be used as a border marker in more rural areas.

Figure 34: Barbed wire across the roads San Gabriele/Erjavčeva ulica in the 1950s. Property of Musei provinciali di Gorizia, Italy.

Even in places where material remains of the border itself do not linger to inform us about their previous presence we can still be reminded of its location through the imprint it has made on the landscape. Looking at Google Earth it is often easy to trace the line of the border even without the actual borderline superimposed. The cut-off point between two states can in this way often be seen through the changes it has made in the landscape, for example through different agricultural use. The agricultural fields around San Pietro/Šempeter, for example, clearly show the variation between the fields on the Slovenian and the Italian side where the border cuts through what was previously larger fields creating smaller and less regular fields around the border line itself. In other places it is represented by a previous road since discontinued on the other side of the border. This is the case near the village of San Pietro the Italian version of Šempeter, located just across the border. The two parts of what used to be one village was previously connected with a road that has since become redundant (Figure 36).

Figure 35a (above left) and 35b (above right): Barbed wire along the border near the San Gabriele/Erjavčeva ulica crossing. Photo: Anna McWilliams 2008.

Figure 36 Picture of discontinued road between Šempeter in Slovenia and San Pietro in Italy once the same village. Photo: Anna McWilliams 2011.

Signs

As we have seen border stones and signs had different purposes with signs aimed at informing. As movement along the borders in the study area was highly controlled it was important to inform people of what areas were restricted and which areas could be accessed. Also it was important to inform people on how to behave within the areas they could access. Although more abundant in the past the presence of signage is still apparent in the landscape and often demonstrates attempts to keep people out of the border area. These signs were installed to inform anyone approaching of the distance to or the exact location of the borderline and were more common in some areas than in others. Especially in areas where people came closer to the border, for example where the border ran near towns or villages, there was an increased need to inform people. From studying photographs from the area at the Goriški Musej Archives it becomes clear that the signs also changed throughout time. During the early period between 1947–1954 when Anglo-American forces were present as peace keepers in the area many of the signs within Zone A were written in English as well as the standard Slovenian and Italian. Later as the Anglo-American forces were removed from the area there was no need for English signs. Although the signs were much more frequent in the past several of them still remain. On the Carso/Karst area near Trieste a sign with information in both Italian and Slovenian and with an empty space where a third, English, sign had been removed is still *in situ* (Figure 37). On the Italian side there were also many signs scattered across the border landscape forbidding photography, filming, drawing or the use of binoculars within the border areas. These signs were written in Italian and had a map to demonstrate the area that was off limits for photographing, filming, drawing or using binoculars (Figure 38). At border crossings there were signs informing on the presence of police and customs and how to approach these.

At the border museum located in Nova Gorica railway station several signs that used to be located on the Yugoslavian and subsequently the Slovenian side are displayed. The signs on the Yugoslavian side were mostly written in Slovenian, apart from signs by border crossings. The most common signs along the border were those warning about the border or indicating the limit of a military area, such as those located by Nova Gorica Railway station. After Slovenian independence the Slovenian coat of arms at the top of the sign was placed on top of the Yugoslavian. The main difference between the signs available today and those in the past is that today there is no need to discourage people from crossing the border. Instead signs are used to inform those crossing of the rules and laws within the territory they are about to enter, such as speed regulations and toll requirements for the motorways. To the contrary many, unofficial signs, from casinos and shops are now encouraging people to cross. Away from the border crossings there are very few signs today informing on the border's presence.

Figure 37: Sign in the Carso/Karst area near Trieste. The former English sign in the middle has been removed.

Photo: Anna McWilliams 2008.

Figure 38: Italian sign warning against photography, filming, drawing or the use of binoculars. Property of Musei provinciali di Gorizia, Italy.

Crossing over

The border crossings were the most commonplace where people came in contact with the border. No matter if the crossing was an indefinite one or if it was only crossing for a few hours, any legal crossing had to go through these points. The layout of the border crossings entitled the guards to investigate documentation and search cars before letting people pass or making them turn back. Apart from checking papers and passports the border guards also checked the vehicles to make sure they corresponded with the paperwork presented through inspecting and registering the chassis number of the cars (Figure 39).

4: CASE STUDY 1: THE ITALIAN/SLOVENIAN BORDER

Figure 39: Car being checked before crossing the border at Casa Rossa/Rožna Dolina. Both registration number and chassis number is being checked. Property of Goriški Muzej, Nova Gorica, Slovenia.

When the border was established in 1947 two types of crossings were opened, one for farmers who owned land on both sides of the border and one for international crossings. In 1955 agreements were reached between the Italian and Yugoslavian governments which allowed people living in a 10 km radius of the border to cross on a more regular basis using a particular pass, Lasciapassare/Prepustnica (Bufon 1996:249). This meant a third type of crossing was created for local traffic. The earliest crossing points consisted of barriers across existing roads with often just a small wooden hut or structure for the guards. At the international crossing points these stations usually had many buildings to house offices, customs and border guards and often several lanes to route traffic through as demands on these crossings were higher. At smaller, local crossings, there was often just one structure with a roofed area extending over the road so that inspections could easily be carried out in any type of weather. Gates and roadblocks were placed in the road.

Name	Type	Comment
San Mauro/Šentmaver	Crossing for farmers	
Salcano/Solkan 1	Crossing for farmers	
Salcano/Solkan 2	Local crossing	
San Gabriele/Erjavčeva ulica	Local crossing	Until 2007 only possible to cross on foot or bicycle
Rafut/Pristava	Crossing for farmers, after 1955 also Local crossing	
Casa Rossa/Rožna Dolina	International crossing	Opened in September 1947
San Pietro/Šeptember	Crossing for farmers, after 1955 also Local crossing	
San Andrea/Vrtojba 1	International crossing	Opened in 1985
San Andrea/Vrtojba 2	Crossing for farmers	
Merna/Miren	Crossing for farmers, after 1955 also Local crossing	

Figure 40: Table of crossings in the study area.

In the study area there were ten crossing points of these three different types, two international, five local crossings and three crossings especially for farmers who owned land on both sides of the border (Figure 40). Until 1985 Casa Rossa/Rožna Dolina was the largest border crossing as it was the main thoroughfare for international traffic in the area. This meant that it was the busiest border crossing and at times, particularly in the late 1940s and the 50s there could be long queues of cars waiting to cross. On the Italian side of the Rožna Dolina crossing, several restaurants and cafes grew up to cater for the people waiting to cross (Figure 42). Since the development of the crossing St Andrea/Vrtojba 1 (Figure 43), which was ready to receive traffic in 1981, created a much more effective link between the major roads of Italy with those in Slovenia, the interest in the area around the Casa Rossa/Rožna Dolina crossing much declined. After the crossing policies changed with Slovenia's entry to the EU and Schengen the traffic that goes through this crossing now pass without any obstacles. What was once a busy place with many travellers passing through is now quiet. Many of the businesses have closed down or moved to more attractive areas.

Figure 41. Border crossing at Salcano/Solkan 1 in the 1950s. Picture taken from Italian side with Mount Sabotin/Sabotino in the background. Property of Musei provinciali di Gorizia, Italy.

Figure 42: Casa Rossa/Rožna Dolina crossing.

Photo: Anna McWilliams 2008.

Figure 43: Site visit to San Andrea/Vrtojba 1 during its construction in 1981. Property of Goriški Muzej, Nova Gorica, Slovenia.

Many of the buildings at the crossings remain today but their usage has mostly changed. Most appear abandoned while a small number have been converted for domestic or official use. At the former crossing points in the study area the buildings are still standing but are no longer used. At the crossings by Casa Rossa/Rožna Dolina and San Andrea/Vrtojba 1 the border police still have a presence but it is much scaled down and the majority of the time there is no staff to be seen. During my two fieldwork visits to the area I passed the border numerous times and was never stopped. Only on a couple occasions did I actually see any border staff near the border. At the Casa Rossa/Rožna Dolina crossing the cars are still directed through lanes but all road blocks and barriers have been removed. At San Pietro/Šempeter most of the crossing infrastructure has been removed on the Slovenian side and the only traces that remain are marks in the ground from the roof that previously stretched across the road here. The building that was previously used for the border guards here now look like any other building in this domestic neighbourhood. On the Italian side the previous customs building is abandoned and deteriorating. The roof that previously covered the road on the Italian side has also been removed. The smaller buildings that functioned as customs and border police headquarters at the two Solcano/Solkan crossings, Rafut/Pristava and Merna/Miren are still present but there is no longer any activity here. At Rafut/Pristava there are still barriers on the Italian side (painted in the Italian colours) to stop traffic getting through at what is now a pedestrian crossing. At the San Gabrielle/Erjavčeva ulica crossing there is still a high roof over the Italian side customs buildings (Figure 44). At this same crossing only one of the previous three small huts placed in between oncoming and going traffic remain on the Italian side. Traces of the two other huts can still be seen in the ground where the tarmac has been patched together. All barriers have been removed and the signs that instruct people to stop for customs have been replaced with signs about the speed limits within Italy.

As the border between what is now Slovenia and Italy is more open, crossing the border has become easier and is also encouraged in places. Many border crossings are now unmanned and vegetation is slowly taking over the structures and tarmacked areas. Shops and amenities such as petrol stations and casinos located near border crossings demonstrate how other actors have moved in to supply a new demand as one actor's control of the border decrease and other actors now influence the behaviour by the border.

4: CASE STUDY 1: THE ITALIAN/SLOVENIAN BORDER

Figure 44: San Gabriele/Erjavčeva ulica crossing. Photo: Anna McWilliams 2008.

Many smaller, portable items related to the border have been put on display at the border museum in Nova Gorica. The majority of the items are connected to the border crossings such as uniforms of the border guards, technology used to check people as they crossed the border such as a ray control device for luggage used until 2004. Most of these actually date from after Slovenian independence suggesting that the border is not just something that is connected with the Yugoslavian period. In fact the border guard stations with Italy and Austria became an important stage in the war for Slovenian independence. On the 25th of June 1991 Slovenian guards raised their own flag along the border and took control of the border crossings starting what was to become the ten-day war that was to end with Slovenia's independence (Benson 2004:161). Many pictures of the new flag being raised at border crossings, such as San Pietro/Šempeter as well as on top of Mount Sabotino/Sabotin, at the Goriški Musej Archives demonstrates the importance that is given to this event. Although drastic changes occurred along the borders further north in 1989 the border here stayed the same until 2004 when Slovenia joined the EU. The border control was, however, much scaled down at this point as a photo of a volleyball game over the border fence taken in 1995 demonstrates (Figure 45).

Figure 45: Volleyball game played over the border fence at the Transalpine Square in 1995. Property of Goriški Muzej, Nova Gorica, Slovenia.

The border as an advertising point

It was not only in 1991 that the border was used as a stage to broadcast political messages. Along the border between these two towns people have used the border to express their views also in the past. You could almost say that the border became a kind of an advertisement board for 'the other side'. Many photos show how during the period directly after World War II different affiliations were clearly demonstrated. Some people showed their wish to belong to either Italy or Yugoslavia very publicly. This was done through erecting signs and placards and through graffiti on buildings. Some of this graffiti survives today although is now uncommon as houses have been torn down or refurbished (Figure 46). Ethnologist Jonas Frykman has recorded similar messages in today's Croatia (Frykman 2007:91). Pictures found in the Goriški Musej Archives also demonstrate that political messages were also written on the roofs of buildings (Figure 47).

Figure 46: Writing displaying affiliations with Yugoslavia still visible on building in 2011. Writing on the front of the building stating: 'This is Yugoslavia' and writing on the side of the building saying: 'Long live Marshall Tito'.

Photo: Anna McWilliams 2011.

Figure 47: Construction of buildings in Nova Gorica and building with writing on roof in the background stating 'Tito's Party'. Property of Goriški Muzej, Nova Gorica, Slovenia.

The border also became a place to advertise ideological messages. As a symbol of socialism a red star depicting the hammer and sickle was placed on top of Nova Gorica railway station facing Gorizia soon after World War II. The hammer and sickle was subsequently removed as Yugoslavia turned away from the Soviet bloc but the red star remained until the late 1980s. When Yugoslavia's socialist government was no longer in control the red star went through another transformation. During the Christmas of 1991 the star was painted in gold to represent the Star of David, and complemented with a comet by its side. As Christmas was discouraged by the communist government this became a way for people to disassociate themselves with communism and to reclaim Christmas. The star has again been painted red and is now located in the Nova Gorica border museum having found new life as a showpiece of the communist era (Inga Brezigar, 2008, pers. comm. 2nd September) (Figure 48).

Figure 48: Picture of red star formerly placed on top of Nova Gorica railway station, now located in the railway museum. Photo: Anna McWilliams 2008.

When I first looked at Google Earth of the area around Nova Gorica I came across an intriguing feature on top of Mount Sabotino/Sabotin, directly inside Slovenian territory. It looked like writing and I thought I could make out the word Tito although it was not very clear. I found this very curious and on my first visit to the area I was given the following explanation. During the socialist period an area on the top of Mount Sabotino/Sabotin was cleared of vegetation and large white stones were used to spell out the words 'Naš Tito', Our Tito. This was positioned to be seen far into Italian territory as well as in Yugoslavia. Later Italy projected a large Italian flag on the mountain, inside their territory but where it could be seen also in Yugoslavia. After the independence of Slovenia a further battle has been fought within Slovenian territory where supporters of the old regime have on several occasions reconstructed the words Naš Tito. At one point somebody changed the words to Naš Fido, a common name for dogs in Slovenia, in order to make a joke of the original text and of Tito himself (Anja, 2008, pers. comm. 3rd September). This type of expression of views or propaganda was not only directed outwards but also towards the own population. This can be seen near the village of Branik, approximately 15 km south-east of Nova Gorica where the name 'Tito' is still very clear on the side of a hill facing east towards Slovenia (Figure 49).

Figure 49: The name 'Tito' written on side of hill near the village of Branik, Slovenia. Photo: Anna McWilliams 2008.

Resisting the border

Walking along the border north of Gorizia/Nova Gorica the border takes a turn through the edge of the village of Solkan. I had already spotted this on maps and Google Earth before my visit but it was also very clear in the terrain. Rather than following a straight line across the fields and across the Insonzo/Soča River the border suddenly heads east causing one of the properties to be separated from the rest of the village. A high concrete wall runs along the border here and as I walk on the Slovenian side I can barely see the building behind it. The occasional openings in the wall are closed with iron rods and on top of the wall an old string of barbed wire is meant to stop anyone from climbing over. I wonder what has caused this situation and start asking around. It turns out there is a local story about this place and the border here, the story about Countess Liduška. She lived on the estate that this rather grand building belonged to. Towards the end of World War II American soldiers arrived to the area and built a series of barracks near her property. The Countess threw many lavish parties at her estate which many of the soldiers attended. After the war when the new border was drawn the entire village of Solkan fell within Yugoslavian territory, so also the property of the Countess. She, on the other hand, had hopes to remain an Italian citizen and used her influences within the American army to make sure that she did. Consequently the border here was redirected around her property separating it from the rest of the village of Solkan (Anja, 2008, pers. comm. 3rd September). Looking at maps of the area it becomes clear that the border has taken a detour around the property, marked on the map below as *Villa Nordis* (Figure 50).

There are also other stories of locals in one way or another influencing the location of the border, with many through going out in the night and physically moving the poles set out during the day to mark the new border. Looking at old photographs taken by what is now the Rafut/Pristava crossing within Gorizia/Nova Gorica we can see the differences in the location of the border from the first line was drawn to what it looks like now. Looking at it we can see that a farm has been divided in two which is obviously something the bull is ignoring standing with his head in Yugoslavia and his rear end in Italy (Figure 51). Looking at the site today it is possible to see that the border has actually been moved a distance of approximately 50 m to the east. How this was done is not known but it demonstrates that adjustments on the ground were possible as the border was established.

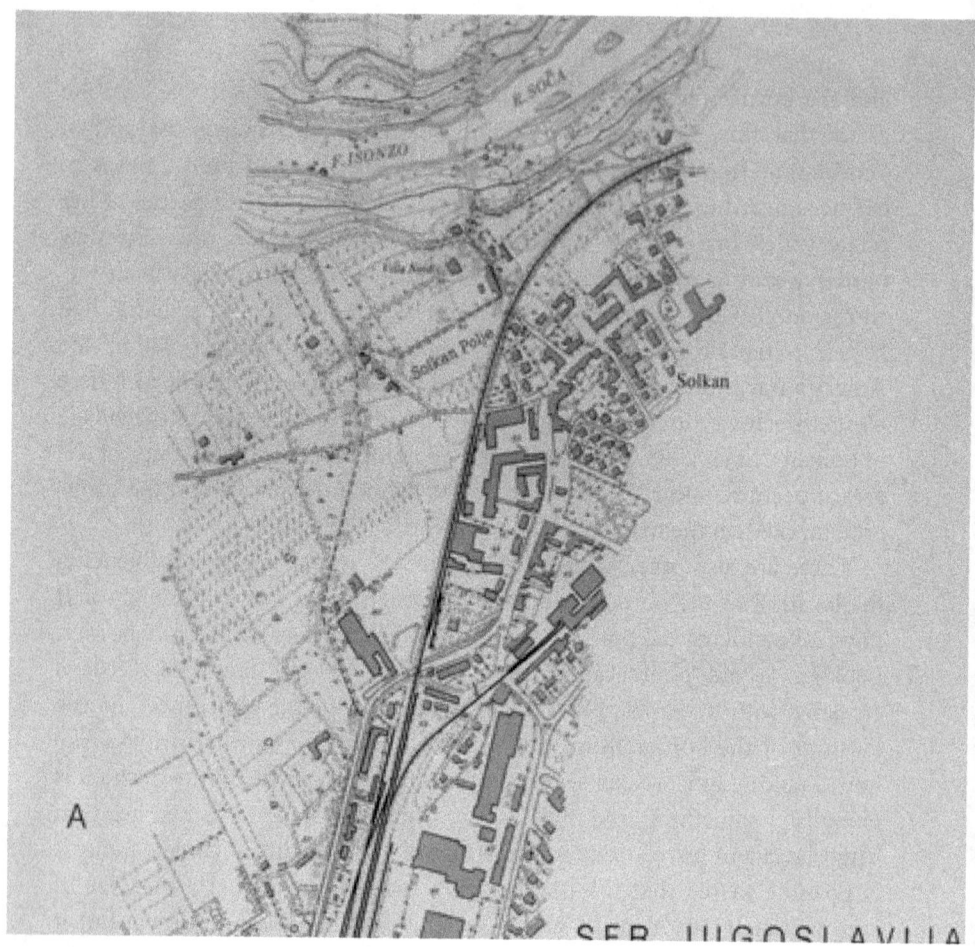

Figure 50: Map demonstrating the borderline (in red) as it runs around Villa Nordis, Countess Liduška's estate. Property of Goriški Muzej, Nova Gorica, Slovenia.

Figure 51: Farm near the Rafut/Pristava crossing divided by the border, 1947. Property of Dino Altran, Gorizia, Italy.

Figure 52: American soldiers marking the new border across Merna/Miren cemetery. Property of Goriški Muzej, Nova Gorica, Slovenia.

Another example of where the new border had almost ridiculous consequences is the village of Merna/Miren, located approximately 2.5 km south of Gorizia. The village was to fall within the Yugoslavian territory but its cemetery, which lay right on the edge of the village, was to be divided. After the new border had been determined a line of barbed wire stretched across the cemetery (Figure 52). One of the stories told here is about a man who lived and eventually died on the Italian side of the border. As he was buried in the cemetery his daughter, who lived over the border in Yugoslavia was allowed to attend the funeral but only if she stayed on the Yugoslavian side (Andrej Malnič, Ingela Brezigar and Jacob Marušič pers. comm. 2008). The border has since been changed here and the whole cemetery now belongs to Slovenian territory but the angle of the former border line is still clear when looking at the markings outside the cemetery. After a period the barbed wire was removed and a system of visiting hours were worked out so that people from Italy could visit during certain times and people from Slovenia during others. One time of year, during All Saints', people could be let in at the same time and these occasions turned into reunions where family and friends met. People also took the opportunity to buy and sell goods (Andrej Malnič, Ingela Brezigar and Jacob Marušič, 2008, pers. comm. 2nd September). Even though the border zone during these times was much more regulated and controlled than it is today it was also, at least at times, a meeting point and a place for people to react against this control. This resulted in there being more activity in the border area than there is today, not just by the military but also by other actors that had an interest here. Wherever you have a border, or any area of control, there will always be people trying to defy that control and push the boundaries. In the study area the new border in 1947 severed a previously homogenous society and caused major difficulties to the people within that society with many trade routes, markets, family ties, and areas cut off. Many people did not let this development happen without pushing the boundaries, sometimes literally, and constantly working towards a more easily manoeuvred border landscape. Sometimes living by a border could be an advantage. When it became easier for locals to cross the border after 1955 people could cross to buy products that may not be available in their own country. Also differences in prices might mean it was cheaper to buy on the other side of the border or to cross it to sell something. For farmers in Yugoslavia, for example, it was more profitable to cross the border and sell their produce in Italy where prices were higher (Janez, 2008, pers. comm. 6th September).

4: CASE STUDY 1: THE ITALIAN/SLOVENIAN BORDER

When I meet with Anja at a café in Solkan she tells me about her own experiences with the border. She was brought up in Nova Gorica and tells me that when she was young in the 1980s her and her friends would always go over to Gorizia to go shopping for branded clothes. This was before outlet shops became common but she tells me of a Benetton store in Gorizia where a lot of the last seasons clothes were put on sale, brought from other Benetton stores in Italy, as people often came over from Yugoslavia to buy them. Shopping is a reoccurring feature when you discuss the border with people and sometimes it appears that the border was a highly useful feature. Cheaper shopping and access to products that would normally not be available is often what people remember. This behaviour is also a type of resistance and manipulation of the border and the authority of the state.

I sit in my hotel room located about 15 m from the border, by the Transalpine Square. The clock has just turned 10 p.m. when I hear tango music drifting into my room. I look out the window and down on the square I see maybe 20 couples dancing to the tango tunes. I walk down to the street and sit down on the curb to enjoy the music and the view of the skilful dancers. "What is this? Why are they dancing here?" I ask a girl next to me. "This border divided people for such a long time", she explains, "We want to show that through peace and passion you can overcome any division of people". A young man comes up and whisks her away to the border that has now been transformed into a dance floor. I realise that resisting the border is not just something of the past, it is still going on.

People and the border

My father was born under Austria, my mother under Italy, me under Yugoslavia and my daughter under Slovenia. We use the word under, not in, as it is meant as being under the rule of. This way of saying under rather than in or from is very typical from this area.

(Andrej Malnič, 2008, pers. comm. 2nd September)

These are the words of Andrej Malnič, director of the Goriški Musej who has grown up in this area. His words demonstrate the mixed background this area has. Looking at the remains of the border structure here I understand that the border has played an important role in the lives of the people in its proximity. I am curious to see what people have to say about it and I meet with Maria and Antonio in Trieste. When I meet Maria she brings along her friend Antonio. They are both Italian and in their 40s. They are both 'Triestini' and know the area well as they were brought up here and they take me to a recreational area near the Slovenian border, on the Carso/Karst, not too far from the town. Their families have very different backgrounds and I notice how that has affected how they speak and think about the border and about Yugoslavia. Maria's family moved here before she was born and although she feels a strong connection with the area she claims not to have the 'hang ups' that she suggests Antonio and many others with a long history connected to the border have. His family had a large farm in what is now Croatia but after World War II they lost everything when they left it all behind and moved to Trieste. He remembers going to visit family in Croatia in the 1960s. "It was about 100 km to get to the town and we only met three cars. It was so poor in Yugoslavia that they did not have cars. Also if you drove in the night it was completely black as there were no streetlights. We brought sugar, spaghetti and coffee with us. They had nothing" (Maria and Antonio 2008 pers. comm. 5th September). Maria's memories about the border are more connected to crossing it in order to buy cheaper food or for example jewellery that was a bit different from what you could buy in Italy. She remembers how their car was always searched when they crossed the border in order to check how much goods they were taking with them. After Slovenia's independence however the situation changed, she says: "when capitalism came into these places it was no longer cheap for us, and there were no good things to buy. The shops were empty so we stopped to go [sic]" (Maria and Antonio 2008 pers. comm. 5th September 2008).

Maria's story, as well as Anja's mentioned above, is not unusual and often told on both sides of the border. This demonstrates that as well as being a divider the border also presented opportunities. People had different relationships with the border. Often people who were affected by the border had to work out a way to relate to it. For example when we walk in the border area of the Carso/Karso, Antonio tells me how people walking on the Italian side sometimes accidently crossed over into Yugoslavia and got caught and questioned by the Yugoslavian border police. He starts laughing and tells me the story of a man who lived near the border here. One day one of his chickens ran away and crossed the border. The man ran after him and was arrested by the Yugoslavian police and put in prison for a while. The fate of the chicken is not explained in the story. Maybe the Yugoslavian authorities were more tolerant towards animals. Similar stories are told in other places along the border. Like a fable or story that projects some kind of moral lesson, it is not the content of the story itself that is important but rather what the story stands for, a way to relate to the border and to people on the other side. For Antonio it is also, most likely, a way to deal with his and his family's traumatic past in relation to the border.

Others have not felt the same need to relate to the border at all. For Angela, a woman in her early 30s brought up in Gorizia whom I also got in contact with through common friends, her interest and focus was always directed westwards, "…my feeling when I was young was to live at the end of something. Our region is at the 'periphery' of Italy, far away from the capital. My attention was all focussed towards the west, towards the rest of Italy, the rest of Western Europe and the 'western world'" (Angela, 2008, pers. comm.). At a group interview conducted in Skofije 2008 with three women and four men in their late 70s and early 80s the early years of the border came back to life through their memories and stories. Many funny anecdotes were told and one of the ladies sang a song about American soldiers. There was a lot of laughter and only the occasional sad story. I wonder if the events were really this uncomplicated or if time passed had soften these people's memories. I ask how they felt when the new border was installed after World War II. They were not worried or upset but they told me that compared to the Iron Curtain this was nothing. It was still possible to cross and there were no high concrete walls. Without reflecting on it they project the image of the Berlin Wall as being synonymous with the Iron Curtain. There were no such thing here, hence, they do not consider this to be part of the Iron Curtain.

Antonio thinks the Italian/Yugoslavian border was part of the Iron Curtain, he says they were poor on the other side, and that they were communists, but Maria is not so sure. Andrej has a complex way of looking at the border in relationship to the Iron Curtain. For two days he drives me around the border areas. He stops and shows me different structures and sections of the border. He uses the term Iron Curtain a lot. He says things like "that watchtower was part of the Iron Curtain" or, "that's where the Iron Curtain ran". When our two day tour of the border areas is finished I ask him if he thinks this border was part of the Iron Curtain and he immediately answers no. I realise that Andrej in his capacity of museum director sees the Iron Curtain as something that sells from a heritage point of view but which also conflicts with his own experiences growing up by the border. The tourist value that is attached to the Iron Curtain is not far-fetched. On the internet there are plenty of travel descriptions of people claiming to be crossing the former Iron Curtain when they cross the Italian/Slovenian border.

A group of British cyclists are hanging out in the Transalpine Square outside the Nova Gorica railway station waiting for a train. They take pictures of each other jumping over the border and standing with one foot in Italy and one in Slovenia. I ask them what the significance of the place is. "It's pretty awesome that you can now just cross over what was once the Iron Curtain," says one of the guys and makes an extra jump over the border line as if to enforce his point.

Some concluding points

The materiality of the border shows the different layers of its history. It provides an understanding of times of division but also of cross border contact and reunion. First and foremost the materiality of the border shows the interaction of people in a highly controlled environment. It also shows the struggle for control in the border landscape by the military but also by other actors connected to the border whether for single crossings or regular interaction. The remains of the military within the border have to a large degree disappeared and at a first glance they may appear non-existent. On closer scrutiny, however, the traces can be seen and different characters appear. The most apparent information gained from the materiality of the border is about its different functions. For example, some remains are more defensive in character, such as bunkers or military stations that are built to withstand attack and supply troops. Related to these are also the remains that point to surveillance activities along the border. Here we see watchtowers, such as the one near the village of Šempeter or the long paths along the border in Nova Gorica. Perhaps most obvious is the surveillance along the ridge of Mount Sabotino/Sabotin where the double paths run along the border.

One of the places where the material of the control exercised at borders is most clear and still remains is at the border crossings. Here many of the buildings, lanes and road barriers still stand, but are now abandoned. With the air of a ghost town the Casa Rossa/Rožna Dolina crossing complex is now quickly passed by traffic no longer held up by congestion caused by rigorous checks. Besides controlling the movement of people these crossings were also part of an important administrative border infrastructure where pre-EU regulations required control of goods in a stricter fashion.

4: CASE STUDY 1: THE ITALIAN/SLOVENIAN BORDER

Trade across border was of importance to both sides and was encouraged to some degree as it helped keep these border areas economically active. Trade was, however, regulated and as such the border crossings had an important function both for controlling people and goods. It was therefore important that the infrastructure functioned in a way to allow for smooth day to day running of the border.

Looking at the material remains in the landscape helps us to understand how this border has changed over time. Through these observations it becomes clear that although the military character of the border itself was severely toned down, for example barbed wire was removed in many areas and replaced by fences in urban areas and mines completely removed, the surveillance was still high. It was higher on the Yugoslavian side but patrol paths also found on the Italian side, such as on Mount Sabotino/Sabotin, show a high presence also from the Italian side. What is interesting here is that we can see the different layers of history so clearly and that they mix more than one might have expected. The lengthy use of Mount Sabotino/Sabotin is demonstrated in the different remains found here but also in the way that remains are reused again and again. Like the monastery on top of the mountain which was not only used by the monks but also by fighting troops during the First World War and again by Yugoslavian soldiers during the Cold War period and tourists today. Now partly restored it is a place that has been reactivated again and again over the centuries.

For people who did not have the possibility of crossing the border legally, other routes had to be found. Due to the border here being more permeable many people chose this route to get to the west. Due to the less militarised character of this border during its latter history it did become a route for people from other parts of Eastern Europe to cross over to the West. In many countries in the Eastern bloc it was often fairly easy to get a visa to travel to Yugoslavia, being a socialist country and not seen as part of the West. The less militarised border here, compared to for example the inner German border or the border between former Czechoslovakia and Austria, made it easier to cross. A ski resort near the village of Bovec was, for example nicknamed the Czech Doors, as many people from Czechoslovakia were given permission to go on holiday to Yugoslavia, drove here and took the ski lifts up the mountain and simply skied down on the other side of the mountain to the Italian ski resort of Sella Nevea. By the end of the ski season many cars remained, abandoned at the car parks on the Yugoslavian side (Janez, 2008, pers. comm).

Through this case study we also gain a glimpse of the people who helped to keep the control here through surveillance. The graffiti scratched, drawn or painted inside watchtowers, lookout points and shelter structures along the border reminds us of the soldiers' presence and their wish for their service to come to an end. From the material we can also learn something about how these guards spent their time off duty, such as in the basketball court at the Yugoslavian border guard station on Mount Sabotino/Sabotin. Apart from a few photos there are few documents about these border guards and the information available from the materiality they left behind therefore becomes all the more important to understand something about their lives here by the border. Other aspects of the surveillance are also dependent on the material traces left such as watchtowers, patrol paths and bunkers as information relating to the Yugoslavian soldiers activities in the area have so far not been possible to access.

Looking at how the new border developed in the landscape after World War II makes an interesting connection between local history and world politics. The route of the border was the result of discussions and decisions on a high political level, worked out as one part of a gigantic puzzle of what post-war Europe was to look like. The local views were officially of importance but in reality the local people had little influence on the decision of where the new border was drawn. The resistance shown on the local level did however have an impact on the physical border and this can be seen in the landscape still today, for example in the detour the border takes around what was once Countess Liduška's property and the previously divided farm near the former Rafut/Pristava crossing. It is interesting that we can still today connect this local history with the world events of the time in such a clear way through the physical remains. This is also something that is done actively by locals in order to connect themselves with a larger historical narrative.

Another way that the material shows interesting links between the local and world history is the display of political and ideological views that has taken place along the border, both before and after its exact location was decided. Although only a few of these survive today pictures from the late 1940s show how people publically demonstrated political and ideological views. Mount Sabotino/Sabotin might not have been strategically important at this point in history but had symbolic value that appears to have been important to both sides. Actions that can be seen as marking the territory seems to have been particularly frequent here, both in projecting national, ideological or political statements or through building bunkers as part of a military statement.

Through this study we can see that the post-World War II border between former Yugoslavia and Italy had a traumatic start and that its beginning stages had a lot of similarities to what can be described as more 'recognised Iron Curtain-style' borders further north, such as the inner German border. Photographs, documents and local stories provide a picture of how the new border was formed and what it looked like. The barbed wire that was first rolled out along the border accompanied by strict surveillance on both sides demonstrates the military character this border had at these early stages. In some places there were even mines (Veluščtek and Medved 2002). One of the important results of this study has been the discussions that it has created of what we consider the Iron Curtain to be, or to have been in the past. The material and other sources show us a highly complex border that has changed over time. It was never the purpose of this study to establish if this was or was not part of the Iron Curtain but rather it was meant to be a starting point for a discussion of what an Iron Curtain is, or was.

This study has demonstrated that people have very different idea of what would constitute an Iron Curtain. A few points are similar in many people's views though and they suggest an Iron Curtain is: high fences or concrete walls; presence of barbed wire; a border impossible to penetrate; a dividing line between capitalist and communist ideologies. This image is very much based on the image of the Berlin Wall. How people see an Iron Curtain and if they see the former Yugoslav-Italian border to be part of one or not is highly dependent on factors such as their own and their family's relationship with the border, or where they are from. Many of the people I have spoken to in Italy claim that people on the Yugoslavian side where much poorer and much more controlled by the authorities than themselves, something they think of as Iron Curtain-like features. For many Italians there is just not much of an interest in looking eastwards, their focus has for such a long time been towards the rest of Italy and Western Europe. This feeling is generally not recognised by people from former Yugoslavia who claim to have, at least in some ways, benefitted from the proximity of the border. You therefore often find that people in Italy are much more likely to consider this border to have been part of the former Iron Curtain than people in today's Slovenia.

The views of what an Iron Curtain is and if the Italian-Yugoslav border was part of it also changes with time and with changing political climate. In what is now Slovenia the use of the term Iron Curtain has in more recent years been connected to politicians for more right wing parties who by claiming that Yugoslavia lay inside the Iron Curtain want to connect socialism and current more left wing parties with a former totalitarian Yugoslavian government.

The term Iron Curtain is also increasingly used by the local tourist and heritage industry, especially in Slovenia, for example at the Railway Museum at Nova Gorica train station, for the advertisement of the watchtower just inside the Slovenian border or proposals of opening a new Border Museum in one of the abandoned crossing buildings. The border here is an important part of the history of the area, the importance of which has only recently been acknowledged and which has led to an increase in interest to the border history and sites related to it. What is interesting though is that the use of the term Iron Curtain has started to make its way into stories, sites and the general history about this border which was not necessarily seen in the past.

4: CASE STUDY 1: THE ITALIAN/SLOVENIAN BORDER

Reference plan and gazetteer of sites

Gazetteer Italy/Slovenia

Figure 53.

Ref. No.	Description	Comment	Figure
1	Cement blocks	Anti-vehicle blocks located on the road leading up to Mount Sabotin/Sabotino.	
2	Gate barrier	Barrier located on the ground next to the former Yugoslavian border guard barracks. Barrier is painted red, blue and white with a red star.	23
3	Former border guard station	Two buildings that were formerly used as a border guard station for the Yugoslavian guards. Now used to house a small museum for First World War history in the area (could not be accessed). In front of the buildings a basketball court and several memorial stones commemorating the First World War.	23, 24
4	Trench system	A series of trenches created and used during the First World War.	
5	Bunker/hut 1	Square structure located just inside Slovenian territory. Constructed of red bricks with cement bonding and covered in white plaster.	
6	Dual paths	Two paths running parallel on either side of the border almost the entire length of the ridge of the mountain. In some places the two paths have merged into one broad path.	25
7	White border markers	As along the entire border there are white border stones also here. As the border follows the ridge and changes directions often the stones are particularly frequent here.	25, 32, 33

4: CASE STUDY 1: THE ITALIAN/SLOVENIAN BORDER

8	Bunker/hut 2	Inside Slovenian territory. Octagonal in shape. Constructed of red bricks with cement bonding and a grey course cement cladding. The inside is painted in white.	
9	Bunker/hut 3	Inside Italian territory. Octagonal in shape. Constructed of red bricks with cement bonding and a grey course cement cladding. The inside is painted in white.	
10	Bunker/hut 4	Inside Italian territory. Round in shape and appears more recent than the other bunker/hut structures. It is constructed in concrete with a cladding of stones. The year 1977 has been written in the concrete steps leading into the structure.	27
11	Italian military station	A small station consisting of one, single story, structure. Could not be accessed.	
12	Memorial	Memorial stone commemorating the lives lost in the First World War.	
13	Information plaque	Plaque informing about the nature park on the mountain top and its flora and fauna.	
14	Ruins of monastery.	Ruins of a 14th century monastery run by Franciscan monks. Closed down in 1782. Church structure, now located inside Slovenian territory, was partially restored in 1999–2000 whilst residential structures, inside Italian territory, are more fragmented and in state of decay.	
15	Cave	Natural cave under monastery reinforced with concrete and used during the First World War and by Yugoslavian border guards.	26
16	Flag pole	Flag pole. This was used to declare Slovenian independence on the 25th June	

		1991.	
17	Writing	"Naš Tito" written in white stones	
18	Changed borderline	Borderline here changed after the Treaty of Osimo in 1975. It was moved closer into Yugoslavian territory.	
19	Osimo Road Corridor	The road corridor here was part of the Treaty of Osimo in 1975 to allow quicker access to Yugoslavian land on the north side of Mount Sabotino/Sabotin. It was built in 1985.	22
20	San Mauro/Šmaver border crossing	Crossing for farmers.	40
21	Barrier gate and stone blocks	Road gate across a path leading to the border from the Slovenian side and old cement road blocks discarded directly north of the gate itself.	
22	Former property of Countess Liduška.	The border was changed in order to include this property within Italian territory after pressure from the owner who wanted to remain in Italy. The property wall, with iron bars across openings and barbed wire on top, therefore became part of the border.	50
23	Salcano/Solkan 1 border crossing	Crossing for farmers.	40, 41
24	Salcano/Solkan 2 border crossing	Local crossing.	40
25	Former American barracks	American barracks used at the end of World War II. According to several oral accounts this was also used as a refugee centre in the years following the new border position. A photo in the archive	

4: CASE STUDY 1: THE ITALIAN/SLOVENIAN BORDER

		may be from here but it was not possible to verify. This site is now closed off and the buildings in a poor state of repair.	
26	Transalpine Square,	This square outside the Nova Gorica Railway station was created after Slovenia entered Schengen in 2007. The fence that once divided the square was removed and several memorials and commemorations have been added here as a sign of a united Europe.	18, 31, 45
27	Nova Gorica Railway station and Railway museum	The railway station was originally built here as part of the Transalpine Railway from Vienna towards the Trieste Coast which opened in 1906. A museum dedicated to the background and history of the border between Nova Gorica and Gorizia is now located within this building.	18, 19, 48
28	Residential building previously used as Italian border police station	Originally built for domestic purposes and has since reverted back to domestic use.	31
29	Transalpine Hotel	Hotel originally built here for those travelling on the Transalpine Railway from Vienna towards the Trieste Coast.	
30	Changed border line	Changed border line following the 1975 Osimo agreement to make more room for the road on the Italian side.	
31	San Gabriele/Erjavčeva ulica border crossing	Local crossing. Until 2007 only possible to cross on foot or bicycle.	34, 40, 44
32	Former patrol path,	Originally a second railway track for the	28

AN ARCHAEOLOGY OF THE IRON CURTAIN

	made into cycle path	Transalpine railway since disused and instead utilized as a patrol path for border guard. Now the path has been made into a cycle path.	
33	Barbed wire along border	A segment of barbed wire is located here.	35
34	Wall enforced with barbed wire	The border here is marked by a garden wall which has been reinforced with barbed wire.	28
35	Rafut/Pristava border crossing	Originally crossing for farmers but after 1955 also local crossing.	40, 51
36	Casa Rossa/Rožna Dolina	International crossing.	39, 40, 42
37	San Pietro/Šempeter border crossing	Originally crossing for farmers but after 1955 also local crossing.	19, 40
38	Former road	A former road between San Pietro and Šempeter, once the same village, severed by the border and hence discontinued.	36
39	San Andrea/Vrtojba 1 border crossing	International crossing	40, 43
40	San Andrea/Vrtojba 2 border crossing	Crossing for farmers.	40
41	Change in field pattern	The different uses of the fields here create a pattern which demonstrates the line of the border even though no other markings are used.	
42	Watchtower	A former watchtower used by Yugoslavian border guards. The construction date of this structure is not known. It now houses a museum about the border guards. Contains graffiti made	29

4: CASE STUDY 1: THE ITALIAN/SLOVENIAN BORDER

		by border guards.	
43	Merna/Miren border crossing	Originally crossing for farmers but after 1955 also local crossing.	40
44	Miren cemetery	Cemetery previously divided by the border. Was divided down the middle with barbed wire but this changed and instead access was controlled so people from Yugoslavia and Italy could only visit at certain times. Border was later moved so cemetery is now fully located within Slovenian territory.	52

CHAPTER 5

Case Study 2
The Czech/Austrian border

> The area with the remaining fortifications felt very lonely – we were the only visitors apart from a Czech police vehicle which drove up the road and looked surprised to see us. Although it was bleak, it was also very compelling – to see the effect on a community of trying to shut the rest of the world out.
>
> (Emma, Australia)

My first encounter with the Podyji National Park, in the southwestern part of the Czech Republic, was through the eyes of someone else. I had been searching the internet and stumbled upon some pictures from the village of Čižov that caught my attention. A line of single barbed wire fencing stretched along the top of a hill and a watchtower stood tall next to it. I contacted Emma who had taken the photos and she explained how this place and its history had fascinated her since her first visit and how she has kept coming back ever since. During the Cold War the area of the park was part of the forbidden zone that stretched along the border between what was then Czechoslovakia and Austria. I first visited the area on a cold December day in 2009. Tourist season was over but occasionally I bumped into a cyclist or a couple of ramblers greeting me with a polite 'Dobrý den'. During season the park is a popular recreational area and with many well marked paths for cycling, walking and horse riding the park draws a lot of visitors. Maps and information points inform the visitors about the vast variety of flora and fauna thriving in the park and how best to experience them. The fact that the area had very limited access during the Cold War made it into a safe zone for many animals as well as for vegetation. This has created a unique flora and fauna that the park is aiming to maintain. Few people that come to the Podyji National Park reflect on the area's turbulent 20th century history. Apart from the fence and watchtower that are left in the village of Čižov there is little indication at a first glance that this area was a closed off military zone. At a closer look, however, there are many scattered traces in the landscape still today. The major infrastructure and manpower required to keep this zone closed from intruders and to stop any attempts of escapes over to Austria have mostly been removed but remains of it still linger occasionally as a reminder of a less peaceful time.

When I first started my research here I assumed that, like in other areas in Europe where I had been working before, the secrecy about the military past would have gone. I had already been to the archives to get the, previously secret, military maps of the area without any problems. I wanted to ask people about the area's past, about how life had been living so close to the border, so close to the Iron Curtain. But interest was low, almost non-existent in fact. I got the feeling I was trying to bring alive a memory that had already been dead and buried for a long time by all involved parties. Occasionally I would be told small bits of information or stories involving the forbidden zones or the border guards but as soon as someone started to open up, they just as quickly shrug their shoulders and said 'Well that's all I know really'. But as the focus of my research centres on the material remains I turned to the park itself to investigate if the materials had a story to tell.

Methods and aims

As with the study area in Italy and Slovenia the aim of the research of the Czech and Austrian border was to understand what this border looked like during the Cold War period as well as what it looks like today. The information gained during the research was then to be used in a discussion of this border's role within the Cold War division of Europe as well as people's attitude towards it today.

On two different occasions I spent time at the Podyji National Park, in December 2009 and in October 2010. Due to the size of the park I had to limit myself to its northwestern section between the villages of Podmyče, Vranov nad Dyji and Lukov. My main method of investigation was walkover surveys in targeted areas in the park itself, and in some surrounding areas, such as the border guard station at Šafov. These areas were chosen after studies of military maps from the 1950s and 1980s, information through written sources and from people having visited the park as well as people currently living in the area. The former fence line was surveyed in its entirety through the park between the villages of Podmyče and Lukov.

5: CASE STUDY 2: THE CZECH/AUSTRIAN BORDER

Archival research was carried out both at the Military Archives, Brno, Czech Republic and at the National Archives, Kew, UK. As with my research in Italy and Slovenia these studies were not meant to be a full archival and documentary study but rather the documents obtained were a way to help understand the material. Language was a problem with the archives in the Czech Republic as I do not speak Czech but this was mitigated to some extent with archival staff translating and explaining some of the material. These studies, however, made it possible to understand the type of material produced about the former militarised borders. I was offered help and information by Czech historian Prokov Tomek at the Military History Institute in Prague and by Pavel Vanek, curator at the Military Archives in Brno.

Another source for this study has been the Army Forum Website. Here former soldiers can discuss and remember their time in the army and as border guards, they can upload photos and images both recent and from their time of service and arrange reunions with soldiers that served at the same time as themselves. This was a useful source as it provided photos taken at the border guard stations that are not available elsewhere as photography was officially not allowed in the border zone. Through this website I was able to get in contact with three former border guards previously stationed at different border brigades along the Czechoslovakian border.

Apart from interviewing people during my fieldwork in the area I have also conducted interviews via email correspondence with three former Czechoslovakian border guards and one Austrian man who had travelled extensively along the border since the early 1990s. The interviewees in this study area were almost exclusively male, ranging in age from their 30s to their 60s, and this is a reflection of the fact that most of the people that were willing to talk to me were those that had a connection with the former militarised border here. Getting in contact with people here I was mostly relying on responses from the Army Forum and through my guide whilst visiting the area, a person who also turned out to himself be a great source of personal stories and knowledge about the area.

My main methods of recording were primarily photography and taking notes occasionally supported by drawings where I felt I needed to make things more clear or put some features in relations to others, for example over the buildings at the border guards stations. Remains in the landscape were recorded on maps in order to document their location and get an understanding of their distribution throughout the area.

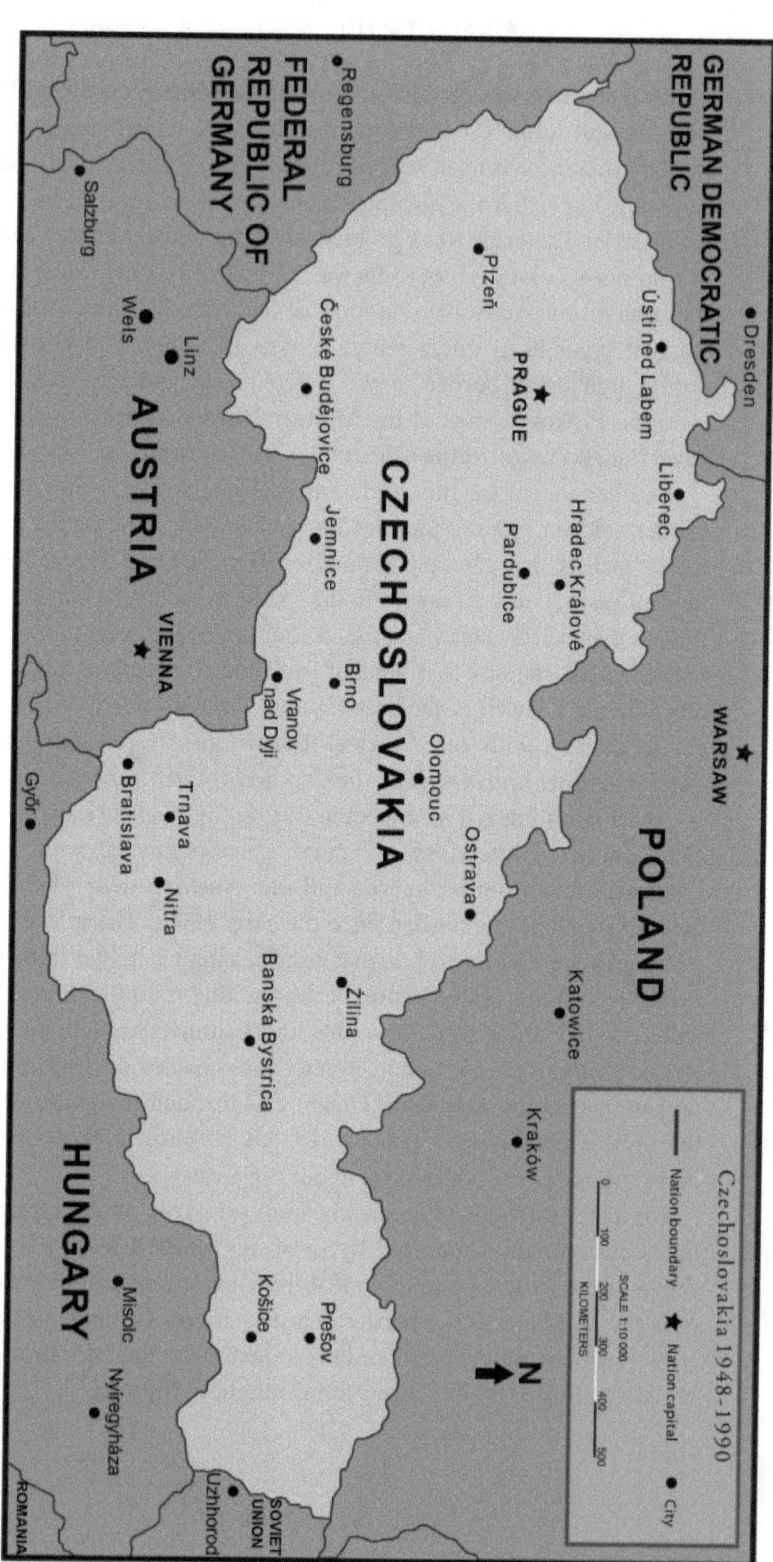

Figure 54: Czechoslovakia 1948–1990. The study area is located by the town of Vranov nad Dyji. Map: Chris Beach.

Figure 55: Bunker near the crossing to Hardegg. Photo: Anna McWilliams.

Figure 56: This map from 1952 shows the different zones. The start of the outer zone being marked in blue and the start of the second zone marked in yellow. The actual border is marked in red. Military Archives Brno.

Figure 57: Photo from 1952 of the first type of fence. Military Archives Brno.

Figure 58: Picture of Jozef as a border guard. Published with kind permission of Jozef.

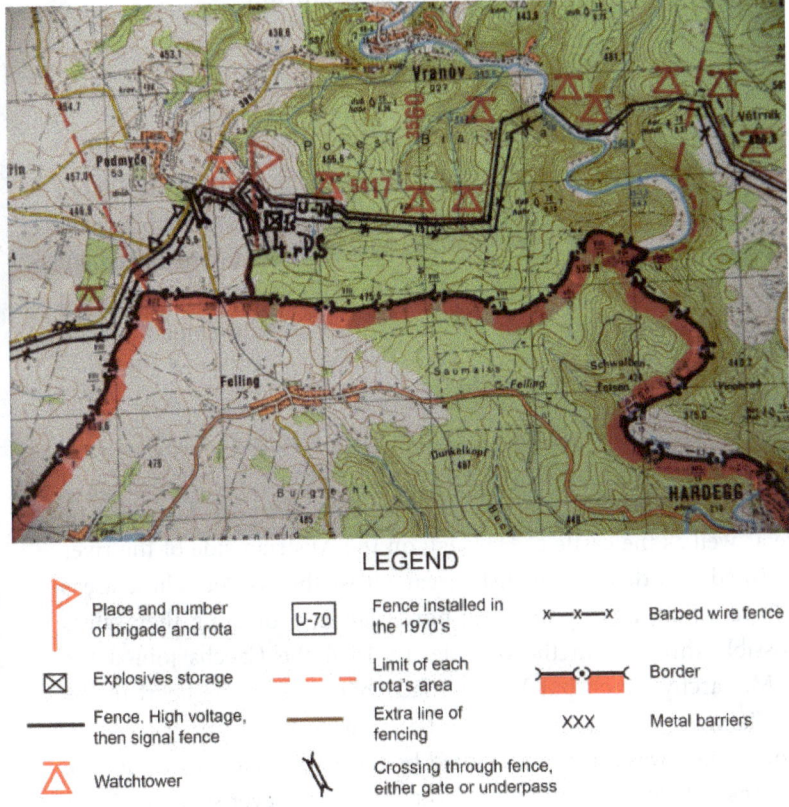

Figure 59: Military map from 1980 of the western part of the study area. Military Archives Brno.

Figure 60: The symbol of the border guard, a dog, on a display stone outside the entrance to the Hajenká border guard station. Photo: Anna McWilliams 2010.

Background

The castle on the rock

The area in which this study has been carried out lies within the Podyji National Park, located in the southwestern part of the Czech Republic right on the Austrian border. The park has a long history of nature management although the motivations behind it and the type of management have varied greatly throughout time. The town of Vranov nad Dyji developed around the castle built on a high rock above the current town as part of a defence system along the river Dyji. It is first mentioned in written records in the year 1100 AD. During the medieval period Vranov was located right on the edge of the Margraviate of Moravia where the river Dyji (in Czech) and Thaya (in German) marked the border with the Duchy of Austria. The castle here as well as the castle at Hardegg on the Austrian side of the river were established as a defence against threat across the border. These areas therefore have a long history of being borderlands, protecting themselves against possible threat from the outside. In 1526 the Czechs joined the Habsburg Monarchy which put Vranov nad Dyji close to the heart of the empire in Vienna only 70 km away. In 1645, during the Thirty Year War, the town of Vranov was seized and looted by the Swedish army but despite several months of trying to invade the castle itself they never succeeded and had to leave Vranov (Vranov Castle website 2010).

Vranov castle was severely damaged by fire in 1665 and was rebuilt into a large Baroque chateau. The study area was part of the large Vranov Castle Estate and became part of the castle's large Forest Park that developed from the middle of the 18th century onwards. One of the first features to be built in the park was a folly located near the village of Čižov which was followed, in the 1780s, by extensive developments of the landscape building the Braitava folly, an English park with pavilions as well as temples and grottoes on Rose Hill, located on the northern side of the Castle. Extensive work was also invested in forest management and cultivation plans. Further development in the 1790s included a wild boar reserve around the already mentioned Čižov folly, a game reserve and a pheasantry. Over time adjustments were made to the park and lookout points and monuments were added, several for and by Helena Mniszek-Lubomirski, Lady of the castle in the mid-19th century, but the character of the forest park stayed similar until the early 20th century. After the 1930s, however, the park suffered neglect and the buildings and monuments within it fell into disrepair (Vranov Castle website 2010).

World Wars

The area was part of the Habsburg Empire until maps were redrawn following the First World War when Vranov nad Dyji and Hardegg yet again became border towns with the river Dyji/Thaya forming the border between them. Following the crumbling of the Ottoman Empire and the defeat of Austria-Hungary and Germany, as well as the Bolshevik Revolution in Russia in 1917 led to great insecurity and the need for new states to be established (Leff 1997:20). The first Czechoslovakian Republic was established in 1918 following the breakdown of the Habsburg Empire. It was felt that the two states were unlikely to gain independence on their own and there was a lot of international pressure on such nation collaboration (Innes 2001:4). The new state consisted of the more industrialized Czech areas of Bohemia, Silesia and Moravia as well as the more agrarian Slovakia. The more economically advanced Czechs took the lead and the first president was the Czech T.G. Masaryk. The Czechs, who had been governed by the Austrian side of the Habsburg Empire, had experienced more independence during this period than Slovakia who, under Hungarian rule, had been much more repressed. Particularly during the 19th century Hungary forced the Slovak minority to assimilate into Hungarian culture and language (Innes 2001:2). In the border areas of Czechoslovakia there was a large German speaking population, the so called Sudeten Germans. In 1919 a large portion of this population demonstrated and campaigned for gaining independence or self-government but the demonstrations were violently fought and the areas stayed within the Czechoslovakian state. Many German speakers continued to live in the border areas of Czechoslovakia. This was also the case within the study area (Zimmermann 2008:11–12).

Following the First World War the Republic of Austria was created, greatly reduced in size from the previous Austrian Empire and the Habsburg Empire before that. Fascism increased its hold in Austria during the early 1930s which led to the installation of the authoritarian rule of an Austrofascist government in 1934 which lasted until Austrian Nazis gained power in 1938 only two days before Hitler established a union with Germany in April 1938 in which Austria was incorporated into the Third Reich.

In Czechoslovakia the increased threat from the Nazis caused the creation of a new defence line built along the borders towards Germany and Austria in the years 1935-38. This defence line of made up of a series of bunkers was modelled on the French Maginot Line. It was especially Czechoslovakia's northern border towards Germany, between the towns of Ostrava and Nachod, where the heaviest defence was built but also the western border towards Germany and Austria was included in the defence line (Kaufmann 1999:240). In the study area 17 bunkers were installed at strategic positions, such as by the crossing over the border river Dyji (Thaya in German), in order to halt any attacks (Figure 55).

In 1938 the French, Italians and British signed the Sudetenland areas over to the Germans in the München Agreements, forcing Czechoslovakia to hand these territories over to the Nazis (Shepherd 2000:15). Even though the majority of the Sudeten Germans were socialist and ready to fight against the Nazis they were sacrificed in hope that this would avoid another war. On the 29th of September 1938 the Sudeten German areas were handed over to become German nationals (Zimmermann 1938:16–18). This deal also meant the majority of the Czechoslovakian defence line now came to lie within German-Austrian territory causing the Czechoslovak state to become completely unprotected against Hitler's troops.

With the Czechoslovakian state in a vulnerable situation Slovakia's demands of autonomy had to be met and on the 6th of October 1938 a second Czecho-Slovak Republic was declared. This was not to last long, however, with pressure from Germany mounting, giving Slovakia the ultimatum of declaring itself an independent state, with Germany's support, or being taken over by Hungary. On the 14th of March 1939 Slovakia declared themselves independent from the Czechs and with that became a Nazi puppet state. It was then easy for the Germans to occupy the Czech lands and making it the 'Protectorate of Bohemia and Moravia', a part of the Nazi Reich (Innes 2001:14). During German occupation many of the Jewish populations were deported to concentration camps. When I visit the town of Šafov, just on the edge of the study area, the old Jewish graveyard demonstrates the large Jewish community that once thrived here.

A new political order

After World War II the allies, who wanted to restore the Czechs and Slovaks as they had been before the war, created a third Czechoslovakia. Through round-table discussions in Moscow, representatives from the Soviet Union and Britain discussed the future of the new state. As the Czech communist party had created strong ties with the Red Army during their strong presence in the country during 1944–45 they found themselves in a fortunate position during the negotiations in Moscow and subsequently in the running of the new Third Czechoslovak Republic (Innes 2001:21).

The fact that the communist groups played an important role in the resistance movements during the war also seemed to give them a moral advantage and respect (Shepherd 2000:21). This combined with general feelings that they had been let down by the West in Munich and the Red Army's liberation of the country helped to spread support for communism. During elections in 1946 the Communist Party won 38 percent of the votes and became the largest party and with that gained the most important posts within the government. Edvard Beneš was elected president. Ahead of the 1948 elections, however, the support for the communists appeared to have fallen and in order not to lose the election the party managed to stage a coup d'état which resulted in a 90 percent win for the party. Beneš retired and Klement Gottwald took on the role as president (Lund 1992:17, Leff 1997:49) The Communist Party soon took control of many of the state's functions such as the police, security forces and the media. Political opposition was brutally fought with tens of thousands sent to prison or work camps during the 1950s. Travel outside the country became strictly controlled and for many impossible (Shepherd 2000:22-24). Following Stalin's death and the condemnation of his politics by Khruschchev at the Twentieth Congress of the Communist Party of the USSR in 1956 there was a general thawing of communist policies throughout the Eastern Bloc. This also happened in Czechoslovakia although at a slightly slower rate than in other states. 1961 saw the release of thousands of political prisoners and censorship was somewhat relaxed (Shepherd 2000:24-26). The election of a Slovak as First Secretary of the Party, Alexander Dubček, in 1968 and the following line of reform which declared a new political climate of "socialism with a human face" was presented in April 1968 (Lund 1992:17). The reforms, referred to as the 'Prague Spring', were to include freedom of media and speech and a move away from planned economy and Stalinism. But these reforms put strain on the relationship with Soviet and on the 21st August 1968 Soviet tanks rolled onto the streets of Prague in an invasion aimed at reeling the power back in. The so called 'Normalisation' that was imposed on Czechoslovakia forced the reformists out of the party and led to a more totalitarian system (Shepherd 2000:30-31). This normalisation which was dominant in the 1970s and 1980s meant a return to the policies that the 1968 reforms were to change. Many of the people at the party's top were forced to resign and given other jobs. Dubček, for example, was given the job as forest worker in Slovakia (Lund 1992:18). A resistance movement, called the Charta 77 after a document published in Western Media criticising Czechoslovakian government, started to take form in the 1980s. The organization was led by, amongst others, Václav Havel. It was their aim to make public the breaches to human rights within Czechoslovakia and its members were constantly under threat and persecution from the Communist Party (Lund 1992:18).

Communism was brought to an end in Czechoslovakia during the so called Velvet Revolution in November 1989. This peaceful revolution, started as student demonstrations, led to the collapse of Czechoslovakia's Communist Party. This followed the announcement of a new Soviet defence doctrine by the Warsaw Treaty Organization (WTO) in May 1987 which stated that global peace was now considered of higher importance than ideology (Tůma 2006:2). Without the threat of Soviet intervention demonstrations were carried out in many of the former Eastern Bloc states and eventually led to the fall of communism in many of these countries. Following the Velvet Revolution the cracks between Czechs and Slovaks started to become obvious. While Slovaks campaigned for a looser federation with more power given to the two republics the Czechs argued for a central government. These issues intensified during elections in 1992 and eventually led to a peaceful split of the two republics into two states, Czech Republic and Slovakia, on 1st of January 1993 (Leff 1997:129-142). Both countries joined the EU in 2004 and Schengen in 2007 opening up the borders towards Western Europe allowing for free travel and much reduced controls at border crossings.

With the new Czech government defence policies changed away from a focus on possible warfare against NATO towards a reorganization which was aimed at eventually joining NATO. Prior to the Velvet Revolution the Czechoslovak People's Army (CSPA) was controlled by and highly loyal to the Communist Party, with 82 per cent of the professional officers being Communist Party members (Tůma 2006:6). Following a major survey of individual officers' attitudes towards the new government led to the removal of almost all generals as well as other staff. Another priority of the new government was also to work towards the withdrawal of the Soviet forces within the country which were finalized by June 1991 when all Soviet forces had left (Tůma 2006:14).

Austria faced other difficulties following World War II. Similarly to Germany the country was divided between the allies: the Soviet Union, United Kingdom, France and the US. Like Berlin, Vienna was also divided into zones. The difference with the case of Austria compared to Germany was, however, that an Austrian government could soon be established even though it took some time to convince the Western Allies who were worried it would become a Soviet puppet regime. During elections in 1945 the conservative party held the majority with the communist party only receiving 5.42 percent of the votes and during the following years the government was to orient its policies more towards the West (Jelavich 1987:249-253). The type of tensions that arose between Western and Eastern zones in Germany therefore never quite happened in Austria. Receiving great assistance and aid from the West, especially the US, in the years 1945-1955 helped to position Austria even further on the Western side of the Cold War divide. In 1955 allied occupation of Austria was ended and the Austrian parliament adopted a policy of neutrality which placed it outside any Cold War engagement. The Austrian Army was only to be used to protect this neutrality and not to engage in other affairs (Jelavich 1987:255-269). Although defence of the state's border was a large part of the army's task, border operations were on a much smaller scale than on the Czechoslovakian, Hungarian and Yugoslavian sides. In the majority of the border areas there was no regular military presence but only at times of uncertainties in the neighbouring countries such as in 1968 or in 1991 during the Slovenian Independence War.

Militarised border in the study area

After World War II the towns and villages closest to the border in Czechoslovakia became heavily monitored and only people that were considered safe, i.e. not likely to attempt escape across the border or help other people across, were allowed to live here. These areas were also severely depopulated after World War II as the large German speaking population living in these areas was forced out of Czechoslovakia as a vengeance against atrocities carried out by the Germans during the war. In total nearly three million people were forced out of areas on the Czechoslovak borders where their families had lived for generations in the 18 months following the end of World War II in what can only be described as ethnic cleansing (Shepherd 2000:16-17). The study area became increasingly militarized and difficult to get through and was soon cut off from its western neighbours. The previously frequent local interaction across the border was brought to an end. The border areas were divided into several different zones with heavier security closer to the border. The outer zones stretching around 3-4 km from the border were restricted to anyone who did not hold a permit to work or visit the area or to people living here. The boundaries of these zones were marked with signs and traffic in and out of here was heavily monitored. For example, the village Vranov nad Dyji within the study area had restricted access during the Cold War period. The main road leading into Vranov nad Dyji from the east was monitored by two watch towers near the village of Onšov and with the help of binoculars the number plate of every vehicle approaching the town was scrutinized. If any unknown vehicles were detected here the soldiers would report this immediately so that they could be investigated on arrival in Vranov nad Dyji (David, 2010, pers. comm. 12th October).

The second protection zone before the border was around 1–2 km wide depending on the landscape and nearby villages (Figure 56). In some areas, such as directly south of the village of Podmyče, the existing road ran only 250 m from the border and the second zone was therefore very narrow here. These kinds of areas were considered weak parts of the defence system and as a result security was particularly high in these places. If single houses were located within this second zone the inhabitants were often moved whilst the houses were either used by the military or raised to the ground making it harder for people to hide within this zone.

The actual border was only marked out in the terrain with white border markers and occasional signs. On the Czechoslovakian side no unauthorized persons were expected to reach as far as the borderline. Two to three lines of fencing were raised sometimes several hundred metres in from the actual border in order to stop any people trying to get through. The first fences that were put up in the early 1950s and from 1952 they were reinforced with mines, first located on the wire of the fence itself and then placed on the ground, in areas that were considered more vulnerable. The first mines on the ground were placed in wooden capsules approximately 6 m apart whilst they soon changed to being placed in concrete capsules which were more explosive. These were located approximately 9 m apart. The mines were dangerous for soldiers that had to keep the fences clear of vegetation and snow and caused many accidents. Consequently, in 1956, they were taken out of service (Vaňek, 2010, pers. comm. 7th December).

The fences had high voltage electricity running through them. These fences were of course highly dangerous and injured not only the people trying to cross but also the border guards who had to keep them clear of obstacles (Figure 57). By the end of the 1950s fences had to be replaced as many sections had been damaged by factors such as weather or mines. The new fence was built in two rows, the first with barbed wire and the second with high voltage current running through it. In order to produce the high voltage current required in these fences transformers were installed and extensive electricity infrastructure had to be developed along the fences. In 1966 the high voltage current was turned off and a signalling fence system replaced it. There is likely to have been several factors for turning off the high voltage current. One was that it was very dangerous to the soldiers maintaining the fences causing many accidents, several with a lethal outcome. The cost of the electrical fences was also very high, for example copper had to be sourced and bought from Hungary, and the government wanted to prioritise other areas of spending (Vaňek, 2010, pers. comm.7th December). It is also of note that the move away from electrical fence towards using a signalling one happened during the period of political thawing when policies were somewhat more relaxed.

Guardians of the border

Keeping the border zones under complete surveillance required large amounts of manpower. The border was constantly patrolled by border guards and border guard stations were located along the entire Czechoslovakian border. These were established in the early 1950s and although they varied somewhat in size they all had a very similar set-up. Some border guard stations were housed in already existing buildings whilst others were built new. In the study area there were three border guard stations: Hájenka, Čižov and Lukov. The compounds had several functional purposes. There were kitchen and storage areas, offices, garages and workshops at the compound. Dogs, mostly German Shepherds and Rottweilers, were used as part of the safeguarding of the borders and the dog kennels were usually located slightly away from the other buildings. There were also sleeping quarters for the soldiers as they stayed at the station during their service. Officers were given accommodation off the compound in nearby villages. Border guards were often placed at a station located far away from their home so that they would not know the local people. Most of the soldiers from Slovakia served in the army in what is now the Czech Republic. Service was part of the obligatory two years of service that had to be served in the army. Service commenced around the age of 18–20 depending on a person's studies. There were two dates to join each year, 1st of April and 1st of October. Special military trains took the men to their place of service.

Jozef, a man in his early 60s answered my note asking to get in contact with former border guards on the Army Forum website and subsequently shared his experiences with me. He was a border guard between 1972 and 1974. He remembers: "A military train left the station in Presov [Slovakia] on the 1st of October in the evening. The station was full of soldiers to be, all saying goodbye to their family and friends. The train took off and stopped in several places along the way letting soldiers on and off. My destination, Budejovice, was around 700 km away and we arrived here in the afternoon of the 2nd of October. At the station there were buses and military lorries waiting for us. A short time later we were behind the barrack gates. Our civil clothes were sent home, our hair was cut, after which we showered and were given our military clothes and equipment. We were also trying to get to know the other new soldiers. We were then divided into groups such as dog handlers, drivers, and cooks or, such as I was, a telephone and radio operator. In the evening we put our clothes and things into the lockers and our first night in green was about to commence..." (Jozef, 2010, pers. comm. 14th November) (Figure 58).

There were different specialisations of border guard such as gunners, dog handlers, drivers, radio operators, engineers, surveillance technicians and cooks. Initial training was given at several training facilities such as in Jemnice which was the training facility for the border guards in the study area (Tomas, 2010, pers. comm. 14th October). Here the future border guards were trained in physical exercise, shooting and gun handling, military tactics, special border training, political schooling (communist propaganda) and particular training required for the different specialisation. This training lasted around 3 months (Marek, 2010 pers. comm.4th November). If you were given more specialised training such as to become a radio and telecommunication operator the training was usually around 6 months (Jozef 2010, pers. comm. 14th November 2010).

A border guard had approximately 10 days off per year with an extra one to three days off in order to travel home depending on the distance. The pay a border guard received was not much more than pocket money but the guards that served directly on the border were paid a bit extra. This did not include people at the border guard station, for example cooks that were not out by the actual border. Work as a border guard could be hard. The guards schedule followed the following pattern: two days on duty then one day of training followed by one day off and then it stated all over again. If, however, the area was under high alert (due to circumstances such as political disturbances in the country or an important political visit) there would not be any days off or time for training at all. A working day was 10 hours and 12 during periods of high alert. Work was not, however, limited to these hours. Marek who worked as a driver with the 12th Company, 5th Brigade at the Chebská border guard station near the border to GDR between 1989 and 1991 had to respond immediately if there was an alarm, day or night. One of the things he remembers most clearly from his time as a border guard was the lack of sleep during his shifts and he often did not get to sleep much for the three days he was on duty (Marek, 2010, pers. comm. 4th November).

The relationship between the soldiers and the officers varied greatly from place to place but was always based on a superior-subordinate relationship. To demonstrate the character of one of his officers who was responsible for political schooling (propaganda) Marek explains how he and the other soldiers were told that they should be proud to be border guards as that meant they could kill a man without any risk of being prosecuted (Marek 2010, pers. comm. 6th November). A previous officer at the Šafov border guard station, Tomas, however, stressed the importance to keep on a friendly foot with the soldiers as this would enable work to run more smoothly. Generally the border guards were conscript soldiers whilst the officers were military professionals (Tůma 2006: 12). There was some possibility of advancing to higher grade also for the soldiers but few border guards were interested in taking this opportunity. The majority of them just wanted to get their service out of the way so they could go back to their regular lives. The border guards could receive awards for good conduct either in the form of a present (a book, diploma, or a photo taken in front of battle flag or wrist watch) or as praise in front of the rest of the unit. The most sought after award was an extra day off but this was very unusual (Marek 2010, pers. comm. 4th November).

All border guard stations were closed in 1991 although border guarding had become much more scaled down and relaxed following the velvet revolution in 1989 (Marek 2010, pers. comm. 4th November). A working day was now reduced to 8 hours per day and 10 if there was an alert. The soldiers were trained to remove the fences at training stations, such as at Jemnice, before they were set to work on removing the actual fences along the borders. Border police took over some of the former border guard stations after their closure, for example in Lukov, but their operations were severely reduced. Most border guard stations were left to decay and the 20 years since their closure have left them in a poor state. The exceptions are those buildings that have been taken over for other purposes.

AN ARCHAEOLOGY OF THE IRON CURTAIN

The material

A changing landscape

My guide David, an official guide at the Podyji National Park, knows the area like the back of his hand. He is now in his mid-30s and since the age of 11 he lived just within the second forbidden zone as his stepfather was a forest ranger managing the woodlands in what is now the Podyji National Park. He takes me to areas that would normally be closed to the public as the woodland is particular sensitive here and to places so well hidden I would never have found them on my own. We talk as we travel around in the park and I ask him about the former border guards but he tells me that he knows nothing about them. They lived separate lives and he only saw them when they came into Vranov nad Dyji to go to a bar on their days off. He shows me patrol paths, a small soldiers hut in what seems like the middle of nowhere, 19th century monuments that have been restored after years of neglect or even vandalism during the Cold War period and border guard stations where soldiers worked, trained, ate, slept and spent their time off trying to entertain themselves until their two years of service was finished. For days we go around the park and although he claims not to know anything of the soldiers that once controlled this area he shows me their history through the traces they have left behind. It is only after a few days he tells me that he as a child with some of his friends visited the Hájenka border guard station a few times. For a young boy there was something exciting about soldiers and the border guards were bored and appreciated the visits from the local children. I ask him what it used to look like and what the soldiers were doing but he says that he does not remember. We walk around the border guard station and he stumbles across materials that are barely visible anymore, such as two cement blocks decorated with yellow dogs, the symbol of the border guard (Figure 60). Although the paint has peeled in places, the yellow colour of the dogs is still vibrant and show little evidence of having spent 20 years slowly disappearing into nature. The cement blocks, which were part of a larger display arrangement, are tilted so that the pictures could be better seen. Between the two cement blocks are several other cement blocks with holes in the middle to support poles of sorts. It is easy to imagine the two bright paintings of the dogs flanking a sign displaying either the name of the station itself or a socialistic slogan to reinforce the importance of the border guards themselves. Placed opposite the main entrance to the border guard barracks this message would have been seen every time a soldier left the building. I suggest to David that he must have known the signs were there as they were so hidden by grass and the overhanging branches that it was not possible to see them. But he claims he did not. He merely stumbled across them now.

The area of what now contains the Podyji National Park has changed dramatically since the end of the Cold War. The material landscape in the area today holds information of a long series of changes that have occurred during the last couple of hundred years. The layout of former Castle Park with its landscaped gardens and woodlands with paths, monuments and viewpoints scattered across it still remain, even though its maintenance has a different goal today, when sustainability and protection of rare species are of more importance than pure aesthetics. The monument, Felicia's well, is one of the monuments that survive from the earlier designed park (Figure 61). It was placed here in what is called Felicia's Valley by count Stanislav Mnizek as a memorial for his mother Countess Felicia in 1806. The white memorial built in neo-classicist style stands out against the green backdrop of trees. The frieze at the top of the structure shows women dancing with amphorae in their hands. The monument was restored in 2001 and there are no traces of the deterioration that took place after the area was closed off after World War II. When the park administration took over the park, however, the monument was in a very poor state from the lack of care for over half a century. The monument had also been used for target practice by the border guards and almost all of the dancing women at the top had had their heads damaged this way (David 2010, pers. comm. 13th October). On this October day when I visit the area the fallen autumn leaves around the monument and in Felicia's Valley, forbidden zones and patrolling border guards certainly feel a long way away.

Fence line

On the hill stretching eastwards from the village of Čižov towards Lukov a 330 m section of the former fence line is still standing *in situ*. The fence that remains is made up of wooden poles and barbed wire and is part of the fence installed in the late 1950s. The second signalling fence that would have been located beyond it has been removed. It took me quite some time to find out why this was still here. I had been shown the order to remove all the traces dated 5th December 1989 by military historian Tomek Prokop (Prokop, 2009, pers. comm. 4th December). Discussions with this historian gave little information as he was not aware of it still standing. Only on my second visit to the study area was I told by one of the staff of the administration office that one of the park rangers who was working in the park as it was handed over from the military had thought it should be kept as a reminder and therefore made sure it stayed.

A watchtower on the top of the hill in Čižov was also kept. Along the fence line in the study area 15 watch towers were located but this is the only one that still remains today (Figure 62). The watchtowers were prefabricated and were assembled on site. A series of photos and plans found in the Military archive in Brno demonstrate how the structures were to be assembled (Figure 63–64).

Figure 61 (left): The monument, Felicia's Well, in Felicia's Valley near Vranov Castle.

Figure 62 (below): Fence, Watchtower and anti-vehicle cement blocks at Čižov.

5: CASE STUDY 2: THE CZECH/AUSTRIAN BORDER

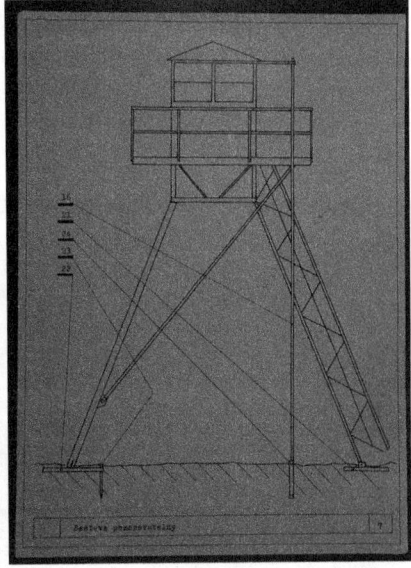
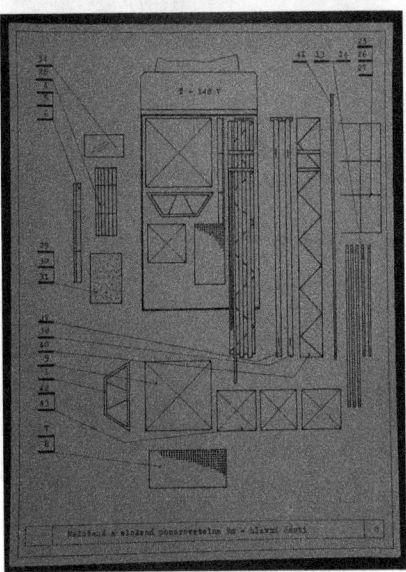

Figure 63-64: Examples of photos and plans from the instructions used when erecting the prefabricated watch towers on site. Military Archives Brno.

Apart from this fence the most obvious mark the fence line has made in the landscape is its effect on the vegetation. Large quantities of pesticides and herbicides were used along the fence line as the ground here and the immediate adjoining areas had to be kept clear to aid visibility (David 2010, pers. comm. 12th October). This has created toxic conditions, not only for the vegetation but also for the park rangers that now look after the park and it is only very recently that it has been possible to plant new trees here. The rangers now take great care to plant and protect trees in these areas in order to erase these low vegetation corridors. An interesting phenomenon has occurred as a result of this in one section of the former double fence line in the park. In sections between the towns of Podmyče and Vranov nad Dyji a new double fence now follows almost exactly in the same line as the former militarised fences, only this time the fence is constructed out of wood and its purpose is to keep animals from eating the new trees, stunting their growth (Figure 65). A dividing fence has now become a protective one. In most sections along the former fence line, however, typically demonstrates an approximately 3–4 m wide corridor of younger trees and lower vegetation compared to the ones growing beyond it.

Figure 65: A protective double fencing around newly planted trees in a corridor of stunted tree growth along the former fence line caused by pesticides. Photo: Anna McWilliams 2010.

The militarised border and the infrastructure that was required to keep it going took advantage of the former layout of the park and used some of the paths and roads that already crossed the landscape. The fence line followed to a large extent already existing roads such as the old road between Vranov nad Dyji to Čížov as well as the former road between Čížov and Lukov. That way the former roads became the patrol paths that followed the fence line. The length of these paths along the former fence line were tarmacked apart from two sections: one on the slope directly west of the river Dyje and one section between Čížov and Lukov. At this latter section 8 cast iron rods, 0.11 m wide, were discovered along the path at the steep slope through the valley between Čížov. The rods either functioned on their own to provide grips for safe walking up and down the slope when the ground was wet or they were part of a larger step construction. One suggestion that there had been iron steps up and down these hills could not be confirmed and no other traces were found.

Figure 66: Sawn off electricity or telegraph pole located along the former fence line. Photo: Anna McWilliams 2010.

In some areas the fence line was diverted from the earlier roads in order to reach a more direct route. Although a large section of the fence line between Vranov nad Dyjí and Čížov follows an older road in one section it takes a more direct route, rising sharply upwards until it again meets the old Vranov to Čížov road again at the top. Today there are some stone boulders placed at the start of this path trying to discourage people from using it. This direct route up the hill is also not indicated as a path on the park's official tourist map. As with most of the former patrol roads along the former fence line this path has been reinforced by asphalt. On my right side as I walk up the hill is the by now so familiar corridor of younger trees stretching out 3–4 m until more mature trees take over. Two faint ridges run parallel with the path in the middle of this corridor. These were created as the fences were pulled up and out of the ground, subsequently keeping their form due to water running down the hill. Directly at the start of this path at its bottom there is a drain constructed in concrete with a wire frame over it to guide the water coming down from the hill away from the patrol path. As I walk up the hill concrete supports for poles or fences and former electricity or telegraph poles cut off near the ground start to appear. It takes me a while to spot the sawn off poles as they have started to assimilate into the background, their colour similar to the trees around it and the moss slowly growing in the circles middle (Figure 66).

On the opposite slope as the fence line ran westwards from the river Dyji towards Podmyče I encounter a completely different picture. This is the second section of the former patrol path along the fence line that does not appear to have been tarmacked. Here the stunted growth of trees is the only sign of the former fence line. There are no signs of a path. A single section of an electricity or telegraph pole is lying on the ground here (Figure 67).

Figure 67: Part of electricity or telegraph pole located along the former fence line. Photo: Anna McWilliams 2010.

At the bottom near the edge of the river there are more traces from the former fence line. Two large electricity poles reach several metres above me but are no longer connected to any electricity network. A remnant of a former electricity supply, now no longer required in the remote woodlands. A lone wire hangs from the pole's outstretched arms, cut off and ending on the ground close to the pole (Figure 68).

Figure 68a and 68b: Electricity pole and connecting wire. Photos: Anna McWilliams 2010.

Close to this electricity pole, right on the edge of the river is the remains of a former bridge. It looks like a slightly raised river bank and could just seem to be a natural phenomenon but a closer look reveals that this bank is constructed by wood. Tall grass covers most of the bank but stretches of barbed wire twist their way in and out around wooden poles. This is part of the footing of the former bridge that crossed the river at this point but was swept away when the river flooded in 2002 (Michael 2011, pers. comm. 15th January) (Figure 69). This bridge followed the line of fencing that stretched across the river and allowed the soldiers to easily cross to the other bank. On the other side of the river there is no constructed bank and the remains of the former bridge are less clear here but a cement footing which served to secure the bridge is visible in the ground. A new footbridge has since been built slightly north of the former bridge. No photographic evidence of the former bridge has been found.

Figure 69: Traces of cement footing of old bridge on the western bank of the river with new bridge in the background. Photo: Anna McWilliams 2011.

A shooting range was located in the vicinity of the river and the former bridge. Today the range consists of a large open L-shaped grassy area. One section is used by a botany university whilst the rest is a large meadow with several rare types of lizards. The fence line previously followed the side of the shooting range and the patrol road, the old road between Vranov nad Dyji and Čižov, is now used as a tourist trail. In the park there are several signs with emergency contact information in case of emergencies, clearly marked with the name of the location. One of these signs has been located at the side of the previous shooting range, its location named Střelnice meaning 'Shooting range' (Figure 70). Although little survives of the shooting range itself the name still prevails. Next to the shooting range there is a reinforced ford across the river Dyji, built in coarse concrete, which was used to get military vehicles across the river (Figure 71). The closest crossing over the river here, the above mentioned bridge, was located on the other side of the fences and facilities to cross the river also in other parts were necessary in case an unauthorized person managed to get across.

5: CASE STUDY 2: THE CZECH/AUSTRIAN BORDER

Figure 70: Sign stating the site's name: 'Shooting Range'. Photo: Anna McWilliams 2011.

Figure 71: Ford reinforced by concrete slabs. Photo: Anna McWilliams 2011.

Searching the landscape

My guide has promised to show me a soldier's hut hidden in the woodland and we are charging through the terrain, jumping over streams, climbing over large, fallen tree trunks and balancing to keep ourselves steady on the sides of the hill. The terrain here can be difficult to manoeuvre around but eventually we reach our destination. Here, along the Dyji River, into the woodlands and away from the tourist trails, is a small guard hut at the base of a slope (Figure 72–74). It is located along an old road between Vranov nad Dyji and Hardegg that is barely decipherable in the landscape today. The small hut was used by soldiers but is now in a poor state. It consisted of only one small room and was kept warm in the winter through the use of a small wood burner. With the exception of the floor the entire hut is covered by graffiti. Most of the writings refer to the end of the soldier's service with many stating how many days they have left. Some of the numbers also have a name and a date next to them. The dates range from 1978 to 1990. The floor of this hut consists of the same tiled floor as at the border guard stations suggesting they were built at the same time. The door has been taken off the hinges and left leaning against the back of the building. There is one window opening but the actual window has been removed from the site. Outside the hut the ground is littered with concrete slabs and iron rods. It is not possible to say exactly what these have been used for but they are likely to have been part of a vehicle obstacle.

Figure 72: Small guard hut located along the river in the study area.

Photo: Anna McWilliams 2011.

As we can see from these remains it is not just traces of the actual fences that help us understand how the former militarised border functioned but also other features that were also important parts of the border infrastructure put in place to keep any unauthorised persons out. There are

5: CASE STUDY 2: THE CZECH/AUSTRIAN BORDER

also many of these other types of remains still visible in the landscape today such as guard huts, steps and training facilities.

Figure 73: Wall inside guard hut demonstrating graffiti left by border guards. Photo: Anna McWilliams 2011.

Figure 74: Part of concrete and iron object outside the guard hut. Photo: Anna McWilliams 2011.

Border guard stations

One of the most obvious remains of the former militarised border is the many border guard stations that were located every few kilometres along the route of the border. These were sometimes housed in already existing buildings but most of them were built for this particular purpose. Although they varied in layout and size they often had similar requirements and therefore similar features and functions.

Figure 75: Hájenká border guard station. Photo: Anna McWilliams 2011.

In the study area there were three border guard stations divided into groups, so called rotas (rPS): Hájenka (4. rPS) (Figure 75), Čižov, and Lukov (both part of the 5.rPS). These border guard stations all belonged to the Znojmo district, the 4. bPS (Znojemská brigade). The station at Čižov was housed in an already existing building which had previously been used as a mattress factory. Hájenka and Lukov were built new. Čižov has been completely renovated and now houses an information centre and a small museum for the Podyji Park. Lukov former border guard station has also been refurbished and has been made into a block of flats but a small structure within the building complex still houses a small police station. Hájenka border guard station, however, was taken over as the premises of the park's maintenance team. As only parts of these premises are used for maintenance purposes a large portion of the buildings here have been left unaltered. It was located only approximately 500 m from the border inside what is now the Podyji Park. It now belongs to the Park Administration and is used for storage and maintenance for the park staff. It is still surrounded by the original fences, the same barbed wire type as the late 1950s fence lines. One section of the complex, the former training ground, is now used as a nursery to cultivate trees before they are planted in the park itself. In the early 20th century a game lodge belonging to the Vranov Castle Park existed in the same location (Anderle and Schmidt 2002:22). The name of the border guard station 'Hájenka', meaning lodge, also reflects this. The border guard compound has been redeveloped and rebuilt during its period of use with the earliest building dating from 1956 (building 4). The buildings varied depending on how many soldiers it needed to house and the different functions they were used for. Although slightly outside the Podyji Park itself I have also looked at Šafov border guard station, 3.rPS, also part of the Znojemská brigade, as it has not been reused and although it has fallen into a poor state of repair it still gives an understanding of how the border guards lived and worked during their service (Figure 76).

Figure 76: Šafov border guard station. Photo: Anna McWilliams 2011.

Similar to the Hájenka border guard station a solider entering the Šafov border guard station was greeted by a message painted on the opposite wall to the main entrance. On the painting's left side we see a man dressed in what appears to be some kind of traditional clothing standing with a German shepherd dog in a rural, tranquil environment. On the right side of the painting two men are standing on a road, one soldier and one man in civil clothing, in the background a watchtower. The text across the top states "We protect the socialist way of life" (Figure 77–78).

When entering the border guard stations now the sense of ruin and abandonment creates an eerie feeling. The grass grows high and bushes and trees are taking over. Nature is reclaiming not only the outside areas but also inside the buildings where fungus, mushrooms, plants and even bushes are gaining grounds. Windows are broken, paint is peeling off the walls and bricks and mortar crumbles under one's feet when walking along the corridors. Most of the furniture, equipment and personal effects have been removed, however there are still enough traces for us to get an understanding of the activities that took place here and the people that inhabited these buildings.

The two border guard stations that were investigated for this study, Šafov and Hájenka, had a similar U-shaped layout with two main buildings connected by a corridor (Figure 79). Different types of areas were distinguished from each other, divided into private and official use. Sleeping quarters, offices, storage areas and kitchens were kept separate from each other. Furthermore dogs were kept in kennels away from the main buildings.

Figure 77–78: Painting inside the front door at Šafov border guard station. Photo: Anna McWilliams 2011.

Figure 79: Hajenká border guard station, entrance to building 1.

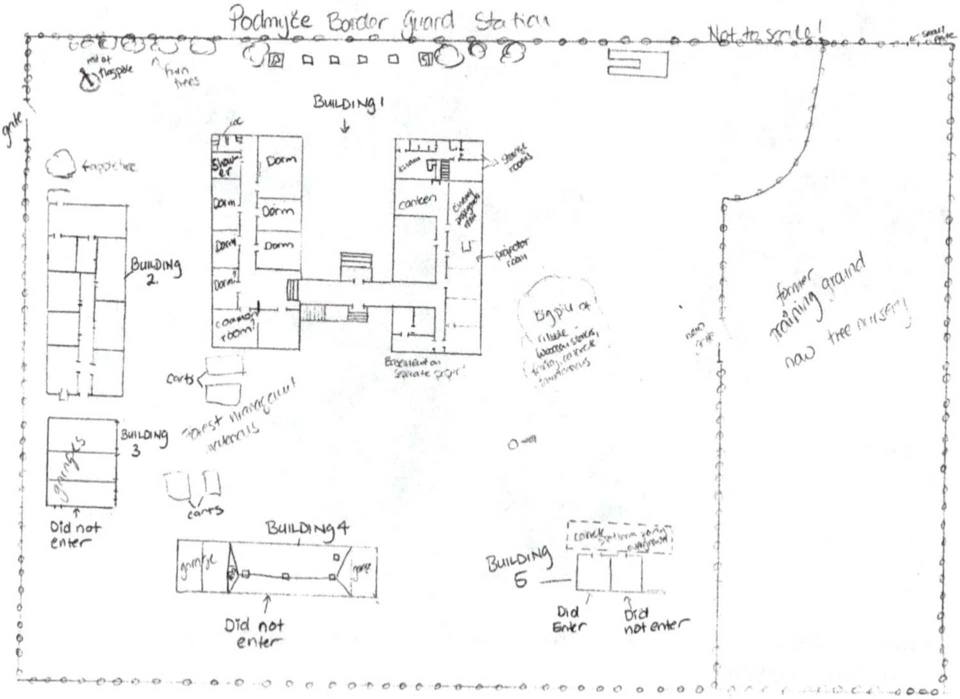

Figure 80: Site plan of Hájenka border guard station drawn during site visit. Plan: Anna McWilliams 2011.

At Hájenka the compound consisted of 5 buildings of varying sizes (Figure 80). The main building, building 1, was built along two main corridors connected by a central corridor. The eastern section of the southern section of building 1 was the kitchen area. This section contained the kitchen, with adjoining storage areas and a canteen. The canteen was connected to the kitchen through two large hatchets which are now walled up (Figure 81).

Figure 81: Closed up hatches to the canteen seen from the kitchen at Hájenka border guard station.

Photo: Anna McWilliams 2011.

Figure 82: Site of former wood burner in the kitchen, since removed at Hájenka border guard station.

Photo: Anna McWilliams 2011.

Signs are much more frequent in the kitchen than in the other parts of the building differentiating between different storage and cooking areas, such as distinguishing between different sections for raw and cooked meat as well as signs explaining how to use the equipment. A wood burner, since removed, heated water for a large water tank (Figure 82). It is possible the wood burner had at some point been used also for cooking but instruction signs on the walls show that an electric fryer and an electric oven were available when the kitchen was last used. The walls in the kitchen had been decorated with labels from among other things canned fruit, beer and bananas (Figure 83).

Figure 83: Labels from food jars on the kitchen wall at Hájenka border guard station. Photo: Anna McWilliams 2011.

Figure 84: Wall in the 'propaganda room' at Hájenka border guard station. The square hole in the wall for the projector located in the adjacent room has been blocked. Photo: Anna McWilliams 2011.

5: CASE STUDY 2: THE CZECH/AUSTRIAN BORDER

The western section of this southern building was used for official purposes as offices, communications rooms and for admin purposes. Some of the rooms are likely to have been used as archives. Seeing the vast amounts of papers generated by the border guard at the Military archive in Brno, storage must have been required for at least some of these reports, something that is easily forgotten in today's digital world. Little evidence survives here to be able to give us an indication of exactly what the different rooms were used for. Between the official and the kitchen areas a communal room was located where official meetings were held. A square hole in the wall and the mountings for a projector in the adjacent room indicates that films were shown here (Figure 84-85). When I enter this room with my guide he refers to it as a 'Propaganda room' as if it was obvious there would be one of those. He explains how most official places and institutions had these types of rooms to show communist propaganda, or 'political schooling' as the official term was (David 2010 pers. comm. 13th October).

Figure 85: Mounts for a projector in room adjacent to 'propaganda room' at Hájenka border guard station.

Photo: Anna McWilliams 2011.

The northern section of building 1 was mainly used as sleeping quarters with at least four of the rooms here used as dormitories (Figure 86). A picture taken in one of these rooms in 1988–1990 shows a minimum of six bunk beds in this room (Army Forum Website Image 1) but it is possible that there were more that could not be seen on the picture. A total of 40 soldiers were housed here at any one time. Only the soldiers lived on the premises with officers provided with houses for them and their families in Vranov nad Dyji (Tomas, 2010, pers. comm. 14th October).

Figure 86: Corridor of sleeping quarters at Hájenka border guard station.

Anna McWilliams 2011.

Graffiti found in two of the dormitories show how the soldiers were counting down the days until they were to finish their service. One of these was written in English, stating 'I very look forward to civilian'. Written in another room was the suggestion "burn the officers' nest". There is also graffiti comparing time spent at the station as being in jail. The dates in the graffiti indicate that the majority of it was written towards the final years of the compound's period of use during the late 1980s and 1990s. In one dormitory some kind of score sheet was kept between people from both the Hájenka and the Šafov stations (Figure 87). It is not clear what the scores were referring to but it does show that there was interaction between the different stations. There were also pictures put up by the soldiers in several of the rooms, especially on the back of the doors. These were typically clippings from papers of half-naked or naked women but there were also numbers counting down the days, action heroes holding guns, as well as stickers from cigarette and filter packages. Some attempts to clean up and remove some of these clippings have been made but many still remain (Figure 88–89).

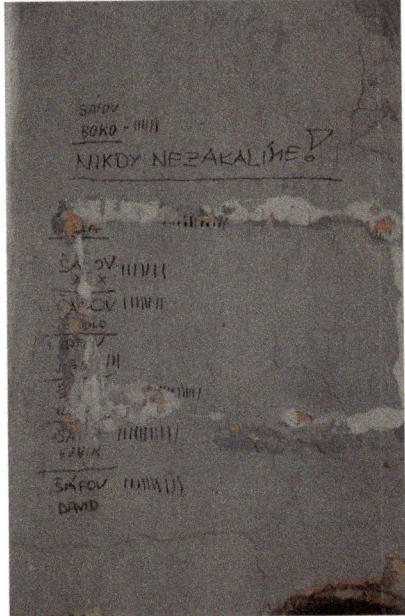 

Figure 87: Graffiti of a score sheet located on the wall in one of the dormitories at Hájenka border guard station. Photo: Anna McWilliams 2011.

Figure 88: The inside of a cupboard door left leaning against a wall in a corridor at Hájenka border guard station. Photo: Anna McWilliams 2011.

Two larger rooms were located at the western end of this building which could have been used as communal areas. Pictures on the army forum show communal areas that were less official that contained comfy seats, pool table and a TV and it is likely some of the rooms also at Hájenka were used for leisure (Army Forum Website Image 8). Dominik who were placed at the Šafov station as chef during two months in November and December 1986 confirms that there were one or two rooms for more unofficial gatherings. He remembers getting permission to watch *Green Ice* with Omar Sharif at the station over Christmas. He explains how he saw the film five times during the Christmas days (Dominik, 2010, pers. comm. 17th December). At the other end of this building were a wet room with six showers and six sinks located (Figure 90). Adjoining to the shower room was a room with toilets with seven cubicles and 8 urinals (Figure 91). No space provided for the private or the individual and probably rather cramped at times with 40 men. It is clear in everything from the layout of the building, the way many soldiers were forced to share a very limited space, to the uniforms and uniformity of the way the soldiers were expected to act that there was very little room left for any personal space.

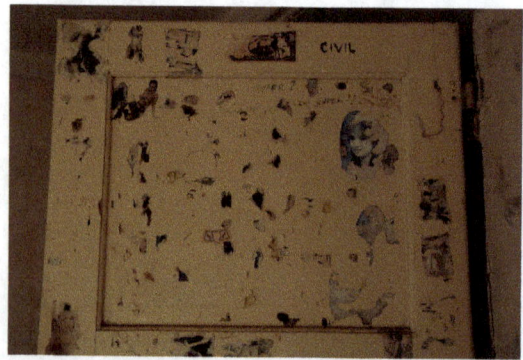

Figure 89: The inside of a door to one of the dormitories.
Photo: Anna McWilliams 2011.

Figure 90: Shower room at Hájenka border guard station.
Photo: Anna McWilliams 2011.

Many of the other buildings within the compound, as well as the basement of the main station building, were also used for storage as well as garages, workshops and maintenance. Some of these buildings are used by the park rangers today for storage and to carry out maintenance. The majority of building two would have been used as workshops but to the eastern end of this building another entrance leads into the smaller section of this building containing one large room and two small rooms (Figure 92). This is likely to have housed communications rooms for technical surveillance as the views from this building extend out across the approaching road. It is also close to the edge of the compound and therefore a suitable place for incoming cables and technology to be placed. This section of the building has no adjoining access to the other part of the same building used as workshops.

Figure 91: Toilettes at Hájenka border guard station.
Photo: Anna McWilliams 2011.

Figure 92: Eastern part of building 2 at Hájenka border guard station.
Photo: Anna McWilliams 2011.

Building three consisted of two large garages now used by the parks administration staff (Figure 93). Building four could not be entered as it was locked whilst at building five, only one section could be entered (Figure 94). Building five is a small structure at the south-west corner of the compound used as part of the dog kennels (Figure 95). No room inside building one or two appeared to have been used for dogs. In old pictures, building five, on the other hand, can be seen with fencing around it (Army Forum Website Image 2). Old pictures also show that at least two watchtowers were located just inside the fencing at the western edge of the compound but there are likely to have been more located at the other side of the compound providing views to the east (Army Forum Website Image 3).

Figure 93: Building 3 at Hájenka border guard station.
Photo: Anna McWilliams 2011.

Figure 94: Building 4 at Hájenka border guard station.
Photo: Anna McWilliams 2011.

Figure 95: Building 5 at Hájenka border guard station.
Photo: Anna McWilliams 2011.

The buildings are now in different states of preservation with building 1 in the best condition. Being maintained by the administration staff has made this border guard station slightly better kept than the one at Šafov.

5: CASE STUDY 2: THE CZECH/AUSTRIAN BORDER

The Šafov border guard station has a similar setup to that at Hájenka with division of areas for private and official use. Here there was, however, somewhat less of a division between the sleeping quarters and the many storage areas both housed in the same wing of the main building. An extra storage section was added to this wing at a later stage. In one of these storage rooms there are traces left of wire fencing within the room which suggests that this was an extra secure storage area, possibly for weapons. In the soldiers' bathroom at Šafov 31 stickers from tins of shoeshine have been stuck to the wall together with a handful of stickers from cleaning products such as toilet cleaner, attesting to the orderly and clean existence expected by the soldiers (Figure 96).

Figure 96: Two low sinks with stickers from shoe shine jars and cleaning products stuck to the wall above at Šafov border guard station.

Photo: Anna McWilliams 2011.

Looking through the photos and drawings posted on the Army Forum one frequently comes across some sort of 'graduate drawing'. It appears that many if not all of the groups of soldiers created one of these drawings when they finished their service. These types of drawings can be seen as having a vague similarity with school graduation materials such as yearbooks, signed T-shirts or school uniforms in which the group identity, friendship and solidarity are confirmed and often kept as a memento. These drawings are produced to varying quality, no doubt depending on the artistic skills of the 'graduating' soldiers. Usually the drawings include pictures or drawings of the soldiers, part of a particular two-year group of soldiers, the years the soldiers were at the site and the name of the border guard station. Almost all drawings have images symbolizing everyday life at the station, such as watchtowers, the border guard symbol of a dog, fences and trees. Some of them even have the castle at Vranov nad Dyji included. From the mid-1980s until the last drawings in the early 1990s the style is changing and there no longer seem to be a great importance attached to including all the soldiers' names and pictures. Instead there is a focus on the artistic, often with a strong, male character included as well as images from the site, such as watchtowers or the border guard station itself. It is not uncommon to also find images of women dressed only in underwear or not wearing anything at all in the drawings. These motifs mirrors the images displayed in the dorms at the stations. Other drawings are also posted on the Army Forum website but it is not as clear if these were drawn as part of the 'graduation' or not (Army Forum Website Image 4–7). Through the materiality left behind by these soldiers, both at the actual site as well as on the Army Forum, gives some insights to the people who worked and lived here. Although asking people in the area was not very fruitful as few people were interested in talking to me but I occasionally met some people who could give me more information.

We walk along the main thoroughfare of Šafov village and at first it seems to be deserted. We have been tipped off that there is a former officer to the Šafov border guard station that still lives here and we have come to see if we can find him. We see a couple who are raking leaves in their garden and we decide to ask them. After the usual Dobrý den and references to the weather they confirm that the man next door to them used to be an officer. Excited by our progress we walk through the front gate and around the house to the entrance. The garden is small but the space is well used and vegetables and flowers take up a large part of its area and a few geese waddle around in the back of the garden. A woman answers the door and when she hears of the purpose for our visit she calls for her husband Tomas to come out. He confirms that he used to be an officer, right up till the closure of the border guard stations in 1991, and invites us in and says he'll try to answer my questions although he does not seem sure that this information can be of any interest. As his wife serves us strong coffee from bright yellow mugs he tells us that his house was built by the soldiers. Although the soldiers were staying at the border guard station the officers and their families were offered accommodation in the village. He himself came here with his family in the early 80s and his wife shows us some pictures from the family album of their first years in the house. "About half of the vehicles used by the army were Russian whilst half were Czech", he explains. "Our car was Russian" he continues and points to a picture with the family gathered around a car. I cannot tell much about the car as it is mostly hidden behind people posing on and around it, children as well as adults, but it is clear from the people that this was not a car to be ashamed of.

"It was important for me as an officer to keep on a good footing with the soldiers. Everything worked much more efficient if there was a friendly atmosphere". He thinks back and starts laughing a bit to himself "Have you seen all the pools around here?" I nod as I have seen the many natural pools in the area and he carries on "sometimes when they were out on their patrols they stopped to have a swim. They thought we didn't notice". It all sounds more like a holiday camp then the army. Almost as if he can read my thoughts he flicks in "Of course it was all serious business but I think compared to other jobs in the army, a border guard had a fairly easy time". He emphasises the fun that was had by the boys and maybe these are the memories he has taken with him.

He explains how the place looked very different then when 50 soldiers were staying at the Šafov station as well as several guard dogs. Many of the soldiers were scared of the dogs but of course they were trained to attack. There were even pigs kept in the yard which were used for food. "Now the place is falling apart". There is no nostalgia or regret within this sentence but merely a statement.

I try to put a few more questions forward but he seems to have lost interest. Instead he shows me some photos of the time all taken at the training facilities in Jemnice. "We were not allowed to take any pictures at the actual border or at the stations. No cameras were allowed." I am allowed to photograph some of his pictures however, and he explains them as I go along. There are pictures of him posing with a small group of soldiers, then one picture with a larger group of soldiers posing in front of a barbed wire fence. Some of the soldiers are holding long poles with double hooks at the end, he explains: "For clearing the fences". I ask about a picture of a boy in uniform posing with a dog and the wife answers that this was one of the soldiers that were originally from Slovakia. They do not know anything else about him. There are also pictures of the officer and the soldiers being instructed in how to dismantle the fences (Figure 97). "The beginning of the end" he says and laughs. This is also the end to our interview and I understand that although he does not so much mind sharing information about his time as an officer this is a chapter of his life that is over and there are many other things he would rather do with his time that dwell on the past. He accompanies us to the door. As we leave the house one of the geese is splashing around in a bucket of water. I look around and to my eye there is little here that would distinguish this house built by soldiers for army purposes from the other houses in the village.

Figure 97: Learning to dismantle of the fences at the Jemnice training facility. Published with kind permission of Tomas.

Archive studies

In the record office at Brno I search through file after file of official reports, maps, photos and best practice guides. I have been told that the files of the border guards stretch 1 km of archive shelves. I have been given the files of what is thought to be roughly the area I am interested in as the files have not been fully sorted. Many people would consider my attempts to understand this material without speaking the language futile. But just seeing the vast amounts of paperwork produced in order to keep the borders secure says something in itself. The constant need for upgrading, for reporting and to train and support the guardians of the border is almost beyond comprehension.

A best practice manual from 1978 demonstrates how soldiers were to respond to an attempt of escape through the border areas (Figure 98). The manual, of 10 pages, of a mock escape situation has some written instructions but is mainly made up of 34 black and white photos glued into the folder demonstrating information like: what equipment to be used, such as weapons, dogs and vehicles; how to trace an escapee, showing soldiers looking for footprints, recording a hat lost by the escapee and allowing dogs to follow the trace; recording the information and reporting to headquarters and eventually the discovery and arrest of the escapee, a scene demonstrated in the picture by a soldier, with a dog at his feet, pointing his gun at a man with his hands up in the air.

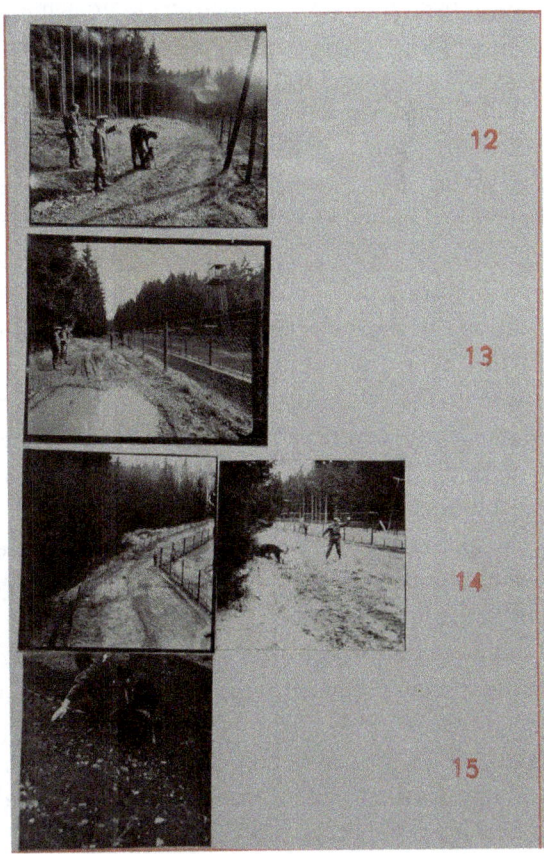

Figure 98: Page from Best Practice Manual. Military Archives Brno.

Some of the material does not need any words. More pictures than I like to remember have showed the failed attempts of people trying to cross the border. Although I find none of these pictures from my study area they appear at times in the archive materials of other parts as I sift through the documents. Their bodies sprawled across the ground or stuck in a fence, arms and legs in awkward angles, dead eyes staring into nothing. The pictures are taken in all directions to make sure not to leave any clues out. These pictures of dead accompanied by detailed maps and descriptions of the persons movement across the landscape in order to upgrade and improve security in the apparently weak points these files were then circulated and eventually ended up in this archive. I have not included any of these pictures as I do not think they would add anything to the study and therefore I do not consider it to be ethically correct. Here I think there is a difference to how we instinctively approach a material that is more recent rather than if we were to excavate or use pictures of an older skeleton where one can question if it is at all unethical to publish photographs of the dead. With prehistoric skeletons it is simply easier to distance oneself (Nordström 2007:20). That we have a complicated relationship with death becomes clear in archaeologist Mike Parker Pearson's example of two news stories published on the same day (24th May 1991): "One is from the *Guardian*, a national newspaper, about the discovery of a 1200–1500-year old skeleton in Southwark in south London, found during archaeological excavations in advance of development. Alongside a close-up photograph of a trepanned skull, the article enthuses about the discovery and what may be learned from it. The other report is from the local *North Norfold News* about 500–1000-year old human bones from a ruined medieval churchyard eroding out of the sea cliff at Eccles. There appears to have been no archaeological involvement but some of the bones had been taken by souvenir hunters. The manager of a nearby holiday camp is quoted to have said that people who took the bones 'must be sick'" (Parker Pearson 2003:183–184). This demonstrates the difficulty we have in our approach to death. The added complication of portraying death in more recent times is the issue of the possibility of friends or relatives of the deceased that can recognise and take offence to the publication of the picture. My approach has, therefore, been to think if a picture would add something imperative to the discussion and on this occasion I found that it would not. This does not mean they did not affect me and the way I looked at my research. The stories of those who did not make it over the border are as important as any other stories that have arisen out of this material. Occasionally, however, I came across a report where a person had actually got through the fine-tuned safety net of the Iron Curtain. The reports contained long descriptions and maps demonstrating the route the escapee are likely to have used (Figure 99–100). But the reports of failed crossings are in the majority. The net was often too difficult to get through.

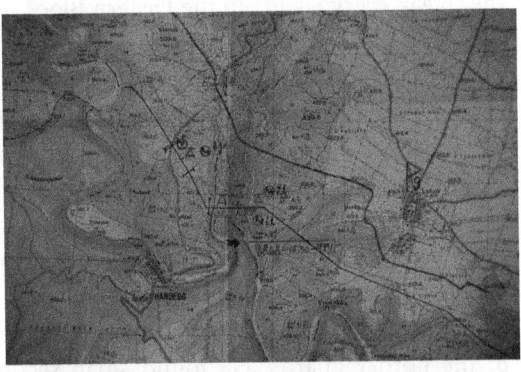

Figure 99–100: Map and photo which were part of a report of a breach through the border zone between Čižov and Lukov in 1968. The person or persons, who scaled the fence using a window frame, made it across to Austria. Military Archives Brno.

Voices from Austria

As the fence line was generally placed several kilometres within Czechoslovakian territory it was often not seen from the Austrian side. The knowledge of its presence was however widespread. From the Austrian side there was generally little interest in the communist neighbour hiding behind secure fencing. As in many other border areas crossing over to buy cheaper products was done occasionally but it depended on the political situation and often it was difficult to cross.

Michael was brought up in Vienna, around 50 km from the border to Czechoslovakia. He is a lawyer by profession but it is in his spare time that he has developed an interest for the former militarised border. He answers my advert on the border guard website for information about the former militarised border as he has always found it interesting. He explains how visits to Bratislava in 1984 and East Berlin in 1987 gave him an insight to the "bleak everyday life in the Eastern Bloc" (Michael 2011 pers. comm. 10th January). He continues to explain the effects this had on him: "This of course left a particular threatening impression on me, but then also certainly some form of fascination, when standing only a few hundred metres away from the fences, the watchtowers and the foot patrols" (Michael 2011 pers. comm. 10th January). In 2008 when Schengen had been extended and the borders of many of the former Eastern countries were open he decided to investigate these areas that had tickled his imagination for such a long time. During weekends and holidays he started walking along the paths following the former fence line to investigate what remained of the border guards. He found small sections of the former fencing at Čižov, at Navary in South Bohemia, Czech Republic, and along a cycle path between Breclav and Potok, near the tripoint of Austrian, Slovakia and Czech Republic. He came across many border guard stations in different stages of ruin. Some have been reused, one even as a brothel, whilst the majority of the sites have been left to deteriorate (Michael 2011 pers. comm. 10th January).

At the National Record in Kew Garden, London I find a story told by a South African woman feeling powerless to help her husband held in captivity by the government on the other side of the border. From the Austrian side she is trying to make the diplomats of the West understand the disastrous results a national border can have. In her letter she writes about her husband who left Czechoslovakia in 1969 because of the political situation and settled down in South Africa. Whilst in Austria in 1972 he went to the border near the town of Mikulov in order to wave to his parents whom he had not seen since he left three years earlier. The wife is suggesting that the phones must have been bugged when arrangements were made with the parents as there were several soldiers at the ready when he turned up. Although he stayed within Austrian territory he was shot and dragged by force over the border. She recalls the event:

> On the road left of my car I noticed a cap belonging to one of the frontier police lying on the ground. Immediately afterwards I heard one single gunshot and then a series of gunshots as if from a machine gun. By this time I had reached the bridge which spans the small canal which is the border and I looked over to the left to see two or perhaps three

Czech soldiers dragging my husband, who was at least 15 or 20 meters inside Austria, towards the border... By the time I reached him the soldiers had him only a few meters away from the small canal. I grabbed my husband's leg (the soldiers had both his arms) and attempted to pull him back towards safety. My husband had a bullet wound on his left leg (thigh) but I was terrified to let go [of] this leg and pull the other leg in case the soldiers jerked him away whilst I was changing legs. The soldier dragged both of us down the back into the canal where I managed to wedge my leg into the side of the canal. Another soldier grabbed my hair from behind and attempted to pull me away from my husband. We battled in the water for what can only have been a few seconds but somehow seemed like a lifetime, and then suddenly my husband was jerked out of my hands up the bank into Czechoslovakia.

(National Archives, London)

It is unclear what happened to the woman and her husband but the incident demonstrates the brutality of the Iron Curtain and the devastating effects it could have on the people around it.

Some concluding points

The Podyji Park is an area of great beauty and it is easy to understand that tourists keep coming back here to enjoy the nature through hikes, bike rides and horse rides. It is difficult to imagine how different the area would have been with fences, watch towers, mines and patrolling soldiers. This study has helped to understand how this area has looked and functioned throughout its history, from Castle Park, to military zone to national park. It has been possible to gain an understanding here of the monumental infrastructure that was the Iron Curtain and an appreciation of the difficulties getting across this landscape as an unauthorized person. Even more than along the Italy/Slovenia border the need for control here was intense. Instead of making sure traffic across the border was controlled the aim here was simply not to have any traffic across at all. Mostly, however, this study has shown an insight into the lives of the many soldiers who served here. When you walk around a site, such as the border guard stations, where so much remains although in a state of ruination it becomes clear that the once major feature of this place, the soldiers themselves, have all long gone. Reading ethnologist Susanne Wollinger's study of a brigade in Sweden

(2000) it becomes very obvious how silent the sites I visit are. Wollinger explains how the noises of TVs, record players and conversations would flow through the corridors in the evening, the sound of military boots against the flooring and the sound of Velcro as someone opens their uniforms as they enter a building (Wollinger 2000:75 and 62). She also speaks of the *smellscapes* of the corridor, particularly on Wednesday evenings, the usual time for a night on the town, when the smell of deodorant and aftershave hung heavily in the air. The sites I visit are silent and where smells are involved they are more likely to be connected with the buildings' degeneration than their previous occupants. But there are still traces left of those who once spent two years of their lives here. Those who patrolled, monitored and guarded the borders but also lived here and carried out their everyday duties, both official and private. Their lives here both on and off duty have come to linger through the remains they have left behind, both at the site itself and through their memorabilia displayed on their website and these things speak loudly. In the absence of people the things themselves become more clear.

Although a lot of the buildings have fallen into disrepair and most of the furniture has been removed walking around in this former guard station still gave a sense of how life here would have been like. It is obvious from graffiti in which soldiers were counting down the days that if they had been given a choice many of them would not have been here. This was part of the obligatory two year military service that all Czechoslovakian men had to do in their late teens and early twenties (conscription to the army took place after they had finished their studies and therefore the age of the soldiers varied somewhat). After an initial month of training at the Jemnice facility the soldiers spent the remainder of the time in one place, transfers being unusual. It is clear from the graffiti but especially the "graduate drawings" that were produced by the soldiers themselves and the many photos displayed on the army forum that a real sense of camaraderie developed and that contacts have been kept also after the soldiers left the camp (Army Forum Website). Of course, one has to remember that the people displaying these pictures and keeping up contacts on this website are a very small part of the all the soldiers that came through these border guard stations. Many of the former soldiers that are not taking part in these kinds of forums may not feel the same. There is a great stigma attached to any act that is related to communism or former communist activities.

The different areas within the study area also display slightly different pictures of the soldiers. What is interesting is that the guard hut located along the river fairly far into the woodlands had a much larger amount of graffiti in it than the structures at the stations. In fact there were few sections of the walls and the ceiling that did not feature writing by soldiers. The writing here also had a much wider spread through time with a lot of much earlier dates. This suggests that the hut in the woodlands were barely visited by higher ranking staff and therefore were considered more of a soldiers' 'free zone' where they could get away with a less strict behaviour. It also suggests that writing on the walls was generally not an accepted practice as there is a relatively small amount of writings on the walls in the dormitories, which could easily be inspected by higher ranking staff. The fact that the writing that we do find in the dormitories is of a later date, not too long before the border guard station was closed down in 1991, suggests that there was less importance placed on strict behaviour or that defying the rules had less consequences.

Different sources – different stories

Three pictures emerge of the border guards: the first of soldiers as defenders and keepers of the socialist ideals, the official line, which becomes clear from paintings, signs, the "propaganda room", the orderly soldier that polishes his shoes; the second image being of border guards as young lads, the private line. Lads who cannot wait for the end of their two year service, as seen in the graffiti left behind, who have pictures of naked ladies on the wall and who, years later, reminisce about their time together on an online forum. But there is also the more brutal view from other sources, of guards shooting people trying to escape over the border. I cannot help but feel that the different images of the border guards clash in my head. On the one hand you have the brutal stories of border guards dragging people into the Czechoslovakian side of the border in order to arrest them, as well as pictures of those they killed and on the other hand you have the images of young men doing their military service counting down the days until they can go home, trying to entertain themselves best they can until that day comes. The different stories that emerge from the different sources do not match but are all equally valid.

Today the area of the Podyji Park is mostly used for recreational purposes and to create a 'utopia' for animals and vegetation. The landscape we see today is the result of many different phases of history. Today a lot of emphasis is put on remembering the days of the area as part of Vranov Castle Park. The monuments from this part of the history has been restored, renovated and given a new lease of life. What material that has survived from the militarized phase of the park's history has been more by accident than by choice. In fact in areas where there are more tourists there has been more of a 'clean up' whilst in areas that are less used or where access is prohibited things have survived better, for example soldiers huts. The park's aim is stated on their website: "The target for a protected land, which is awarded the statute of a national park, is primarily to develop the natural values towards a near-natural state and the protection of biodiversity" (Podyji National Park Website). It is clear that the emphasis for the park is on the nature aspects rather than the history. They are however strongly linked with the last two centuries history having created the park as it is today. In fact, had it not been for the militarised borders here nature would probably not have been left as undisturbed as it was. The only part of the former militarised landscape that has been left alone on purpose is the fence and watchtower at Čižov although this appears to have been done not through an official decision but rather through the initiative of one employee. Through new usages of the park as a recreational area and a protected natural zone the everyday actions of new users, tourists, guides, locals, park rangers, create a new landscape by reusing the old, walking the old Castle Park paths walked by border guards, peeking into World War II bunkers, or resting by the former shooting range.

Apart from the material remains that we found in the park itself which tells us of the practical everyday running of the former militarized border we have other sources that sometimes tell a rather different story. The stories may not contradict each other as such but they do show very different aspects of the Iron Curtain, for example between Austria and Czechoslovakia. The physical remains tells us the story of the practical, everyday running of a highly militarized area where the main aim was to stop anyone trying to get through. The memories of former officers and soldiers, both in direct communication and through the Army Forum, tell the story of lads doing their military service, making the best of a time when they would probably have rather been somewhere else. The archival sources in turn also has a different story to tell and here it depends somewhat on what archives one looks at – are we getting the view from the East or the West? From the vast information from archives in the Czech Republic and reports produced by the communist regime we see a rather cold representation of people trying to cross and how to avoid this. We have best practice manuals and a large proportion of escape reports, both successful and unsuccessful. These reports included description of the events, photos and maps in order to learn from every escape attempt and tighten up the security. In archives from the West, such as those examined from the National Archives in London, another story emerges which often tells of border incidences and of the often frightening behaviour at the border. These different stories are difficult to reconcile into one history but they all help us understand the many faces of one monument.

AN ARCHAEOLOGY OF THE IRON CURTAIN

Reference plan and gazetteer of sites

Gazetteer Czech Republic/Austria

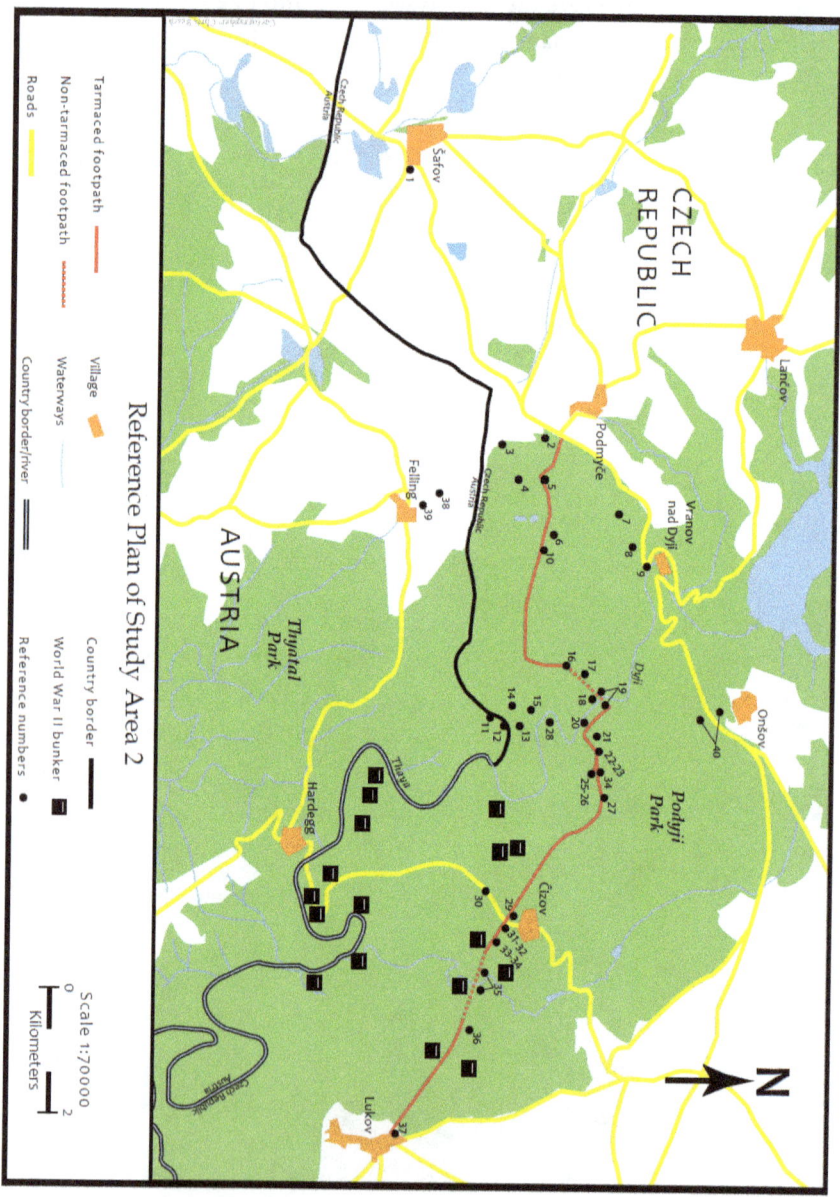

Figure 101.

5: CASE STUDY 2: THE CZECH/AUSTRIAN BORDER

Ref. No.	Description	Comment	Figure
1	Šafov border guard station	Part of the 3.rPS Znojemská brigade. Still holds part of its original fencing. Buildings in varying degree of decay.	76
2	Remains of gate	Formerly located across former access road.	
3	Former road to Felling (Austria)	This former road to Austria was cut off by the Iron Curtain after World War II and could not be crossed.	
4	Hajenka border guard station, officially referred to as 4bPS.	Now used by the park administration. Still fenced off with original border fencing. Buildings in varying degree of decay.	75, 79, 80
5	Electricity transformer along the former fence line.	No longer connected to anything.	
6	Storage facility built into the ground.	Storage facility of unknown origin. Likely to pre-date WWII.	
7	Felicia's Well	Built in honour of Countess Felicia in 1806. Used by border guards for target practice and was much deteriorated when it was restored in 2001.	61
8	Hunting Lodge	Built in the 19th century. Refurbished in the early 21st century.	
9	Vranov Castle	Castle built in 1100 and since refurbished and rebuilt during different periods. Currently functions as a museum.	
10	Newly fenced in area	Two recent wooden fences have been raised along the lines of the former	65

		fence line, to promote vegetation growth.	
11	Information plaque	Indicating the highest point in the park	
12	Memorial stone	Commemoration of people who have extradited from the area throughout history.	
13	Lusthaus	Constructed in the 19th century.	
14	Ziggurat	Construction in the shape of a ziggurat constructed as a monument in the 19th century.	
15	Lookout point	A wooden platform. Views from here are extensive over the river Dyji/Thaya	
16	Turning point for vehicles	Partially tarmacked.	
17	Wooden electricity pole	A small section of electricity pole lying on the ground.	67
18	Cement electricity pole	Electricity pole still standing with cables cut off.	68
19	Remains of former bridge	The former bridge was destroyed during flooding in 2002. Consists of timbers, and soil with cement platforms. Barbed wire was entangled in its base, probably stretching across and possibly in the water.	69
20	Ford	Ford across river reinforced with cement blocks	
21	Former shooting range	Site of former shooting range for border guards.	71
22	Large stone boulders blocking former patrol	Visitors encouraged through blocked entrances to take alternative routes.	70

5: CASE STUDY 2: THE CZECH/AUSTRIAN BORDER

	path	Not marked on tourist maps.	
23	Large drain construction	Cement drainage with metal mesh lid located at the bottom of a steep slope.	
24	Memorial stone	Memorial to Vladimír Urbášek born 1967 and died 1990. No further information about this memorial could be gained.	
25	Cut off wooden poles	A line of electricity poles cut off between 0–20 cm above ground.	66
26	Indents in the ground	Two linear features most probably caused by the former fence and maintained after its removal by water running down the slope.	
27	Cement poles	Remains of additional, smaller, fence located on the north side of the patrol path. This was a lower fence, judging from the approximately 1.20m high cement poles. It is likely it was used to stop stones falling onto the patrol path and fence line from the northern slope.	
28	Border guard hut	A small border guard hut near an old ford across the river. The structure is in poor state of repair. Inside, the walls and ceiling are covered with graffiti.	72–74
29	Building formerly used as Čížov border guard station	The building functioned as a factory before WWII. It now houses an information centre run by the Park Administration and a small museum (nature theme).	
30	Road to Hardegg	Road leads to border crossing by Hardegg (now a pedestrian crossing)	
31	Information board	Added here between my visits in 2009	

		and 2010 with information about the area including some information about the fence and watch tower.	
32	Concrete blocks	Anti-vehicle cement blocks. Their exact original position is not known but is likely to have been placed to stop vehicles along the road to Hardegg.	62
33	Remains of fence	One row of former fence line has been kept here which consists of wooden poles and barbed wire. One gate is located within this fence.	62
34	Watch tower	The only watch tower to remain in the area.	62
35	Iron rods	A series of cast iron rods (11cm wide) are located at the very steep slope through the valley. This suggests there was never a tarmacked road here and that these rods were required for safe stepping when the ground was wet.	
36	Clearing in woodland	Clearing in woodland at the site of a former watch tower.	
37	Lukov border guard station	Was made into a police station after the fall of the Iron Curtain and is now a domestic building.	
38	Memorial stone	A commemoration of people extradited from Vranov	
39	Memorial stone	A commemoration of people extradited from Šafov	
40	Former location of watch towers	Former location of watch towers on route into Vranov.	

CHAPTER 6

An archaeology of the Iron Curtain

Artefacts, text and everything else in between

To utilize a familiar archaeological metaphor, I suggest that we think about the present as a surface – a physical stratum that contains not only the present, but all its physical and imagined pasts combined.

(Harrison 2011:153)

Historical narratives, myth, metaphor and materials; they are all parts of an iron curtain. All intertwined and sometimes separate. My research of the former Iron Curtain was firmly embedded within the historical accounts of the Cold War as I have been brought up with it. Ideas that started forming there on the shore of the Baltic in the 1980s and that have been influenced by the books I have read, the news reports I have heard and the films that I have seen. But what stood out most in the places I visited was not the way the places helped me get a better understanding of the Cold War, how they helped to confirm or contest historical events or the way they connected world history with the local (although they of course had this effect as well). What became most obvious was how the sources from these places had so much to say and how my interaction with these sources created stories far beyond what I had expected. I had planned to let the different sources mix, to take them all into account and to create something from this mixed material, an account of the Iron Curtain. I had expected the sources to say different things, at times to tell the same story and at times to tell different ones and to give different perspectives. What I had not accounted for was the way the different sources were capable of saying so much on their own. I have realised that by really appreciating a source for what it is, not only for how it fits in with other sources, new insights can be made. This was especially true for the physical materials I encountered. I wrote in the introduction chapter that to an archaeologist it should not come as a surprise how important the materials are for how we view history but it still did. Considering that materials are the main source of information for an archaeologist and that it has always been at the heart of this study that may sound ludicrous. But still here I am at the end of the study surprised at the materials' ability to act and interact.

When dealing with a history close to our own there are often more sources available for information than when we are dealing with earlier archaeological periods. Archaeologist Anders Andrén discuss what he calls *the dilemma of the in-betweeness*, created by the specialisation within modern science and means that archaeology of historical periods can find itself in an ambivalent space between material culture and text. He suggests that we have to acknowledge that they are part of two different discourses and although we should attempt to decrease the distance between them we will not solve the problem by seeing objects and texts as the same thing (Andrén 1998:14). Instead we need to approach the material across the disciplines through methodological discussions. Often discussions regarding different sources concentrate on contradictions between them and if one story is more correct than another. In other cases it is the many stories or angles of an event, a period or a place that are in focus and the sources certainly do tell different stories. Within my research, for example, this could be discussed through: the archives from East and West showing official documents from governments with different ideological views; the oral accounts of people who have had very different experiences of the border, as well as the material which often has been altered after its use as a militarised border. When dealing with material from the 20th and 21st century it is, however, not enough to discuss the sources from just the discourses around materiality and text. In my research I have had to deal with both objects and texts but also other sources such as film, news reports, oral accounts, song lyrics and art. All these sources are important in the understanding of the materials that we encounter today and need to be recognized. It is also clear from my fieldwork that it is very difficult to define these different sources in order to fit them into a source category. Is writing on a wall a text or material? How do we classify a memory awakened by an object or a photo accompanied by an oral account? Although they may be ontologically different in their makeup they are still all sources that face us as we approach our material. At times they require different methods but at times they appear surprisingly similar. If anything they demonstrate the different traditions of method and theory that the division between different disciplines has produced and although we often speak in terms of materials versus text it often really comes down to archaeological tradition versus historical tradition. Although I have had my starting point in the material I have tried to take a holistic approach where I acknowledge all material that has come my way despite its ontological background. Although it has not been possible to follow all these leads further, and one is forced to make a selection, this has not been done as a result of seeing one source as less valuable than others. The relationship between the different sources is therefore complex. It is not my aim to go into detail on the relationship between text and material here (although see Andrén 1998) more than to highlight the discourses surrounding these two. Instead I want to focus on the discussion of an alternative to history. Although alternative histories may have been sought within archaeology there has not been much attention paid to reaching something other than, or alternative to, history as noted by archaeologist Þora Pétursdóttir (2012:587), Nandy 1995). "We seek other histories and alternative histories – but we rarely seek beyond it. And while we are concerned with what things remember it is mostly because we believe they give us an alternative perspective on history (which they surely do), but not that their memory may also *differ from history*"(Pétursdóttir 2012:587, emphasis in original).

In the 1980s and 1990s we saw what is referred to as the 'linguistic turn', a part of the post-processual theoretical strand in which the world was to be seen as a text to be interpreted, the material to be used to reach the people behind it (for example: Hodder 1982, Miller and Tilley 1984, for more background see: Johnson 1999, Trigger 2007). It is the social, cultural and symbolic meanings behind the objects themselves which have been considered of most importance. Recently several researchers have claimed that a new 'material turn' is on its way (for example: Burström 2011, Olsen 2012:20, Pétursdóttir 2012:577, Pétursdóttir 2013:32). Within this new 'turn' of archaeology materials are to be seen for what they are and not "[load] them with interpretative burdens they mostly are unfit to carry" (Olsen 2012:22). Archaeologist Bjørnar Olsen writes in his critique of the linguistic paradigm: "[a] boat is never a boat; a reindeer is never a reindeer; a river is always a "cosmic" river" (Olsen 2012:22). "It is possible that our recent persistent efforts to make our silent objects speak – in order to make them meaningful – have made us forget that they actually don't" (Pétursdóttir 2013:47). Both Pétursdóttir (2013) and Olsen (2012) discuss the term 'speaking' in relation to materials, something also brought up also by archaeologist Mats Burström's question: "[W]hat language(s) do things themselves speak?" (Burström 2012:43). Olsen proposes that if objects were actually to speak they would say things like "..."walk here", "sit there", "drive like this", "use that entrance"....." (Olsen 2012:102). He suggests that although this may appear banal this reflects our everyday interaction with materials and as such they are important since they involve our senses, as we touch, smell, taste things and through this everyday encounter with the materials we "create affinity with the world; they evoke the symmetry crucial for our common being *in* it" (Olsen 2012:102–103, emphasis in original). As Burström points out the material turn that can be discerned within archaeology, as well as social sciences as a whole, is not a return to an empirical archaeology but rather a "theoretically well-founded research" in which lessons from the post-processual period are recognised (Burström 2011:54). This is a vital observation as we need to appreciate that a turn to more empirical perspective does not mean we should not try and reach further than using materials to date, to explain providence and usage etc. but we also have to appreciate the materials for what they are and that this is also important. What is important to me is just this: things do not have to have a symbolic meaning or cultural value to be important. Instead, they can be important for what they are and the role they play.

Archaeologist Laurajane Smith has discussed materiality from a heritage point of view and suggests that there is no such thing as heritage but that it is just a discourse (Smith 2006:13). This is a trend that is highly noticeable within the heritage literature (see, for example, Chouliaraki and Fairclough 1999, Fairclough 2003, Fairclough et al. 2008, Harrison et al. 2010, Benton 2010). Intangible values have been recognised and raised most prominently by UNESCO's adoption of the Convention for the Safeguarding of the Intangible Cultural Heritage in 2003 where intangible cultural heritage is described as for example "oral traditions, performing arts, social practices, rituals, festive events, knowledge and practices concerning nature and the universe or the knowledge and skills to produce traditional crafts" (UNESCO website). This focus on the intangible heritage is a reaction against a long prevailing thought in western heritage management, especially within its legal and policy framework, of an intrinsic value of an object, place or practice (Harrison and Schofield 2010:25). As part of a discourse of tangible heritage Smith argues that instead of such a heavy emphasis on tangible heritage we need to focus on the intangible, that it is in our practices that heritage really lies, not in the objects themselves, hence suggesting that there is no such *thing* as heritage (Smith 2006:13). Smith suggests, therefore, that there is nothing inherent in the material itself that is valuable and uses the provocative example of Stonehenge to make her point that it "is basically a collection of rocks in a field" (Smith 2006:3). Criticism of this statement from archaeologist Brit Solli on the other hand counterclaims that "Stonehenge's essence is its durable 'stoniness'" and that there is something inherent in its materiality and permanence (Solli 2011:45). What is missed in this discussion, as shown by Pétursdóttir, is to recognise the hierarchy that is implied within these discussions of tangible or intangible, with one seen as better than the other. Pétursdóttir agrees with Smith that Stonehenge is exactly that, a collection of rocks in a field but what she disagrees with is Smith's way of seeing this to be meaningless and instead she claims that the 'stoniness' should be seen as valuable and important (Pétursdóttir 2013:47). She writes "Conversely though, it is not her [Smith's] statement that 'Stonehenge... is basically a collection of rocks in a field'... that is problematic; *that is in fact exactly what it is*. The problem, however, is to see that as meaningless. What characterizes the intangible heritage discourse (or even heritage discourses in general), as well as much of interpretative archaeology, is not only that meaning, value and significance are seen as inevitably subjective, but also that meaning is confused with or restricted, rather to symbolical or other modes of derivative meanings... is it so that Stonehenge itself, in its simple 'stoniness'... brings nothing of value to the encounters with the subjective experiences that for centuries have circulated around it?" (Pétursdóttir 2013:47, emphasis in original). Although the example of Stonehenge may appear exaggerated it is exactly because of its status as a monumental heritage that it becomes interesting and brings several questions forward. Most of all, I believe, it makes it clear that the discussions in which we place tangible and intangible against each other are not really going to bring the discussion of heritage forward. Similarly to discussions of the different sources we deal with in our research we have to be open to the different types of heritage we are faced with, tangible or intangible, and recognise the value in both. It is here that I fear this material turn is slipping over into the wrong type of focus in which strengthening the value and status of physical objects also means intensifying the divide between objects and other sources even further and with that we risk falling down in Andrén's in-betweeness even further. I believe this material turn has its strength in the way it helps us interpret our sources in order not to load them with cultural and social values they are unfit to hold. It can help us to have an open and holistic methodology towards our sources so that we do not subject our narratives and metaphors to the material that we study and by making sure we do not make objects mere props in our history writing.

Moving in memories

In a story where we start at the materials themselves time is less relevant. We can see in the landscape today how the materials from all periods are intermingled and mixed, all there in the present. Archaeologist Laurent Olivier highlights archaeology's close and problematic affiliation with history and that through this affiliation we are used to seeing time as unilinear. He suggests that the objects that archaeologists study are "memory recorded in materials" (Olivier 2004:211) and should be understood rather for their similarity to memory rather than to narrative history writing. This follows the Freudian idea of memory as fragmented and constantly created and recreated in the past and in the present. He means that the past exists in the present as "fragments of the past [...] embedded in the physical reality of the present" (Olivier 2004:209) as well as the present exists in the past as we read it through our own horizon and our own behaviour (Olivier 2004:210). This idea of the present as multitemporal has also been expressed by archaeologist Gavin Lucas as he moves the attention of *prehistory* from its chronological emphasis to an ontological one and suggests that "prehistory was, above all, history studied through material culture, not through texts" with the consequence that "even archaeologists studying the material culture of the historic past ... are doing prehistory, not history" (Lucas 2004:111). This is true to some extent and an important observation within historical archaeologies that are often so highly dependent on historical sources and narratives. At the same time we cannot, and neither should we want to, escape from the fact that in a period closer to our own we will always be affected by other sources apart from the physical ones. It is not in the distinction between the different sources that the problem lays but rather it is in our way of valuing them differently that the issues arise. We have to appreciate our past as fragmented, that all its pieces does not match up, and that sometimes it creates constellations that we do not expect.

In the Podyji Park time intermingles. The monument to Felicia was constructed as a memorial by Countess of Mniszek and has stood there ever since but it has acted in different situations since its inception: as a memorial in the 1800s, reborn to become the target of the border guards' shooting practice linking two parts of the park's history that are otherwise unlikely to be connected, since reborn again in our present following a restoration and again acting as a memorial but now in a different capacity to a different audience (see Chapter 5). Olivier writes that: "[l]ike memory, archaeological material bears the mark of repetition... it is essentially the same site which is reproduced, similar and yet different every time, because unique at each moment in time" (Olivier 2004:210). Paths lead my feet here just as it has allowed others to walk along it before me. Paths that stretch across the Podyji Park but which continues, almost indefinitely through the landscapes of the former Iron Curtain. Along its route it connects the past and the present through those who have travelled along here before and whose remains can still be seen along its route. On Mount Sabotin/Sabotino the paths take me past structures from the First World War, reused by the border guards and then by myself during a sudden shower, and the trenches the fighters in this war have left behind in the ground; they take me past ramblers who walk along dual paths without knowing their origin on their way to see the remains of a 14th century monastery which has fallen apart over time, its ruination quickened by the destruction during the First World War; the paths take me down along the mountain past flagpoles in which the Slovenian flags were first raised on 25th of June1991; they take me past border crossings, sleepy ones partially used still and deserted ones; they take me past the Countess Liduška's former residence firmly located within Italy, just the way she wanted it when she persuaded the American soldiers to influence the establishment of the border in 1947 (see Chapter 4).

During my field surveys of my study areas I walk through the fragments of the past and the present, all here now for me to see: paths walked by monks, pilgrims, tourists, soldiers, landowners, border guards; bunkers; war trenches; remains of a monastery and church; information boards and graffiti. All fragments from the past intermingling and reactivated in the present. Also the sources that I encounter intermingles: the pictures of poles being hammered into the ground by Nova Gorica railway station, the way the square outside the station building looks today and the way a cyclist waiting for a train jumps over the former Iron Curtain, the dancers across the border that I witnessed one evening. Or the words of Cold War division presented in a news programme, preserved pieces of Berlin Wall, tourists enjoying the well preserved nature of the Podyji Park, an actor on a film set making his way through a barbed wire, a stretch of barbed wire fence in Čižov left by chance, and double paths high up on a mountain between Italy and Slovenia. Or barrack buildings, the writing left within them, official reports by soldiers at the archives and the images of dead people. Documents, objects, photos, people, accounts etc. they are all fragments that sometimes mix and intertwine, sometimes stand on their own. As individual pieces they have their own value, their own story. Sometimes they hook onto each other and create something bigger, something that reaches further, and sometimes they do not. What is important is to not force them into a bigger picture or chronology, to lose track of their individual voice, whatever language they may speak, and to allow ourselves to follow their paths and see where it takes us.

My emphasis on seeing beyond the narrative should not be seen as a way to completely move away from it. Narratives have important functions within the way we write our history. One of the most basic roles of a narrative is to create order and help us organise the information at hand. Chapters 3–5 in this thesis all start with a historical background, all written in a highly narrative style. When we look at the material the narratives can help us understand what we are looking at and to understand why, for example, a fence was changed or removed at a certain point. Narratives are also important as they are a well-established way of writing history and as we have seen in my research, especially in Slovenia, a way for people to connect to others and other people's history. What is important is not to expect to find all the answers in the narrative, or to exclude material that does not fit with it and to be aware that there can be different motives behind using one particular narrative instead of another.

The experience of things

In 2012 I posted a question on the Contemporary and Historical Archaeology in Theory (CHAT) discussion list asking about walkover surveys (McWilliams 2012). This is a term that is used regularly in archaeological reports, articles and texts, but there are no real descriptions or definition of what these entail. I was curious as to what people considered them to be. An array of answers demonstrated that people had very different views, not only of what a walkover survey is but also in the confidence shown in these types of surveys. For many they were just a first step ahead of excavation. Archaeologist Paul Graves-Brown picked up the question and brought it into his presentation "Wandering about" at the 2012 CHAT conference in York and comments on that there is no formal methodology more than English Heritage's reference to reconnaissance as a Level 1 survey seen as a preliminary step ahead of other investigations (English Heritage 2007:3, Graves-Brown 2012:1). But according to Graves-Brown, since excavation is often not the primary approach in contemporary archaeology "walking around is not a preliminary step; it is the methodology" (Graves-Brown 2012:1 emphasis in original). Walkover survey certainly has been a cornerstone in my fieldwork but the lack of formal methodology has at times made me question the validity of what I was doing. Somehow it seemed less legitimate than excavation or other 'proper' archaeological methods. Archaeologist Alfredo Gonzalez-Ruibal rightly points out that we as a profession are the only ones to have "developed a whole methodology to see what is beneath the surface" and this is certainly something that should not be disregarded, neither as a metaphor nor as a methodology but this heavy emphasis on the excavation process itself has caused other methods to appear less valid. As mentioned in the introduction chapter archaeologists Laura McAtackney (2008), Rodney Harrison (2011) and Paul Graves-Brown (2011) have all questioned the way archaeologists often use archaeological techniques such as excavation or buildings recording to validate their practice even in cases where it does not actually bring much to the research. Surely it is in our interaction with the material, whether under or over the surface of the ground, which matters and which provides validity to our research?

Archaeologist Matthew Edgeworth writes about the encounter with the material during excavation and that we should take more note of the importance of our bodies' interaction with the material. He suggests that "[o]ur basic stance in the world and orientation towards things is given in part by directionalities and flows that emerge from our encounters with material evidence" (Edgeworth 2012:91). Edgeworth is particularly describing the process of excavation, following a cut, but the same happens when we encounter materials on the surface, when we wander around the landscape. In our interaction with materials, whether singular objects, ruins, landscapes or archaeological sites our own experiences and our bodies through which we experience become vital. In his *Phenomenology of Landscape* (1994) Archaeologist Christopher Tilley writes: "[p]henomenology involves the understanding and description of things as they are experienced by a subject" (Tilley 1994:12). Archaeological practice, in which practice and theory are in their nature so intertwined, is not just a gathering of information to be theorised over at a later date. The practice itself involves us in a way that we cannot distance ourselves from.

Tilley as well as other archaeologists such as Barbara Bender and Vicky Cummings have been criticised for their efforts to use phenomenology in landscape studies as a way to reach the thoughts of people in the past and understand the motivations behind changes to the landscape carried out in the past (Barret and Ko 2009). As pointed out by Barret and Ko it is not necessarily our own contemporary engagement with the material, in order to describe and understand a site, a series of objects, a larger landscape, that is problematic in itself. Rather, it is when we believe that our own experiences can tell us something about people's experiences in the past that it becomes problematic (Barret and Ko 2009:279). The use of phenomenology within an archaeological framework should be seen as more 'basic' and bodily than this in that it is in the bodily encounter with the material we investigate that it resides, not in our later reflection of it. As Edgeworth suggests it is in our engagement with the materials that the meaning of it is created (Edgeworth 2012:76) but still our interaction with the sites that we investigate is rarely discussed in the reports later written. The writing of Michael Polanyi Graves-Brown speaks of embodied knowledge as a transaction between actors and materials as non-linear but rather more in the form of constellations, "[e]mbodied knowledge is tacit precisely because it exists as constellations, not narratives" (Graves-Brown forthcoming) and as such it escapes words. "[W]e can know more than we can tell" (Polanyi quoted in Graves-Brown, forthcoming). It is in this direct interaction with the material, whether through excavations or other interaction, that our engagement with it helps us create a knowledge of what we study.

Several researchers have written about the way ruins affect us (Van Reijen 1992, Edensor 2005a, Edensor 2005b, DeSilvey 2006, Andreassen *et al.* 2010, Pétursdóttir and Olsen forthcoming, for an historic overview of the subject see Woodward 2002). Something happens when people leave the scene and the objects are allowed to take centre stage. In ethnologist Susanne Wollinger's description of a brigade in Sweden the things are non-existent, overshadowed by the humans that use them, walk amongst them and depend upon them (Wollinger 2000, see Chapter 5). Andreassen *et al.* note on their interaction with the former Soviet mining site of Pyramiden that in a post-human state "[t]hings suddenly 'appear' to us in ways never noticed previously, exposing some of their own unruly 'thingness'" (Andreassen et al. 2010:23). Pétursdottír (2012) lifts the importance of the materials themselves, independent of our archaeological interpretation, and it is often in the abandoned and the leftover that the things get a chance to stand on their own, to be seen for what they are. DeSilvey has, in her studies of a derelict homestead in Montana, shown how the decay of material, often seen as something negative can "be generative of a different kind of knowledge" (DeSilvey 2006:323) letting "other than-human agencies to participate in the telling of stories about particular places" (DeSilvey 2006:318). In a similar way the objects and the 'thingness' of the decaying border guard stations allowed for new stories, new perspectives. Something that would not have been noticeable when the border guards were here crowding these spaces or something the texts and documents in the archives could never convey. This is also what we somehow 'expect' from an archaeological site, for the people to have left, a hangover from studying periods where people are long gone and all that remains are pieces. Here studies of a more recent past do differ from studies of earlier periods. Often we study the abandoned, such as ruins, which we in some way seem to be more comfortable with. We know what to do here, our methods just work. But what happens with those sites that are still used?

Archaeologists are used to dealing with the abandoned. In fact one of the criteria for protecting an archaeological site through policy and legislation in Sweden is that it has been abandoned for a considerable amount of time (varaktigt övergiven) which means it is no longer in use and will not be taken into use again (SFS 1988:950). Even though this definition may not be present as such in other countries' heritage laws it demonstrates a general attitude within archaeology of how we deal with that which is abandoned and no longer in use. But what does this mean when we are pushing the materials that we study further and further into the present? I do not believe it to be a coincidence that the sites that contemporary archaeologists, including my own research, tend to search out are the places that are deserted and uninhabited (although see Kiddey and Schofield 2011 for a different approach). This is what we are used to and what our methods generally allow us to look at. Andreasson et al. as well as Pétursdottír and DeSilvey make a very good case for how the material stands out clearer when not crowded by people. How in the abandoned we can see the 'thingness' of the objects left behind. But what happens in places where people are still present? Where materials and humans are still acting together creating networks and connections? Do we ask people to leave the scene or should we wait until a place have been abandoned? Something that has become clear during my research is that we need to develop and adjust the methods that we use to allow people and objects both to take centre stage without one crowding the other. Surely this emphasis on things in a 'material turn' should not increase the divide between things and humans; rather it should bridge it by putting them on equal terms?

Of course ruins often entice our imagination. Political scientist Anca Pusca (2010) writes of how the decay of buildings is often connected with the notion of dystopia and explains that as spaces and buildings were often highly important for the communist utopia their subsequent fall and ruin has come to symbolise the demise of this ideology. Walking in ruins also awakens a sense of curiosity within us. Edensor describes the feeling as: "movement in ruins becomes strangely reminiscent of childhood sensory immersion and of the pleasurable negotiation of space largely denied to adults" (Edensor 2005a:838). As I walk through the abandoned border guard stations I am spurred on by my curiosity and sense of adventure and I move through the rooms and the corridors eager to find out what is hiding behind the next corner. Is this how one should react when investigating Cold War remains? Should I not be more taken back by the severity of place? But this is exactly the paradox that is with me through many of the visits along the former Iron Curtain. My knowledge of these places' history and a hindsight perspective tells me that I should experience the serious reality behind the Cold War metaphor but what I mostly come across is the traces of the mundane and the everyday. Things that are easy to relate to as part of the ordinariness of life, we sleep, we eat, we have obligations and we try and entertain ourselves. The military remains we often hear about such as bunkers and fortifications, airfields, graves, nuclear research sites and missile bases are important to the understanding of war, but so are the smaller sites, the places of the everyday activities for a large part of those who participated within the war. These sites will provide an understanding of the many different angles and perspectives a war or a conflict can be experienced through.

I could be criticised for producing a too 'nice' portrait of the Iron Curtain, that the severity and cold bloodedness of this monument and of the Cold War is understated to give way to the everyday stories of a more harmless character. But it is not a conscious decision from my side to angle the stories in this way. Instead this is the result of the material that I have encountered. I have no doubt that if I had used different sources and different focus that the picture would have been different. If I, for example, had based my research mainly on personal stories including people from all over the former Czechoslovakia or even the former Eastern Bloc in general or of those that had crossed over or have relatives and friends that have tried to cross over the border the picture of the Iron Curtain would have been a different one. But I wanted to start at the sites and at the materials and work from there to see what stories that emanated from these. This showed a slightly different side of the Iron Curtain than what we know from history writing. From the archives a few stories and pictures gave a glimpse of the horrors that these militarised borders could entail. Mostly, however, the sources provided a more mundane picture. This demonstrates the strength of these types of studies in their ability to provide different stories that do not necessarily fit with our historical narratives but which instead demonstrate an important other aspect of history. It also demonstrates the problems that could appear from just relying on one type of source. Instead we need to appreciate that all stories and fragments of history are important even if they do not necessarily fit together.

The sites may seem more unusual to some than others. They will be more familiar to those who have done military service, for example, than to those who have not. For me and my preconceived ideas of the severity of the Iron Curtain the clashes between the official and the private were quite strong. For others who were once young men being trained as soldiers or conscripted into military service, the clashes that I experienced in trying to fit the pictures of the official line and the soldiers being and acting like young lads may not be as strong. We all bring our preconceived ideas with us into our research.

To go with the flow

To archaeologist Rodney Harrison (2011) the relationship between depth and surface is a metaphor for the relationship between archaeology and modernity. He claims that the metaphor of depth and stratigraphy creates a distance between the present and the past. In contrast, he suggests that the use of the metaphor surface instead draws the past and present together to exist in the same time and space, a kind of surface assemblage. By referring to Walter Benjamin's 'Jetztzeit', 'now-time', Harrison suggests that we are "no longer dealing with a historical present, but a series of localized and hence spatialized presents and pasts that are generated by the relationships between the particular people and things contained within them" (Harrison 2011:183). In her studies of an entertainment complex in the Japanese city of Osaka social scientist Albena Yaneva emphasises the importance of Actor Network Theory (ANT) for the idea of surface assemblage as it studies "assemblages of humans and non-humans jumbled together in the present" and that "ANT methodologies can help to create a space in which the past, present and future are combined and are still in the process of *becoming*" (Yaneva 2013:25 emphasis in original).

This is not an ANT study. There are many points where I am too far from an ANT perspective, maybe most fundamentally as the perspective I have used when taking on this material is from myself, my body. The way that objects impact upon each other is less explored. In this sense one can say that I hold an anthropocentric perspective that is not compatible with

ANT and that in my research the balance between humans and non-humans are unequal. But influences from ANT have still made their way into my research and at times with a quite strong presence.

The first influence that ANT has had on my research is an opening of my eyes to the role of things. Instead of just seeing objects as props on the stage of history or as a means of reaching beyond it, ANT has helped me see how objects in themselves are important actors who can stop a tank from crossing a border, facilitate everyday life for soldiers or allow for easy crossing through a border crossing. But it is not necessarily just the material objects that should be seen as actors but all parts of the past that we encounter today have to be seen as important influences of the past in the present, whether fences, newspaper articles, films, photos or accounts. In the creation of the Iron Curtain I encounter today they have all had a role to play.

The second point of influence that I have taken with me from ANT is to 'go with the flow' and to follow the material. ANT can be seen as a kind of methodology for tracing the associations between the different actors within a so called network. The term Actor Network Theory is not unproblematic and has been used, buried and resurrected by its users, for example Latour who claims that "'actor-network-theory', a name that is so awkward, so confusing, so meaningless that it deserves to be kept" (Latour 2005:9). The word network should be seen more as associations and not structured or set networks and as Law (2009) points out ANT is not a theory as theories generally tries to explain why something happens and ANT can be seen more as a descriptive methodology (Law 2009:141).

Latour suggests that instead of ordering the social beforehand into convenient categories we should try to understand how the actors (human and non-human) themselves act and interact by tracing the connections between them (Latour 2005:23). Archaeologist Jonathan Westin brings Latour's thoughts into archaeology when he writes: "…a single letter of [an] inscription is not accountable for the meaning of those words or sentences it helps form, political or religious as they may be. […] It is not a process where the primary movement is that of cultural values trickling down and affecting the parts, but a process where the greater movement is that of parts soaring upwards" (Westin 2012:39). Within post-processual archaeology the aim has been to reach beyond the objects to the people behind them, to translate the objects into the cultural and social symbolism that they are presumed to represent. By doing this, making the objects symbolise the trends and the cultural values that we are researching, we take in advance that which we are researching and place it in an already established order or structure. In this way, for example, I could have demonstrated several ways in which communism and its oppression trickles through the many layers of people and objects all the way down to the barbed wire still present in Čižov. Instead I have taken ANT as an inspiration in the way I am turning, firstly, to the materials themselves and letting them and the connections between them and the people involved with them guide me towards an understanding of their whole and to see them as building blocks that together may, or may not, create a larger network.

Yaneva demonstrate two methodological approaches to material culture in her case study of an entertainment complex (Yaneva 2013). She does this through the eyes of the 'hasty sightseer' and the 'slow sightseer', the first of which, through hurrying through the ethnographical fieldwork only has time to gain an impression of the material and reproduce concepts of society and culture rather than, the second who through a slower methodology can understand the material through experiencing it (Yaneva 2013:11). She writes: "ANT gives us one more tool, with which to follow the painstaking ways humans interact with objects and environments, and shape dynamic contemporary cultures at different scales" (Yaneva 2013:25).

I have already mentioned how the fence and the watchtower in the village of Čižov demands attention, and they really do. It was images of these that drew my attention to this location in the first place. When I first saw these pictures on the internet I thought this tower and the fence represented the dark past of the Iron Curtain in an acute way. I had that with me when I arrived here. Yet when I climbed up the watchtower, and got over my initial dizziness of the distance between me and the ground, I was taken by the beautiful view across the park and down towards the valley of the Dyji River. I wondered how much this landscape had changed over the last few centuries. I wondered if the border guards enjoyed the view during their shifts up here. Early one morning as I walked along the fence the sun started pushing through the moody looking clouds and I took several pictures capturing the dark clouds, the sun slightly against the lens of my camera and the barbed wire almost glistening in the sun's rays. At this moment the fence was almost beautiful (Figure 101).

My preconceptions tell me that I am not allowed to think such a thing at all. This is a monument that lifts the memory of people killed trying to cross it, it is a witness of oppression, it is a testament of a divided Europe, a symbol of the Cold War. But I find that this is not enough. I find that the material has more to say. The watchtowers were prefabricated in a factory and transported to the site to be assembled here, the material to these towers reached the factory in which they were made from yet another place. The person who put together the IKEA-like instructions was maybe placed at the same factory, maybe somewhere else, the paper produced from wood felled at another site. The trucks that brought them here were probably serviced regularly by a mechanic. These networks of people and things demonstrate that the making and assembling of these watchtowers involved many different people, vehicles, tools which can all be seen as actors in their construction. What becomes clear through following these connections is how the totalitarian and dark oppression of people that I first wanted to place on a symbolic piece of barbed wire extended so much longer, further to include so much more, and in that making it somehow stronger. None of these different elements can be seen as responsible for the oppression of the people but they were all part of a system that held this oppression together, even though it might have been unknown to them. These were people who got up in the morning and headed off to their job in a factory or a mechanics, a job like any other. I came here to find the barbed wire of the metaphor I had got to know as I grew up but what I find is something else. As I climbed down the metal steps of the watchtower I realized that this is not monumental, in fact, it is rather mundane.

One can see this as a sort of material correlation to Hannah Arendt's observations of how networks in society can create circumstances where evil can be found in the ordinary, the 'banality of evil' (Arendt 1963:252). In *Eichmann in Jerusalem: A Report on the Banality of Evil* Arendt wrote about the former SS officer Adolf Eichmann who was put on trial in Jerusalem and subsequently found guilty and hung for his role in "the final solution of the Jewish question" (Arendt 1963:5). Arendt's observations as she looks closely at his role in the Nazi machine show that by breaking down events, people and places into smaller pieces when studying them it becomes clear how they can appear much more banal and ordinary than first thought. She described how people expected to see a monster in court, something encouraged by the prosecution (Arendt 1963:54), but instead they saw an ordinary looking man: "medium-sized, slender, middle-aged, with receding hair, ill-fitting teeth, and nearsighted eyes" (Arendt 1963:5) who was more a clown than a monster. Even if our historical knowledge makes us look at a person, a material or an event through particular glasses, creating expectations of what we should find, it often becomes clear when looking at the smaller pieces that what we see as evil can be found in the most ordinary and banal.

Figure 102: Fence and Watch Tower at Čížov. Photo: Anna McWilliams.

Arendt makes a distinction between the *doer* and the *deeds*: "The deeds are monstrous, but the doer (Eichmann) is *not* a monster; 'he is terrifyingly normal'" (Bernstein 2010:133). Philosopher Richard J. Bernstein, who has suggested that Arendt's use of the term 'banality of evil' has been much misunderstood in part as many has taken this to mean that she considered Eichmann to be just an innocent cog in the Nazi system, which she did not (Bernstein 2010). Her descriptions of Eichmann and of the trials clearly show that she thought he was guilty. Instead through looking at all the pieces of his life within the Nazi system she demonstrates that he is rather ordinary and that it was more out of thoughtlessness or "inability to think" (Arendt 1971:417) that he committed these crimes rather than being a monster. Bernstein also suggests that people have thought she was trying to create some sort of theory or thesis on the nature of evil to which he refers to a lecture given by Arendt in 1971, *Thinking and Moral Considerations* in which she claims that: "...reporting the trial of Eichmann in Jerusalem, I spoke of the "banality of evil" and meant with this no theory or doctrine but something quite factual, the phenomenon of evil deeds, committed on a gigantic scale, which could not be traced to any particularity of wickedness, pathology, or ideological conviction in the doer, whose only personal distinction was perhaps an extraordinary shallowness" (Arendt 1971:417, Bernstein 2010:133).

To discover the mundane is therefore not the same as finding the trivial. It is not my intention to go into the question of guilt or where evil lies within a system as the one Eichmann functioned in as much of the discussions about Arendt's observations have come to focus on this (for a discussion of this discourse see Bernstein 2010:131) or within the communist system in Czechoslovakia at the time. Instead my observations are to make clear that by starting with the materials themselves we can see how the networks that connect these with other materials, places, people, and events can extend in a way that we would not expect. I also want to demonstrate in what we may see as traces of the mundane and the everyday how we can also find clues that can help us understand a system from the bottom up. It is neither my intention to go into the details of what ordinary life in Czechoslovakia at the time was like or the Eastern or Western bloc more generally for that matter. What I want to demonstrate is what the materials from the sites that I have investigated reveal and that it is only by starting within these small pieces that it is possible to extend such research through the networks outwards and upwards in order not to load the materials with meanings that they are not fit to hold. It is in the discovery of the smaller components, however mundane, that we can gain a better understanding of the bigger picture.

The mundane war

In his review of Andreassen, Bjerck and Olsen (2010) archaeologist John Schofield writes about the importance of the mundane within the pictures they display in the book. He writes: "… it is not views and sight-lines that matter so much as the mundane, the everyday details of the place – objects, surfaces and their sometimes odd juxtaposition" (Schofield 2012:133). The most common find at excavations of sites from any period are those of the mundane, the everyday and even the banal. We find broken pots, ceramics, stone axes, glass bottles, clay pipes, all finds that have been part of everyday, mundane activities. The finds from a time closer to our own have a habit of finding their way under our skin, more so than those of older periods, partly because they fit easier into our own understanding. They remind us of the things we have around us in our own mundane lives. As there are more sources remaining it can be easier to follow the different leads and understand the relationship between different parts.

When we think about remains of the Cold War we often refer to large military installations or sites connected with the nuclear arms race. This is clear also in most of the sites related to the Cold War that have so far been studied by archaeologists which have consisted of sites noted for their monumentality and significance in relation to the Cold War narratives we are so familiar with (for example Cocroft 2003, Schofield and Cocroft 2007, Burström *et al.* 2011). This is also true for my own research. There are few symbols or monuments cited as often within historical narratives of the Cold War as the Iron Curtain and as many others I started with a view of the monumental and what seemed most significant. My previous historical knowledge also informed me in my choice of study areas and what materials to approach during the early stages of my research. But what has become very clear during my fieldwork is that the sites and the objects that stand out the most are the leftovers of the mundane. The majority of the sites linked in some way to the Cold War are often smaller sites, places seen less important to the world in general but in fact probably more significant than they have been credited for. These are the sites that make up the intrinsic network of actions, people, objects that created the solidness of the Cold War. What I have always found so interesting about the Cold War is exactly this, that it is not only about the large military installations or the sites that had the worlds eyes focused on them during much of the second part of the last century, interesting as they may be, but it is also about the way that Cold War, ironically, came closer to the people than many other wars in the past had. The constant threat of war was hanging heavy over the population in both East and West and reached us through media, through information packs delivered by the government in some countries of how to act in case of nuclear fallout and through emergency drills to prepare the population further. Growing up in a small town on the east coast of Sweden I knew exactly where our closest fallout shelter was located, at three o'clock on the first Monday of every month I heard the warning sirens as they were tested and I had seen the government issued brochures "In case of war" (*Om kriget kommer*), a handbook sent out to all citizens which explained evacuation plans, what to pack and other useful information of what to do in case of war. Similar handbooks were also issued in Denmark (*Hvis krigen kommer*), West Germany (*Jeder hat eine Chance*), East Germany (*Was jeden über den Luftschutz wissen muss*) and in Switzerland (*Défense Civile*) (Cronqvist 2008:452). News on the radio and on TV reported on the latest update on the US and USSR flexing their muscles and on the suspected sightings of yet another submarine within Swedish territory in the Baltic Sea whilst spy films and novels described the division between East and West as concrete, barbed wire and diligent guards who would not hesitate to shoot. The Cold War was all around and at the same time nowhere to be seen. As a child I asked my parents on a regular basis if we were at war yet. Their response was always a look of surprise and they would ask where I got such an idea from. I could never give them a very good answer, but as I think back now I find it less odd that one of my biggest fears as a child was one of war, seeing the whole society around me was one of total war preparation even though this was not explicitly stated, at least not in a 'neutral' Sweden.

Even in places that were seemingly more involved in the Cold War than Sweden such as those on the border between the Eastern and Western blocs, the sites connected with this war were mostly made up of smaller military installations, protective zones and no-man's land areas. Important as they were for sustaining the Cold War and the division that characterised it, they were often rather banal in their character. It is exactly this mundaneness that becomes evident when you visit these places. The stories that come from these sites are far less known. This is of course not exclusive to military sites. About her visits to an abandoned herring station in Iceland about which long accounts had already been produced, Pétursdóttir writes: "…while Eyri and the herring history appeared to be so well known, all these things I encountered on my first visit were unknown, unaccounted- and uncared for"

(Pétursdóttir 2012:584). The material we encounter in the places of the Cold War may not look like we expect them to and this is an important point to make. As they may tell other stories they may not fit into our known narratives and accounts. Narratives can be seen as a consequence of the 'linguistic turn' and according to Solli "[c]onsidering the legacy of the linguistic turn nothing is proving more resilient than narrative" (Solli 2011:43). Criticising this narrativisation can therefore be seen as a quite natural part of a 'material turn' in which there is less stress on translating objects and the study thereof into narratives. It is an important point to make as it has consequences for the material that we study. In trying to fit them into our known accounts and narratives we can actually cause damage to these sites in the process. By excluding those fragmented objects and the memories they entail because they may not fit into our narratives we are actively forgetting them. Pétursdóttir demonstrates through her research that "archaeological remembering of this site, and its inclusion in historical narration, can in fact easily result in the active forgetting of things, their fragmented and discontinuous memory and their utter silence" (Pétursdóttir 2012:577). The sites and materials that are not included in the historical narratives are therefore in danger of disappearing altogether. Maybe this is not an issue in itself, not everything can remain, but will be if we think that what we have left in our historical narratives and accounts is representative of a particular time, period or event.

How the material of the former borders has been treated in Slovenia/Italy, Czechoslovakia/Austria and Berlin varies. In Berlin the historical narratives of the Cold War and the metaphor of the Berlin Wall and the Iron Curtain are highly established. Here the story of Cold War division became so physical and obvious and as shown in Chapter 2 the idea of the Iron Curtain intertwined with the physical Berlin Wall. Through history writing, politics, popular culture and media the story of the Berlin Wall as the Iron Curtain was created. The treatment of sites and objects of the Berlin Wall therefore have to relate to this narrative and metaphor. To allow the remains to stand on their own as different fragmented stories that do not relate or fit into this grand narrative causes problems. On the Slovenia/Italy border the remains have not really been connected to the larger historical narratives in the same way and have therefore not been burdened with such a heavy requirement. Instead we find smaller, more local stories connected with the changing of the border line, smuggling and trade across the border etc. Interestingly, the local narratives here appear to be in a process of trying to connect with the European Cold War history, possibly as a wish to connect to European narratives. In this process the border is used to connect to a wider historical narrative of the Iron Curtain and here the physical remains of the border such as the watch tower made into a museum and the images and remains of the former more militarised border at the Railway Museum are being lifted forward as a link and possibly as a way to authenticate this connection. In the Czech Republic the stories of the border is as fragmented as the materiality that remains. The different parts do not really fit into a clear narrative even though it is of course possible to relate parts of it to the general historical narratives of the area as well as to more regional and global accounts. The three cases I have used have very different contexts. The study area by the Slovenian/Italian border has always belonged to a living community with traffic across it and a relationship across the border. Berlin has even more of a living community and the border here no longer exists. It has returned to be one town, one homogenous society. Yet again, in the Czech Republic/Austria these areas have been depopulated over long periods of time and are still sparsely populated today. Here there is much less interaction over the border today despite EU and Schengen memberships. But despite their different contexts, or maybe just because of these differences, a comparison between them still demonstrates the different processes that are involved in how we write our history and create our heritage.

It is impossible to study everything. 'Stuff' will inevitably disappear unnoticed and the historical accounts that we have got used to ordering our past into within our post-modern society will be written, but by being aware of this process and by taking a different approach to the sources and the materials that we study we can try and challenge this method of creating archaeology in a historical way even when we are dealing with historical archaeology. As mentioned above Olivier suggests that we should understand archaeology more in relation to memory, as more fragmented than the historical chronology as "memory-time functions in a way which has nothing to do with history-time" (Olivier 2004:211). Through really looking at the material, through experiencing it and describing it we can see different constellations than those we encounter in the history writing. We have to be able to see that the narratives are an important part of how we see the past but it is not the only way of seeing the past. Materiality, for example, often provides different constellations than historical narratives and these should not be valued any less.

An archaeology of a metaphor

The metaphor of the Iron Curtain, as demonstrated in Chapter 2, is strongly connected to the narrative history created through historical accounts, media, films, novels, materiality etc., but how does this connect to the materials? The impact of popular culture can be seen to have had a major effect on the idea of the Iron Curtain as well as the Cold War. The effects of historical films have, for example, been discussed by historians Robert Rosenstone (2006) and Alun Munslow (2007) who suggest that film production is also a way to write history that needs to be taken seriously and not be dismissed as less legitimate. It is recognised that film can have a cognitive mechanism and "create experiential and emotional complexities way beyond the printed page" (Munslow 2007:572). The idea that experiences are becoming increasingly important to people has been raised by several researchers such as archaeologist Cornelius Holtorf (2007). Similarly to other researchers, of which many of them are active within marketing studies such as Pine and Gilmore (1999), he claims that the importance lies in "*engaging* people sensually, cognitively, socially, culturally and emotionally"(Holtorf 2007:6). Much of the influences of Holtorf, Pine and Gilmore's work come from the thoughts of sociologist Gerhard Schulze (1993), who claimed that society was becoming increasingly focussed on how things feel, a "commodification of the eventful" (Löfgren 1999:14). Ethnologist Orvar Löfgren, whose interest lies in tourism, suggests that Schultze's claims of this being a completely new phenomenon is not really true as these ideas have been around for quite some time within travel and tourism (Löfgren 1999:16). But as Holtorf also points out this 'experience value', has now extended into almost every field including archaeology and heritage and suggests that it is the experience of the sites and the stories that are more important than the acquisition of new knowledge (Holtorf 2007:4). Although not true for everyone we have to understand that some people are more interested in using the sites and the materiality to confirm and authenticate their already existing view of history. This can be seen as one of the issues with the two Berlin museums, where one, Documentation Centre, corresponds better with material story (possibly a bit less impressive and more fragmented) whilst the other, Haus am Checkpoint Charlie, corresponds more to the metaphor and the historical narratives of the Berlin Wall, of the Iron Curtain and of the Cold War that have been created and recreated since World War II. This can also be seen on a much smaller scale in Slovenia where the 'idea' of an Iron Curtain has started to make its way into the history writing in that it is used to connect the local history to world history through the materiality of the border. This is mainly, at least so far, lifted forward at the museum of the former watch tower and to some extent in the border museum in Nova Gorica railway station but was also picked up and used by media in 2004 when Slovenia entered EU and Schengen when headlines like "Towns dismantle Cold War fence" were used (BBC News 2004). When we deal with a material closer to our own time there is therefore a need to consider not just the materials and the historical texts that have been produced but also an array of other influences, for example popular culture. It is of course not only the sites and materials of recent periods which have been affected by these types of influences. One example is the case of the Vikings and how the study and portrayal of them in history writing, popular culture, media and heritage and tourist sites has affected the way they are seen. In his doctoral thesis archaeologist Fredrik Svanberg argues that "the core of "the Viking Age" is a system of related axiomatic ideas that was put together about 130 years ago by some of the founding fathers of Scandinavian archaeology" and means that the idea of the Viking was constructed under the heavy influence of nationalism (Svanberg 2003:11). From these early nationalistic influences the image of the Vikings has since come to evolve. Chris Halewood, active in the field of Environmental Studies and geographer Kevin Hannam suggests that the image of the Viking has been heavily influenced by heritage tourism and popular culture. They suggest that the Viking is often portrayed as a bloodthirsty barbarian in the Anglo-American stereotypical representation of the Vikings, using films such as the Kirk Douglas' film *The Vikings*, novels such as *The Longships* by Frans Bengsson and the cartoon strip *Hagar the Horrible* as examples. Instead, they suggest, the Scandinavian image of the Vikings in popular culture rather stresses that although they were seen as pirates abroad they were living in well-ordered societies at home and that this is still the way they are portrayed in popular culture such as films as well as in many heritage sites (Halewood and Hannam 2001:566). They claim however, that it is the bloodthirsty image that tends to draw most visitors to the heritage sites (Halewood and Hannam 2001:566). Remains and stories of older periods are therefore also affected by the later portraits produced by them but what can be seen to distinguish the sites and materials of later periods is that it may be easier to study more in detail how these developments have taken place and what the influences are from their conception until the present.

6: AN ARCHAEOLOGY OF THE IRON CURTAIN

Holtorf suggests that it is not necessarily the public that need a better understanding of archaeology but the archaeologists that need a better understanding of the public (Holtorf 2007:6). If we do not understand how the past that we see in the present has been created we cannot understand different people's connections with it and why people interact with it the way they do.

There is also an issue of how we value these different parts of the puzzle. In Berlin the stories that have arrived out of the narratives and the metaphor have a very high significance to the story of the Berlin Wall. But still the narratives and the metaphor have a need to be authenticated with material 'proof' such as barbed wire on a film poster, the objects in museums, the remains left in the landscapes in Berlin and to some extent in Slovenia where it is used, especially at the watchtower museum and the remains in the railway museum, to connect with a wider European history. These items are there to confirm the narrative. Not to provide another type of story. This is very common. In a way, in the Czech Republic where some remains have just been left they are easier to follow and understand as they have not been clearly put into a historical narrative. Here they just stand without being forced into a story or trying to fit in with the Iron Curtain metaphor.

What happens when the metaphor and the material do not correspond? Often there is a need to make them match which raises the question: is it easier to change an established narrative or the material? So strong are the narratives that we create and so difficult is it for us to think in other terms that the two have to be made to fit together, even if it means changing the physicality behind it or at least the stories of which they speak. It is clear, through looking at this research, that the metaphor and historical narratives of the Iron Curtain have had a major impact on not just its own story but also on Cold War history in general. It is a problem when the material does not fit into the narrative and it therefore appears we need to change and adapt to make it fit better. The problem is therefore not that they tell different stories but rather that we are not allowing them to. As conservation architect Leo Schmidt demonstrates there are no sections of Berlin Wall left today that corresponds with people's views (Schmidt 2005:16, see Chapter 2). This has created major tension in discussions of managing the remains of the Berlin Wall today. The problem, as I see it, is not the fact that there are different stories that appear from different sources, the problem arises when we insist on forcing them together even when they do not fit. Like trying to piece together many different puzzles into one, sawing and filing at the pieces until they fit, inevitably losing parts of them in the process. In doing this it also becomes much more difficult to understand how it came to be and it becomes difficult to trace all the different influences that helped to shape the material that we see today, that has been part of their 'becoming', the constructions of structures, the developing ideas of these intermingled with politics, propaganda, popular culture and sometimes just pure randomness which results in materials being left, changed or removed.

The end of a journey

The abundance of sources generally available when dealing with a period closer to our own and the opportunities and problems that this brings is clearly demonstrated in this research. However we classify our sources as photographs, objects, written reports, films, oral accounts, maps etc. we still have to address them. Our methods for how we approach the different materials may differ but the problem does not lie in the ontological difference in the sources that we use but rather when we value them differently and when we place an historical narrative account against the archaeological material and try and join them into one coherent story. Instead we have to appreciate the sources for what they are and recognise the roles they may or may not have played. Andrén makes an important point when he says that differences between text and objects need to be recognised (Andén 1998:14) but by concentrating too hard their differences we risk missing what connects them.

Of course we have to limit ourselves. When the sources are abundant it is just not possible to follow all the leads. I wrote in the introduction to this thesis that my start and point of return have been archaeological and my focus has been on the physical remains. However other sources and the interaction with these should not in any way be seen as un-archaeological. The abundance of information about the places we study force us to draw boundaries of what to include and what we have to leave be. Some of these decisions are more obvious than others. What has become evident throughout my research is that the different sources are not just a means to an end, something that have to be gathered in order to reassemble a past, but rather the sources and the tracing thereof are an important part of the stories that emerge and are themselves active both in the past and in the present. In our research we follow the actors of the stories we tell, they are all part of the material that we track. They do not always act in the way we want or expect them to but instead of discarding the parts that we do not think fit or which we think cannot create enough of an interesting discussion in relation to the accounts that we know we need to let them stand by themselves. Instead of taking the view of Yaneva's 'hasty sightseer' discussed above, who only reproduces concepts of society and culture, we need to go with the flow and follow the connections. An archaeology of surface should not be seen as equivalent to superficiality but should instead be seen it as an opportunity to stretch our research in all directions, horizontally as well as vertically. When we follow the different tracks and paths that the sources lead us through we can make connections and find stories we were not expecting. We can see how materials and periods are intertwined in often unexpected ways and that the past that we see in the present is here for us to see as a result of a long list of influences. For the Iron Curtain these influences involve many factors such as the materiality, the narratives, the metaphors, people's attitude in the past and today, media, popular culture and how different people interact with the material today. It is important to see all these factors in order to understand *how* the material was created. It is a long and at times rather random process which is constantly recreating the material and the attitudes of it.

One of the consequences of following the material of the Iron Curtain is that I have been led to sights that were so much less monumental and much more mundane than what I had expected. Starting from one of the most monumental of Cold War icons and metaphors, the Iron Curtain, I found smaller sites that at first may appear rather insignificant but when you look at them, really look at them, they surprise you in the way that they connect with so much more such as different time periods, physical places, people, objects, histories, stories etc. and it becomes clear how significant these places really were during the Cold War. How these different connections extend into today varies. Those parts that do not fit are often forgotten, consciously or not.

The observant reader is likely to have noticed the heavy emphasis in this thesis on the eastern side of the borders, especially in my fieldwork studies where remains in Slovenia and the Czech Republic has come to figure much more than the remains in Italy and Austria. This was not intentional but was a result of the material that I studied. It is also something which demonstrates that the physical side of the Iron Curtain, the militarised borders, were in fact here, on the eastern side, sometimes a few kilometres inside the East/West divide. This puts it in an interesting contrast to the idea of the Iron Curtain which is, as we have seen, much of a Western idea. So the friend, whom I mentioned in the beginning of this thesis, who pointed out that the Iron Curtain never existed was in part right, at least from his western point of view. From this angle it was merely a metaphor. But had he lived in the Eastern bloc during the Cold War his view would most likely have been another and he would have claimed that the Iron Curtain was indeed a very real thing, a prison wall keeping people in rather than a protective barrier keeping the enemies out. The term may be of western origin but its presence was certainly an eastern reality.

I have used my research, in particular the process of my fieldwork, in two main ways: firstly to connect to Harrison and Schofield's call for more research of the contemporary past in order to test methods which are still seen as experimental (Harrison and Schofield 2010:88). In this work I have noticed that there is indeed great insecurity within the validity of some of the methods often used within contemporary archaeology, something that I have tried to highlight and in part address in this thesis. The research should also be seen in relation to Harrison's ideas of archaeology as a surface in which past and present exists 'now' which also connects with Olivier, Olsen, Pétursdóttir and others' discussion of the past within the present. I have also wanted to use my research to demonstrate the complex process of how the past that we see in the present can be created and recreated and how open we need to be in our approach in order to see this process, to see that the influences can be so much more extensive than what we first might think. If we carry out our research as hasty sightseers we will only reproduce those narratives which are known to us. I started at the monumental, at the metaphor of the Iron Curtain. I came across plenty of barbed wire and concrete but I found that loading this with all the symbolism of the Iron Curtain was not enough. Instead of confirming the known narratives of the Cold War with the objects that I found I followed the material and let it show me other types of connections and fragments.

Finally, and possibly most importantly, I have wanted to shine a light on this amazing material that is the archaeology of the Iron Curtain, an archaeology of a metaphor.

Sammanfattning
(Summary in Swedish)

Ett vanligt förekommande uttryck i diskussioner om kalla kriget är begreppet "järnridå". Man talar om läget "bakom järnridån" eller vad som hände "efter järnridåns fall". Men vad är det egentligen man menar när man använder sig av denna liknelse? I ett berömt tal från 1946 beskrev Winston Churchill hur en järnridå sänkts över den europeiska kontinenten, från Stettin vid Östersjön till Trieste vid Adriatiska havet (Wright 2007:43). Detta uttalande har bildat utgångspunkt för avhandlingens fokus: att undersöka de materiella lämningarna längs de forna militariserade gränserna genom Europa. Med undantag av den inre tyska gränsen, och då i synnerhet Berlinmuren, är dessa lämningar ett i stort sätt outforskat område i tidigare forskning och litteratur.

Syftet med avhandlingen är att utforska vad de fysiska spåren av järnridån kan berätta, och vad dessa lämningar betyder eller har betytt för människor i dess närhet. I undersökningen jämförs också de materiella spåren av järnridån med de idémässiga föreställningar om järnridån som växte fram i väst under kalla kriget. Hur förhåller sig metaforen järnridån till den fysiska järnridån? Är det samma historia som återspeglas?

En annan fråga som behandlas i avhandlingen är järnridåns status som kulturarv. Med tiden har många av lämningarna längs den forna militariserade gränsen omförhandlats, och på flera platser har miljöerna redan etablerats som obestridliga kulturarv. Men det finns också platser där det anses uteslutet att betrakta järnridåns lämningar som kulturarv. Vad är det för kulturarvsprocesser som pågår? Vad är det som påverkar hur detta kulturarv skapas?

Ett annat syfte med studien är att bidra till den fortgående diskussionen om samtidsarkeologisk metodutveckling. Inom arkeologiämnet har samtidsarkeologins metodik gjort sig känd som experimentell och nyskapande (Harrison och Schofield 2010:88). Att studera material från senare tid med hjälp av arkeologiska metoder har visat sig vara ett bra sätt att utvärdera och utveckla den arkeologiska verktygslådan. Samtidsarkeologins något annorlunda utkikspunkt har även lett till nya arkeologiska perspektiv och omprövning av vissa arkeologiska tankeaxiom.

Rodney Harrison (2011) har diskuterat de nära sambanden mellan arkeologi och utgrävning och visat hur detta grundlagt en förståelse av det förflutna som något som är dolt, isolerat och överlagrat av senare epoker. Han menar att vi behöver skifta fokus, och i stället för att fokusera på djup tänka på de arkeologiska spåren som olika ytor, som alla utgör en del av vår samtid och befinner sig i samspel med varandra. Att erkänna det förflutna som en del av samtiden och studera det som något som finns här och nu ligger också i linje med Laurent Oliviers betonande av att vi borde se arkeologi mindre som narrativ historieskrivning och mer som minnesfragment, som konstant skapas och omskapas (Olivier 2004:209–211).

För att utforska dessa perspektiv och för att förstå hur järnridåns platser utvecklats och hur de ser ut idag har jag vänt mig till tingen. Bjørnar Olsen (2003, 2010) har framhållit att tidigare arkeologisk forskning sällan sett föremål som betydande i sig själva, utan snarare betraktat dem som representationer för något annat. Min föresats är istället att undersöka vad vi kan förstå utifrån lämningarna i sig själva. Som hjälp i detta arbete har jag använt Actor Network Theory (ANT). Nätverksteori erbjuder ett bra ramverk för att synliggöra såväl människor som ting som aktiva och skapande, och tydliggöra relationer dem emellan.

Arkeologiska studier som ligger närmare vår egen tid tenderar att hamna i en gråzon mellan discipliner som till exempel etnologi, historia, konsthistoria, antropologi och kulturgeografi. Människors berättelser vävs ihop med det materiella på ett sätt som gör det svårt att separera de olika källmaterialen från varandra och som ställer nya krav på valet av metod.

Att materiella lämningar och människors berättelser är tätt sammanflätade och snudd på förutsätter varandra framgick med all tydlighet i samband med mina intervjuer och fältstudier. För att nå dessa berättelser krävdes ett reflexivt förhållningssätt, där man måste vara flexibel och beredd att anpassa sig, men samtidigt vara erfaren nog att avgöra vilken metod som är bäst i de olika situationerna. Jag har huvudsakligen använt mig av arkeologiska metoder, framför allt inventering, tillsammans med mer etnologiska metoder och förhållningssätt.

SAMMANFATTNING

En fysisk metafor

I kapitel två diskuterar jag hur uttrycket järnridån har vuxit fram. Från att ha varit ett fysiskt skydd som förhindrade att bränder spreds på teatrarna i London under 1800-talet har det utvecklats till att åsyfta något helt annat. Under första världskriget användes begreppet för att poängtera skiljelinjerna och motsättningarna mellan de stridande sidorna. Under och efter andra världskriget blev uttrycket en metafor för de växande klyftorna mellan de allierade. Winston Churchill omnämnande av järnridån i sitt tal i Missouri i USA 1946 banade väg för en bred spridning av uttrycket.

Rent fysiskt växte de militariserade gränserna i Europa fram efter andra världskriget. Sedan Tyskland delats upp stegrades spänningarna i gränszonerna, framför allt mellan de västallierade (USA, Storbritannien och Frankrike) och Sovjetunionen. Motsättningarna mellan de olika sidorna ökade, samtidigt som svarthandel, olagliga övergångar och våld gjorde det allt svårare att upprätthålla lugnet i gränsområdena. För att få bättre kontroll började snart både öst- och västmakterna att bygga barriärer (Sheffer 2008:91). Bland lokalbefolkningen fanns det ett visst stöd för dessa barriärer, eftersom de tillsammans med militära sanktioner skapade stabilitet i gränsområdena. Barriärerna fick generellt sätt inte mycket uppmärksamhet i medierna, eftersom de till viss del följde tidigare gränser och uppdelningar och dessutom var relativt gömda för insyn.

När Berlinmuren började byggas 1961 var däremot medias och befolkningens reaktioner mycket starka. Trots att man var medveten om de militära gränser som växt fram både i Tyskland och längs med andra gränser genom Europa, så framstod denna barriär i en annan dager. Med byggandet av Berlinmuren klövs en tidigare homogen stad itu, och delningen mellan öst och väst blev väldigt påtaglig. I Berlin kunde man till och med röra vid muren! I väst blev muren en viktig symbol för östblockets förtryck och en ofta använd referens i retoriken mot kalla kriget. Den användes bland annat som bakgrund vid den amerikanske presidenten Ronald Reagans tal i Berlin 1987. I östblocket hyllades istället barriären – åtminstone i den offentliga retoriken – som en antifascistisk skyddsvall.

Det var inte bara i media och politik som Berlinmuren gjorde sig känd som en symbol för kalla krigets delning. Genom musik, film och skönlitteratur (och då i synnerhet i spiongenren, som fick stort genomslag under 1960-talet), smög den sig också in i populärkulturen. Järnridån och Berlinmuren blev allt mer sammanlänkade i det allmänna medvetandet, och till slut sågs de nästan som synonyma. De skildringar av muren som förmedlades i media, politisk retorik, populärkultur och litteraturen påverkade alltså inte bara förståelsen av Berlinmuren själv, utan i förlängningen också bilden av järnridån. Förståelsen för hur denna barriär och andra militariserade gränser genom Europa fungerade har till stor del gett vika för den metaforiska, mer stereotypa bilden av Berlinmuren, med dess betongväggar, taggtråd och vakttorn.

Berlinmurens materialitet

Eftersom Berlinmuren är så central i den rådande idén om järnridån finns det anledning att uppehålla sig lite vid dess materialitet och historia. I kapitel tre beskrivs översiktligt den historiska bakgrunden och de fysiska lämningarna av muren, som de ser ut idag. Beskrivningarna och diskussionerna om murens materialitet bygger dels på egna observationer, gjorda under två besök i Berlin, dels på de arkeologiska undersökningar som gjorts vid Brandenburgh Tekniska Universitet i Cottbus, Tyskland (Klausmeier och Schmidt 2004).

Trots att stora delar av Berlinmuren revs under tidigt 1990-tal är den fortfarande ett högst närvarande minnesmärke i staden idag. Muren gör sig inte bara gällande i de lämningar som finns kvar, utan också genom ett omfattande minnesarbete som kommer till uttryck i form av museer, minnesplatser och olika slags installationer. Den forna muren kastar också skuggor i staden genom de tomrum som den efterlämnat; platser där gränsens infrastruktur rivits och fortfarande inte ersatts med något nytt. Frågan om murens värde som kulturarv och hur det historiska minnet av den ska bevaras har varit omdiskuterat sedan 1989, när berlinborna själva började riva ner den framför världspressens kameror.

Under 1990–1991 gjordes stora ansträngningar för att utplåna muren, och en hel del av dess infrastruktur revs. Mycket av det som brukar ses som själva muren, det vill säga de betongväggar som sträckte sig igenom stadslandskapet, är numera borttaget. Ändå finns det många fysiska lämningar av muren kvar. Några av betongväggarna har återanvänts som konstinstallationer både i och utanför Berlin. Det finns också mindre uppmärksammade betongväggspartier – företrädesvis sådana som vette mot öst – som helt enkelt blivit kvar. Andra spår av murens infrastruktur är till exempel vakttorn, belysning och stora öppna områden som ännu inte bebyggts.

Upplevelserna av Berlinmuren under kalla kriget var högst varierande mellan olika människor. Efter murens fall blev det tydligt att det rådde delade meningar om hur dess kvarlevor och det historiska minnet runt dessa skulle hanteras. I Berlin finns det idag flera minnesmärken för håg-

SAMMANFATTNING

komst och kunskapsförmedling kring Berlinmuren och kalla kriget i stort. Dessa har inte sällan skapat debatt, då det finns skiftande uppfattningar om hur de borde se ut och vad de borde representera.

Att det finns olika perspektiv på muren och dess historia är inte minst tydligt i de två museer som handlar om just Berlinmuren, men som presenterar två ganska olika berättelser. Gedenkstätte Berliner Mauer är ett kunskapsmuseum som bygger på och förmedlar forskning om muren och dess historiska sammanhang. Haus am Checkpoint Charlie är istället mer fokuserat på upplevelse, och utgår från den idé av järnridån och av Berlinmuren som framhävts av media, populärkultur och till viss del den litteratur som finns om perioden (som diskuterats i kapitel två).

Fallstudie 1: den italiensk/slovenska gränsen

Kapitel fyra är en redogörelse för det fältarbete, som utfördes vid gränsen mellan Italien och Slovenien 2008 och 2011. Att studera denna gräns blev en viktig del av förståelsen av vilken betydelse lokalsamhället lägger i begreppet järnridå och vilka egenskaper som ansågs vara centrala. Kommentarer som "Det var en del av järnridån för de var kommunister på den andra sidan och kapitalister på denna" eller "Detta var aldrig en del av järnridån för att det gick att ta sig över" hjälpte till att synliggöra allmänna uppfattningar om vad järnridån var och inte var, hur den definierades och hur den upplevdes på plats.

Det primära syftet med fältstudien var att skapa en bättre bild av hur gränsen sett ut under kalla kriget och hur den ser ut idag. Under det första fältarbetet (2008) undersöktes översiktligt gränserna mellan Italien/Slovenien och Österrike/Slovenien. Det andra fältarbetet (2011) fokuserade mer i detalj på ett område i och runt städerna Gorizia (i Italien) och Nova Gorica (i Slovenien). Dessa städer växte fram bredvid varandra som en konsekvens av den nya gräns som efter andra världskriget drogs mellan Italien och forna Jugoslavien. Den stad som tidigare funnits här, Gorizia på italienska och Gorica på slovenska, hamnade nu helt inom italienskt territorium, medan stora delar av det odlingslandskap som försåg staden med mat hamnade i Jugoslavien. På den jugoslaviska sidan anlades snart ett nytt Gorica, Nova Gorica, för att skapa ett nytt centrum för det omkringliggande området.

Gränserna i det aktuella området har ändrats åtskilliga gånger under det senaste århundradet. Området har tillhört både Österrike, Italien, Jugoslavien och Slovenien. Efter andra världskriget reviderades gränsen av de allierade och en kommission fick i uppdrag att utföra arbetet med att staka ut gränslinjen i landskapet. Lokala berättelser gör gällande att ortsbefolkningen under de första dygnen försökte påverka gränsdragningen. Nattetid smög sig markägare ut och flyttade helt enkelt de stängsel som satts upp, för att få så stor del som möjligt av sin mark i ett och samma land. Snart började dock gränsen patrulleras hårt på båda sidor, vilket omöjliggjorde vidare försök att rucka på gränsdragningen.

När denna gräns växte fram hade den först likheter med gränsen mellan Öst- och Västtyskland, med intensiv patrullering och gränsövervakning. Men till skillnad från den inre tyska gränsen, som med tiden blev mer och mer militariserad, så började snart gränsen mellan Italien och Jugoslavien öppnas mer och mer. Denna utveckling var i linje med Jugoslaviens avståndstagande från det kommunistiska Kominform och landets alltmer västvänliga politik. Eftersom många andra gränser längre norrut i Europa var svårare att ta sig igenom (till exempel den forna tjeckoslovakiska gränsen) blev den jugoslaviska gränsen ofta ett sätt att nå Västeuropa för invånarna i länder med hårdare kontroll. Det var jämförelsevis lätt att få semestervisum till Jugoslavien, eftersom det sågs som ett socialistiskt ickevästerländskt land, och härifrån fanns det sedan bättre möjligheter att ta sig över gränsen. Gränsen förblev dock bevakad fram till 2004, då Slovenien gick med i Europeiska Unionen. Den revolution som 1989 ledde till öppnande av flera andra gränser i Europa hade med andra ord inte samma effekt i detta område.

Mina arkeologiska undersökningar av Gorizia/Nova Goricaområdet har frilagt flera lager av historia, som interagerar med varandra. Lämningarna här är av olika typer och stammar från olika tider. De återspeglar människors agerande, eller förbud från att agera, i ett högst kontrollerat område. Trots att merparten av lämningarna från den tidigare militariserade gränsen inte finns kvar, finns det ändå spår av övervakningen, i form av bland annat vakttorn och patrullvägar. Vid övergångarna är gränserna som mest framträdande, även om de är långt mindre sammansatta idag än tidigare. Här finns fortfarande gränspolisens byggnader kvar, även om de i de flesta fall nu står tomma. I asfalten kan man skönja markeringar från tidigare vägfiler och det finns även rester av de forna barriärerna. De större gränspassagernas gynnsamma effekt på handeln har lämnat avtryck efter sig i form av tomma affärs- och restauranglokaler. Många av lämningarna, till exempel soldaternas graffitti i de övergivna vakttornen, ger också en viss inblick i tillvaron för de som kontrollerade dessa gränser. Därtill finns ideologiska slogans, som textats på hus och bergssidor. Dessa spår är i mångt och mycket på väg att försvinna.

SAMMANFATTNING

Fältstudier av lämningarna i detta område gjorde det tydligt att järnridåns faktiska materialitet är mer komplex än vad man i allmänhet föreställer sig. Samma sak kan sägas om den mentala kartan av järnridån. Generellt sett tycks det vara vanligt att föreställa sig järnridån som näst intill omöjlig att forcera, med höga murar och taggtråd. Denna visualisering är i huvudsak baserad på den bild som skapats av Berlinmuren. De intervjuer som jag utfört inom ramen för fältarbetet visar att uppfattningarna om huruvida denna gräns har varit del av en järnridå eller inte beror på informanternas bakgrund och deras ålder. De som upplevde gränsen under dess tidiga skede tenderar att koppla samman gränsen med järnridån, medan de som är födda senare snarare sett gränsen som en tillgång för handel med andra sidan. De som kommer från det italienska området menar oftare att detta en gång tillhörde järnridån, medan de som kommer från Jugoslavien och Slovenien mer sällan delar denna upplevelse.

Något som också blev tydligt genom fältstudierna var hur det materiella kalla kriget-landskapet expanderar i tid, både bakåt och framåt. Mycket av det som konstituerade gränsen och dess infrastruktur var i själva verket återanvända rester av tidigare verksamheter, till exempel ruinerna från ett medeltida kloster eller anläggningar från andra världskriget. Många av gränsens lämningar har också återanvänts senare, i nya sammanhang. Patrullvägar har till exempel blivit vandrings- och cykelleder. Fragmenterade och återanvända representerar lämningarna en lång tidshorisont.

Fallstudie 2: den tjeckisk/österrikiska gränsen

I kapitel fem presenteras det fältarbete som utfördes vid gränsen mellan Tjeckien och Österrike under 2009 och 2010. Syftet med denna fältstudie var att skapa en förståelse för hur gränsen sett ut under kalla kriget och hur den ser ut idag. Det första fältarbetet, som utfördes 2009, hade ambitionen att grundlägga en översiktlig förståelse av den tjeckisk/österrikiska gränsen. Det andra fältarbetet, som genomfördes året därpå, fokuserade mer detalj på ett område i den tjeckiska nationalparken Podyji, vid staden Vranov nad Dyji.

Nationalparken Podyji utvecklades delvis som en konsekvens av det militariserade gränsområde som etablerades här efter andra världskriget. Stora områden närmast den österrikiska gränsen lämnades då i stort sätt orörda, bortsett från stängsel och annan infrastruktur. Efter det att den militariserade gränsen försvann under tidigt 1990-tal gjordes området om till en nationalpark, för att ta vara på det unika natur och djurliv som skapats här under flera århundraden. Områdets historia som park sträcker sig dock längre tillbaka än så. Från 1700-talet och framåt var det en del av Vranovs slottspark och inkluderade bland annat en engelsk park med paviljonger, hägnader med djur och monument. Innan andra världskriget byggdes bunkrar i området. Dessa utgjorde en del av den försvarslinje som dåvarande Tjeckoslovakien etablerade som skydd mot det växande nazistiska hotet i Tyskland och Österrike. 17 av bunkrarna finns idag kvar i studieområdet.

Under kriget drevs många av de judar som bott i området ut. Efter kriget tvångsflyttades stora mängder tysktalande och andra som ansågs vara ett hot mot säkerheten i de känsliga gränsområdena. Detta är en utveckling som går igen i flera av gränsområdena i regionen. Befolkningsminskningen gjorde gränsområdena relativt glesbebyggda och därmed lättare att militarisera.

Gränsernas infrastruktur sträckte sig åtskilliga kilometer in i landet, från de faktiska gränserna räknat. Den egentliga gränsen var däremot inte markerad med annat än enkla gränsstenar. Det var helt enkelt inte meningen att någon från Tjeckoslovakien någonsin skulle komma så pass nära den egentliga gränsen. En serie stängsel, minor och patrullerande soldater skulle stoppa de som försökte ta sig över till väst. Inga officiella gränspassager fanns i studieområdet.

Lämningarna i landskapet är av många olika slag. Tillsammans berättar de om den infrastruktur som skulle stoppa rymningar över gränserna västerut, och om de soldater som skulle skydda just dessa områden. Även om soldaterna har försvunnit så finns deras närvaro kvar i de ting de lämnat efter sig. Intervjuer med före detta gränssoldater och en officer har också hjälpt till att befolka dessa platser och förstå något av vad som utspelat sig här.

De flesta av de gränsvaktsstationer som etablerades här för soldaterna står fortfarande kvar. Inom ramen för min studie har jag undersökt de två stationerna Hájenka och Šafov. Trots att många av inventarierna har tagits bort så finns det ännu spår kvar som upplyser oss om soldaternas liv i gränsområdet. Som exempel kan nämnas graffiti på väggar som vittnar om hur soldaterna räknade ner dagarna på sin tvååriga militärtjänst. Andra spår från soldaternas vardag är etiketter från skoputsburkar som klistrats upp i ett av tvättrummen samt dekorerade logementdörrar.

Under dessa fältstudier har det blivit tydligt att olika källor visar på olika sidor av vår historia och olika berättelser. Mest påtagligt blir detta när det gäller bilden av soldaterna. I det fysiska landskapet framträder bilden av unga värnpliktiga, som putsar sina skor och fördriver tiden i väntan på dagen då man fullföljt sin tjänstgöring. I arkivens dokument framträder en helt annan bild – de vittnar om hur samma soldater utan att tveka skjuter de

SAMMANFATTNING

som försöker ta sig över gränsen. De källor vi använder har utan tvekan en stark påverkan på vilken historia vi i slutändan berättar.

I den offentliga framställningen av parken idag har man valt att koncentrera sig på dess natur och djurliv. Till viss del uppmärksammas också de monument som finns kvar från tiden som slottspark. Däremot finns det nästan ingen information alls om parkens historia som militariserad gräns. I de områden som turister mest rör sig i verkar man till och med ha försökt städa undan de fysiska rester som finns kvar av platsens förflutna som militariserad zon.

I fallet med nationalparken Podyji och den tjeckisk/österrikiska gränsen har de olika källorna tillsammans skapat en djupare förståelse av både lokal- och världshistorien, även om bilderna delvis är fragmentariska och motsägelsefulla.

Järnridåns arkeologi

I det sjätte och avslutande kapitlet diskuteras resultaten av de olika fältstudierna i relation till det problemområde som tecknats i de inledande kapitlen. Det blir tydligt att historiska narrativ, myter, metaforer och fysiska lämningar alla är delar av järnridåns kulturella konstruktion.

Min forskning har i hög grad påverkats av de historiska narrativ om kalla kriget som jag växt upp med. Mest påtagligt har detta kanske varit i valet av empiriskt fokus, att undersöka platser där järnridåns konturer kunde förväntas klarna. Men de platser som jag undersökt har visat sig rymma mer komplexa och betydligt vidare berättelser än jag kunnat föreställa mig. Det blev tydligt hur mycket källorna kunde ge och att de ofta berättar olika historier, som inte alltid passar ihop. Att se dem som de fragment som de är kan hjälpa oss att förstå en plats, en tid eller en händelse på ett mer nyanserat sätt.

Den materiella vändning man kan skönja inom arkeologin under senare år, framfört av bland andra Bjørnar Olsen (2003, 2010) och Þora Pétursdóttir (2012, 2013), försöker höja tingens status som källmaterial. Man menar att tingen inte bara ska ses som passiva redskap för människan och – inom ramen för historievetenskapen – användas som kunskapskällor till kulturella sammanhang och meningar, som ligger bortom tingen själva. Det är viktigt att komma ihåg att tingen inte bara har ett symboliskt eller kulturellt värde, utan att de också är spelar en egen aktiv roll, som de ting de är.

När man börjar se tingen som viktiga i sig själva träder andra berättelser och konstellationer fram. Vi kan se hur föremål från olika tidpunkter samexisterar, vilket gör den kronologiskt avgränsade tiden mindre intressant. Laurent Olivier (2004) har påpekat att arkeologins starka beroende av historieskrivningen är problematisk. Han menar att vi måste börja se de objekt och platser som vi studerar som mer fragmentariska, och i den bemärkelsen mer lika minnen än narrativa berättelser. I studieområdena är det tydligt hur olika tidsavsnitt blandas genom att tingen återaktiveras, rekontextualiseras och återvinns. Samma beståndsdelar av vad som en gång var ett medeltida kloster har genom historien använts av munkar, soldater och turister. Samma stigar har nötts av olika människor under olika perioder.

I det avslutande kapitlet diskuterar jag också samtidsarkeologin från ett mer metodologisk perspektiv. Undersökningar av mer recenta material brukar inte ha samma fokus på utgrävning som andra arkeologiska undersökningar. Man arbetar helt enkelt med mer ytligt belägna lämningar. Rodney Harrison (2011) har argumenterat för att den gängse arkeologins fokus på djup, och synen på det förflutna som något dött och begravet, skapar ett mentalt avstånd mellan det förflutna och samtiden. Han föreslår att man istället ska visualisera det förflutna som olika närvarande ytor, och se det förflutna som del av samtiden.

Laura McAtackney (2008), Rodney Harrison (2011) och Paul Graves-Brown (2011) har alla ifrågasatt varför arkeologin är så förknippad med utgrävning som metod, och varför andra metoder generellt anses mindre tillförlitliga. Samtidigt finns det en viss osäkerhet för giltigheten av de alternativa metoder som används inom samtidsarkeologin. En metod som används flitigt inom studiet av mer samtida lämningar är inventering. Traditionellt sätt har inventering sätts som något preliminärt – inte minst som förberedelser inför utgrävning – och inte som en giltig metod i sig själv. Detta blev också tydligt när jag ställde frågan om vad en inventering är på Contemporary and Historical Archaeology in Theorys forum (McWilliams 2012), där svaren blev väldigt varierande.

Jag har i min studie använt ett reflexivt förhållningssätt för att pröva några av de metoder som är vanliga inom samtidsarkeologin. Jag har diskuterat det nära förhållandet mellan samtidsarkeologin och dess granndiscipliner, främst etnologi och historia. Att röra sig i gränsområdena mellan olika vetenskaper kan vara en tillgång, då olika material och källor kan ge olika information och belysa olika aspekter. Samtidigt finns det en risk att just sådana gränsområden inte tas i anspråk av forskningen, eller att forskningen inte drar nytta av den mångfalden av källor och metoder som står till buds. Anders Andrén (1998) har i en diskussion om skillnaderna mellan materiella och skriftliga källor varnat för det han kallar "mellanrummets dilemma". Han påpekar att även om vi behöver minska klyftan mellan skriftliga och materiella källor så löser vi inte problemet genom att se text och ting som identiska.

Men det finns också andra källor förutom just ting och text som måste tas i beaktande, källor som filmer, nyhetsrapporter, bilder, muntliga berättelser, sångtexter och konst. Alla dessa har varit viktiga i min forskning och har visat sig vara en tillgång för att förstå olika aspekter av järnridån. Det kan vara svårt att dra upp rågångarna mellan dessa källor, och sortera dem i olika fack. Är till exempel graffiti på ett föremål enbart att betrakta som text? Hur ska vi klassificera ett minne som väcks av ett ting? Ibland kan källorna te sig annorlunda och kräva andra metoder än de vi som arkeologer är vana vid, men ibland kan de i allt väsentligt också vara väldigt lika. När vi talar om skillnaderna mellan text och ting kan man se att det ibland snarare handlar om olikheterna mellan historiska och arkeologiska traditioner. Skillnaden ligger därför inte alltid i källornas ontologi utan i hur vi betraktar dem och i de metoder vi väljer att studera dem.

Min forskning ska inte ses som en ANT-studie, men jag har hämtat inspiration från ANT:s tankar om tingens mer aktiva roll. Jag har inte velat reducera tingen till rekvisita åt historieskrivningen, utan försökt nå och följa alla aktörer – mänskliga såväl som materiella – på de platser jag studerat. ANT har också varit viktigt rent metodologiskt. I linje med ANT:s arbetssätt har jag valt att utgå från det lilla för att sedan arbeta mig utåt och uppåt genom de nätverk som aktörerna bildar. Det jordnära perspektivet tvingar oss att stanna upp och verkligen se det material vi har framför oss. Det som blir tydligt är att denna metod möjliggör för andra berättelser än de stora, erkända och förväntade att komma fram. Ett av de påtagligaste exemplen på detta i min forskning är hur jag hittar fragment av en berättelse om vardagliga lumparkillar, en berättelse som inte passar ihop med vår vanliga bild av järnridån, som en mur av förtryck och våld.

I sökandet efter en av de mest välkända ikonerna för kalla kriget – järnridån – fann jag en rad vardagliga platser som vid första anblicken kan te sig oviktiga, men som vid närmare betraktelse skapar nätverk som kopplar ihop tidsperioder, platser, människor, ting och berättelser.

Bibliography

Literature

Anderle, W. and Schmidt, W. 2002, *Frain, einst die Perle im Thayatal*, Band 1.

Anderson, J. 2004. Talking Whilst Walking: A Geographical Archaeology of Knowledge. In: *Area* 36 (3): 254–61.

Andreassen, E., Bjerck, H., and Olsen, B. 2010. *Persistent Memories: An Archaeology of a Soviet Mining Town in the High Arctic*. Trondheim: Tapir Akademisk Forlag.

Andrén, A. 1998. *Between Artifacts and Texts: Historical Archaeology in a Global Perspective*. New York: Plenum Press.

Arendt, H. 1994 [1963]. Eichmann in Jerusalem: A Report on the Banality of Evil. Penguin Books.

Arendt, H. 1971. Thinking and Moral Considerations: A Lecture in: *Social Research* 38, No. 3

Arvastson, G. and Ehn, B. (eds.) 2009. *Etnografiska observationer*. Lund: Studentlitteratur.

Ashworth, G.J. 2003. Heritage, Identity and Places: for Tourist and Host Communities. In: Singh, S., Dallen, J. T. and Dowling, R. K. (eds.) Tourism in Destination Communities. Wallingford: CABI Publishing.

Baer, A. 2001. Consuming history and memory through mass media products. In: *European Journal of Cultural Studies*. Vol. 4(4), p. 491–501.

Ballinger, P. 2003. Imperial nostalgia: mythologizing Habsburg Trieste, Journal of Modern Italian Studies, 8:1, p. 84–101

Barret, J. C. and Ko, I. 2009. A phenomenology of landscape: A crisis in British landscape archaeology in: *Journal of Social Archaeology*. 2009 9:275.

Bateman, J. 2005. Wearing Juninho's shirt: record and negotiation in excavation photographs. In: S. Smiles and S. Moser (eds.) *Envisioning the past: archaeology and the image*. Oxford: Blackwell.

Benson, L. 2004. Yugoslavia: A Concise History. Gordonsville: Palgrave Macmillan.

Benton, T. 2010. *Understanding heritage and memory*. Manchester: Manchester University Press.

Berggren, Å. 2001. Swedish Archaeology in Perspective and the Possibility of Reflexivity. In: *Current Swedish Archaeology* 9, 9–23.

Berggren, Å. 2002. Reflexivitet inom arkeologin. In: Å. Berggren and M. Burström (eds.) *Reflexiv fältarkeologi?* Riksantikvarieämbetet and Malmö Kulturmiljövård.

Berggren, Å. and Hodder, I. 2000. *At the Trowel's Edge: An Introduction to Reflexive Field Practice in Archaeology*. Westview Press Inc.

Berggren, Å and Hodder, I. 2003. Social practice, method and some problems of field archaeology. In: *American Antiquity*, Vol.68(3), p.421–434

Bernstein R. 2010. Is Evil Banal? A Misleading Question. In: *Thinking in Dark Times*. R. Berkowitz, J. Katz, and T. Keenan (eds.). New York: Fordham University Press.

Boulton, A. 2007. Cood bay Forst Zinna. In: J. Schofield and W. Cocroft (eds.) *A Fearsome Heritage: Diverse legacies of the Cold War*. Walnut Creek: Left Coast Press.

Breitner, L. and Lagerwall, K. Spionutpekade svenske prästen: Jag ångrar mig. *Dagens Nyheter*, 28 July 2012. Front page and p. 8–9.

Brück, J. 2005. Experiencing the past? The development of a phenomenological archaeology in British prehistory. In: *Archaeological Dialogues* Vol. 12 (1): 45–72.2007/2008, 21–36.

Bruner, M. S. 1989. Symbolic Uses of the Berlin Wall, 1961–1989. In: *Communication Quarterly*, Vol. 37, No. 4, Fall 1989, p. 319–328.

Bufon, M. 1996. Social Integration in the Italo-Slovene Gorizia Transborder Region. In: *Tijdschrift voor Economische en Sociale Geografie*. Vol. 87, No. 3, p. 247–258.

Bufon, M. and Minghi, J. 2000. The Upper Adriatic borderland: From conflict to harmony. In: *GeoJournal*. 52: p. 119–127

Burström, M. 2009. Looking into the Recent Past. In: *Current Swedish Archaeology.* Vol. 15-16.

Burström, M. 2011. Humankind: Family and Future. Comments on Brit Solli: Some Reflections on Heritage and Archaeology in the Anthropocene. In: *Norwegian Archaeological Review*, 44:1, p. 54-57.

Burström, M. 2012. If we are quiet, will things cry out? Comments on Bjørnar Olsen Archaeological Theory, Christmas Pork and Red Herrings. In: *Current Swedish Archaeology.* Vol. 20, p. 41-45.

Burström, M., Gustafsson, M. and Karlsson, H. 2011. *World Crisis in Ruin. The Archaeology of the Former Soviet Nuclear Missile Sites in Cuba.* Lindome: Bricoleur Press.

Chouliaraki, L. and Fairclough, G. 1999. *Discourse in late Modernity: Rethinking Critical Discourse Analysis*, Edinburgh: Edinburgh University Press.

Cocroft, W. 2003. *Cold War: Building for Nuclear Confrontation, 1946-1989*, Swindon: English Heritage.

Cocroft, W. D. and Wilson, L. 2006. Archaeology and art at Spadedam Rocket Establishment (Cumbria). In: J. Schofield, A. Klausmeier, and L. Purbrick (eds.) *Re-mapping the Field: New Approaches in Conflict Archaeology.* Berlin: Westkreuz-Verlag.

Cronqvist, M. 2008. Utrymning av folkhemmet. In: *Historisk Tidskrift (Sweden)* 128:3

DeSilvey, C. 2006. Observed decay Telling stories with mutable things. In: *Journal of Material Culture* 11 (3) p.318-338

Dolff-Bonekämper, G. 2002. The Berlin Wall: an archaeological site in progress. In: J. Schofield, W. Gray Johnson and C. M. Beck (eds.) *Matériel Culture. The archaeology of twentieth-century conflict*, London: Routledge. p. 236-248.

Drechsel, B. 2010. The Berlin Wall from a visual perspective: comments on the construction of a political media icon. In: *Visual Communication* Vol. 9: 3 p. 3-24.

Edensor, T. 2005a. The ghost of industrial ruins: ordering and disordering memory in excessive space. In: *Environmental Planning D: Society and Space.* Vol. 23, p. 829-849.

Edensor, T. 2005b. Waste Matter – The Debris of Industrial Ruins and the Disordering of the Material World, in: *Journal of Material Culture*. Vol. 10(3): p. 311–332.

Edgeworth, M. 2012. Follow the Cut, Follow the Rythm, Follow the Material. In: *Norwegian Archaeological Review* Vol. 45, No. 1.

Edizioni Della Laguna. 2006. *Transalpina 100 anni (1906–2006). Un binario per tre popoli in immagini d'epoca*. Gorizia: Centro Studi Turistico Giorgio Valussi.

Ehn, B. 2009. Lära sig se på nytt. In: G. Arvastson and B. Ehn (eds.) *Etnografiska observationer*. Lund: Studentlitteratur.

Ehn, B. and Löfgren, O. 1996. *Vardagslivets Etnologi: Reflektioner kring en kulturvetenskap*. Stockholm: Natur och Kultur.

English Heritage 2007. *Understanding the Archaeology of Landscapes: A guide to good recording practice*. London: English Heritage

Fägerborg, E. 2011. Intervjuer. In: L. Kaijser and M. Öhlander (eds.). *Etnologiskt fältarbete*. Lund: Studentlitteratur.

Fairclough, G. 2003. *Analysing Discourse: Textual Analysis for Social Research*. London: Routledge.

Fairclough, G. 2007. The Cold War in context: Archaeological explorations of private, public and political complexity. In: J. Schofield and W. Cocroft (eds.) *A Fearsome Heritage Diverse Legacies of the Cold War*. Walnut Creek: Left Coast Press.

Fairclough, G., Harrison, R., Jameson Jnr, J, H. and Schofield, J. (eds.). 2008. *The Heritage Reader*. Abingdon: Routledge.

Feversham, P. and Schmidt, L. 1999. *The Berlin Wall Today*. Berlin: Verlag Bauwesen.

Feversham, P. and Schmidt, L. 2007. The Berlin Wall: Border, fragment, world heritage? In: J. Schofield and W. Cocroft (eds.) *A Fearsom Heritage: Diverse Legacies of the Cold War*. Walnut Creek: Left Coast Press.

Frykman, J. 2007. Monument som väcker obehag. In: J. Frykman and B. Ehn (eds.) *Minnesmärken, Att tolka det förflutna och besvärja framtiden*. Stockholm: Carlsson Bokförlag.

Gerber, S. 2011. *Öst är Väst men Väst är bäst. Östtysk identitetsformering i det förenade Tyskland*. Stockholm Studies in Ethnology 5. Stockholm: Stockholm University.

Gilles, B. 2009. Understanding a literary site of remembrance: *Témoins*, by Jean Norton Cru. In: N. Forbes, R. Page och G Pérez (eds.) *Europe's Deadly Century*. English Heritage: Swindon.

Gonzalez-Ruibal, A. 2011. In praise of depth. Response to Harrison, R. 2011 Surface assemblages. Towards an archaeology *in* and *of* the present. In: *Archaeological Dialogues* Vol 18 (2).

Graham, B. and Howard, P. (eds.) 2008. *The Ashgate Research Companion to Heritage and Identity*. Aldershot: Ashgate Publishing Limited.

Graves-Brown, P. 2011. *Archaeology. A career in ruins*. Response to Harrison, R. 2011. Surface assemblages. Towards an archaeology *in* and *of* the present. In: *Archaeological Dialogues* Vol 18 (2).

Graves-Brown, P. 2012. *Wandering about*. Presentation at the Contemporary Historical Archaeology in Theory conference 2012.

Graves-Brown, P. 2013. Authenticity. In: *The Oxford Handbook of the Archaeology of the Contemporary World*. P. Graves-Brown, R. Harrison and A. Piccini (eds.). Oxford: Oxford University Press.

Halewood, C. and Hannam, K. 2001. Viking Heritage Tourism: Authenticity and Commodification. In: *Annals of Tourism Research*, Vol. 28, No. 3, p. 565–580.

Hamberg, P. 2009. *Släpp ingen levande förbi*. Stockholm: Natur och Kultur.

Hamilakis, Y. and Anagnostopoulos, A. 2009. Postcards from the Edge of Time: Archaeology, Photography, Archaeological Ethnography (A Photo-Essay). *Public Archaeology*: Archaeological Ethnographies, Vol. 8 No. 2-3.

Hansen, K. 2003. The sensory experience of doing fieldwork. In: J. Frykman and N. Gilje (eds.) *Being There: New Perspectives on Phenomenology and the Analysis of Culture*. Lund: Nordic Academic Press

Harris, O. and Sørensen, T. F. 2010. Rethinking emotion and material culture. In: *Archaeological Dialogues* 17(2), p. 145–163.

Harrison, Hope M. 2005. The Berlin Wall – a Symbol of the Cold War? In: Schmidt, L and von Preuschen, H. (eds.) *On Both Sides of the Wall.*

Preserving Monuments and Sites of the Cold War Era. Cottbus: Westkreuz-Verlag.

Harrison, R. (ed.) 2010. *Understanding the politics of Heritage.* Manchester: Manchester University Press.

Harrison, R. 2011. Surface assemblages. Towards an archaeology *in* and *of* the present. In: *Archaeological Dialogues* Vol. 18 (2).

Harrison, R. and Schofield, J. 2010. *After Modernity: Archaeological Approaches to the Contemporary Past.* Oxford: Oxford University Press.

Harvey, D. 2001. Heritage Pasts and Heritage Presents: temporality, meaning and the scope of heritage studies. In: *International Journal of Heritage Studies,* 7:4, p. 319–338.

Harvey, D. 2008. The History of Heritage. In: B. Graham and P, Howard (eds.) *The Ashgate Research Companion to Heritage and Identity.* Aldershot: Ashgate Publishing Limited.

Hodder, I. 1982. *Symbols in Action: Ethnoarchaeological studies of material studies.* Cambridge: Cambridge University Press.

Hodder, I. 1997. Always momentary, fluid and flexible: towards reflexive excavation methodology. *Antiquity* 71, p. 691–700.

Hodder, I. 1999. *The Archaeological Process. An introduction.* Oxford.

Hodder, I. (ed.) 2000. *Towards reflexive method in archaeology: the example of Çatalhöyük.* McDonald Institute Monographs. BIAA Monograph No. 28. Cambridge.

Hodder, I. 2003. Archaeological Reflexivity and the "Local" voice. In: *Anthropological Quarterly,* Vol. 76, No 1 (Winter 2003), p. 55–69.

Högdahl, E. 2009. Välja sina ord. In: G. Arvastson and B. Ehn (eds.) *Etnografiska observationer.* Lund: Studentlitteratur.

Holtorf, C. 2007. *Archaeology is a brand! The meaning of archaeology in contemporary popular culture.* Oxford: Oxford University Press.

Hutchings, F. 2004. *Cold Europe: Discovering, Researching and Preserving European Cold War Heritage.* Cottbus: The Department of Architectural Conservation at the Brandenburg University of Technology.

Huyssen, A. 1997. The Voids of Berlin. In: *Critical Inquiry.* Vol. 24. No. 1, p. 57–81.

Innes, A. 2001. *Czechoslovakia: the short goodbye*. New Haven and London: Yale University Press.

Jelavich, B. 1987. *Modern Austria: Empire and Republic 1815–1986*. Cambridge: Cambridge University Press.

Johnson, M. 1999. *Archaeological Theory: An Introduction*. Oxford: Blackwell.

Kaijser, L. and Öhlander, M. (eds.) 2011. *Etnologiskt fältarbete*. Lund: Studentlitteratur.

Kaufmann, J. E. 1999. *Fortress Europé: European fortification of World War II*. London: Greenhill Books

Kiddey, R. and Schofield, J. 2011. Embracing the Margins: Adventures in Archaeology and Homelessness. *Public Archaeology* Vol. 10 No. 1, p. 4–22.

Klausmeier, A. and Schmidt, L. 2004. *Wall Remnants – Wall Traces: A Comprehensive Guide to the Berlin Wall*. Berlin: Westkreuz-Verlag.

Klausmeier, A. 2009. Interpretation as a means of preservation policy or: Whose heritage is the Berlin Wall? In: N. Forbes, R. Page, and G. Pérez (eds.) *Europe's Deadliest Century: Perspectives on 20th century conflict heritage*. Swindon: English Heritage.

Latour, B. 2005. *Reassembling the Social*. Oxford: Oxford University Press.

Law, J. 2009. Actor Network Theory and Material Semiotics. In: B. Turner (ed.) *The New Blackwell Companion to Social Theory*. Blackwell Publishing.

Le Carré, J. 1963. *The spy who came in from the cold*. London: Hodder & Stoughton Ltd.

Leff, C. S. 1997. *The Czech and Slovak Republics: Nation Versus State*. Boulder: Westeview Press.

Löfgren, O. 1999. *On Holiday. A History of Vacationing*. Berkeley: University of California Press.

Lucas, G. 2004. Modern disturbances: on the ambiguities of archaeology. *Modernism/modernity*. Vol. 11: p. 109–120.

Lund, H. 1992. *Tjeckoslovakien Runt*. Stockholm: Berghs Förlag AB.

Lundén, T. 2004. *On the Boundary: About humans at the end of territory*. Huddinge: Södertörn University

Manghani, S. 2008. *Image Critique and the Fall of the Berlin Wall*. Bristol: Intellect Ltd.

McAtackney, L. 2008. *An historical archaeology of political imprisonment: Long Kesh/ Maze prison, Northern Ireland.* Unpublished PhD thesis, University of Bristol.

McWilliams, A. 2011. All Quiet on the Eastern Front. In: D. Mullin (ed.) *Places in Between: The Archaeology of Social, Cultural and Geographical Borders and Borderlands.* Oxford: Oxbow Books.

Medved, F. 1993. Slovenien – en lägesbeskrivning in *Östeuropas omvandling.* Stockholm: Svenska sällskapet för antropologi och geografi.

Mihelj, S. 2012. Drawing on the East-West Border: Narratives of Modernity and Identity in the Northeastern Adriatic (1947–1954). In: A. Vowinckel, M. Payk and T. Lindenberger *Cold War Cultures: Perspectives in Eastern and Western European Societies.* New York: Berghahn Books.

Miller, D. and Tilley, C. 1984. *Ideology, Power and Prehistory.* Cambridge: Cambridge University Press.

Moodie, A. E. 1950. Some New Boundary Problems in the Julian March. In: *Transactions and Papers (Institute of British Geographers),* No. 16 (1950), p. 83–93.

Munslow, A. 2008. Film and history: Robert A. Rosenstone and History on Film/Film on History in: *Rethinking History: The Journal of Theory and Practice,* 11:4, p. 565–575.

Nandy, A. 1995. History's Forgotten Doubles. In: *History and Theory* Vol. 34, No. 2: p. 44–66.

New York Times. 11 June 1972. Girl, 9, Survives Napalm Burns.

Nordström, N. 2007. *De odödliga: Förhistoriska individer i vetenskap och media.* Vägar till Midgård 10. Lund: Nordic Academic Press.

Olivier, L. 2004. The past of the present. Archaeological memory and time in: *Archaeological Dialogues* Vol. 10, Issue 02: 204–213.

Olsen, B. 2003. Material culture after text: re-membering things. In: *Norwegian Archaeological Review,* 36:2, p. 87–104.

Olsen, B. 2010 *In Defence of Things.* Plymouth: AltaMira Press.

Olsen, B. 2012. Archaeological Theory, Christmas Pork and Red Herrings. In: *Current Swedish Archaeology.* Vol. 20.

O'Reilly, K. 2005 *Ethnographic methods.* Abington: Routledge.

Parker Pearson, M. 2003. *The archaeology of Death and Burial*. Stroud: Sutton Publishing.

Pétursdóttir, Þ. 2012. Small Things Forgotten Now Included, or What Else Do Things Deserve? In: *International Journal of Historical Archaeology* 16: p. 577–603.

Pétursdóttir, Þ. 2013. Concrete matters: Ruins of modernity and the things called heritage. In: *Journal of Social Archaeology* 13, p. 31–53.

Pétursdóttir, Þ. and Olsen, B. (Forthcoming) Imaging Modern Decay: The Aesthetics of Ruin Photography.

Pine, B. J. and Gilmore, J.H. 1999. *The Experience Economy: Work is Theatre & Every Business a Stage*. Boston: Harvard Business Press

Pripp, O. 2011. Reflektion och etik. In: L. Kaijser and M. Öhlander (eds.). *Etnologiskt fältarbete*. Lund: Studentlitteratur.

Pusca, A. 2010. Industrial and Human Ruins of Postcommunist Europe. In: *Space and Culture* 13(3), p. 239–255.

Rosenstone, R.A. 2006. *History on Film/Film on History*. Pearson: Harlow.

Rottman, G. 2008. *The Berlin Wall and the Intra-German border 1961–89*. Oxford: Osprey Publishing.

Schindler, J. 2001. *Isonzo. The Forgotten Sacrifice of the Great War*. Praeger Publishers: Westport.

Schmidt, L. 2005. The Berlin Wall, a Landscape of Memory. In: L. Schmidt and H. von Preuschen (eds.) *On Both Sides of the Wall. Preserving Monuments and Sites of the Cold War Era*. Cottbus: Westkreuz-Verlag.

Schmidt, L., and von Preuschen, H. 2005. *On Both Sides of the Wall: Preserving Monuments and Sites of the Cold War Era*. Berlin: Westkreuz-Verlag.

Schofield, J. 2012. Book review of Andreassen, E., Bjerck, H. and Olsen, B. 2010. *Persistent Memories: An Archaeology of a Soviet Mining Town in the High Arctic*. In: *Norwegian Archaeological Review* Vol. 45. Issue 1.

Schofield, J. and Morrissey, E. 2007. Titbits Revisited: Towards a Respectable Archaeology of Strait Street, Valletta (Malta). In: L. McAtackney, M. Palus and A. Piccini (eds.) *Contemporary and Historical Archaeology in Theory. Papers from the 2003–2004 CHAT conferences*. BAR International Series 1677.

Schofield, J. and Cocroft, W. (eds.) 2007. *A Fearsome Heritage: Diverse Legacies of the Cold War*. Walnut Creek: Left Coast Press.

Schofield, J., Cocroft, W., Boulton, A., Dunlop, G. and Wilson, L. 2012. 'The aerodrome': Art, heritage and landscape at former RAF Coltishall. In: *Journal of Social Archaeology*. Vol. 12 No. 1, p. 120–142.

Schofield. J. and Schofield, A. 2005. Views of the Wall – Allied Perspectives. In: L.Schmidt, and H. von Preuschen (eds.). *On Both Sides of the Wall: Preserving Monuments and Sites of the Cold War Era*. Berlin: Westkreuz-Verlag.

Schwartz, R. V. 2013. Film and History. In: *Histoire@Politique. Politique, culture, société*, No 19, janvier-avril.

SFS: 1988:950. *Kulturminneslag*. Stockholm: Kulturdepartementet.

Sheffer, E. 2007. On Edge: Building the Border in East and West Germany. In: *Central European History*. Vol. 40, Issue 02: p. 307–339.

Sheffer, E. 2008. *Burned Bridge: How East and West Germans Made the Iron Curtain*. Unpublished PhD thesis, University of California, Berkeley.

Shepherd, R. 2000. *Czechoslovakia: The Velvet Revolution and Beyond*. New York: Palgrave Macmillan.

Sluga, G. 2001. *The Problem with Trieste and the Italo-Yugoslav Border*. Albany: State University of New York Press.

Smith, L. 2006. *Uses of Heritage*. New York: Routledge

Solli, B. 2011. Some Reflections on Heritage and the Archaeology in the Anthropocene. In: *Norwegian Archaeological Review*, 44:1, p. 40–54.

Svanberg, F. 2003. *Decolonizing The Viking Age 1*. Stockholm: Almqvist & Wiksell International.

Talbot, G. and Bradley, A. 2006. Characterising Scampton. In: J. Schofield, A. Klausmeier, and L. Purbrick (eds.) *Re-mapping the Field: New Approaches in Conflict Archaeology*. Berlin: Westkreuz.

Taylor, F. 2006. *The Berlin Wall. 13 August 1961– 9 November 1989*. London: Bloomsbury.

Tilley, C. 1994. *Phenomenology of Landscape*. Berg.

Trigger, B. G. 2007. *A History of Archaeological Thought* (Second Edition). New York: Cambridge University Press.

Tůma, M. 2006. *Relics of Cold War: defence transformation in the Czech Republic*. Solna: Stockholm International Peace Research Institute.

Van Reijen, W. 1992. Labyrinth and Ruin: The Return of the Baroque in Postmodernity. In: *Theory Culture Society* 1992 9:1.

Vecchiet, D. 2008. Il confine – metamorfosi di una città. Trieste: Universita Degli studi di Trieste.

Westin, J. 2012. *Negotiating 'culture', assembling the past the visual, the non-visual and the voice of the silent actant*. Gothenburg: Acta Universitatis Gothoburgensis.

Wollinger, S. 2000. *Mannen i ledet: Takt och otakt i värnpliktens skugga*. Stockholm: Carlsson Bokförlag.

Woodward, C. 2002. *In Ruins*. London: Vintage.

Wright, P. 2007. *Iron Curtain: from Stage to Cold War*. Oxford: Oxford University Press.

Yaneva, A. 2013. Actor-Network-Theory Approach to the Archaeology of Contemporary Architecture. In: P. Graves-Brown, R. Harrison and A. Piccini (eds.) *The Oxford Handbook of the Archaeology of the Contemporary World*. Oxford: Oxford University Press.

Zimmermann, G. 2008. *Österrikare, tjeck och tysk utan att behöva flytta: En berättelse om Sudetentyskarnas öde under 1900-talet*. Mjölby: Atremi AB.

Electronic sources

Aktion Reinhard Camps website http://www.deathcamps.org/sabba/ [Accessed on 2011-11-09]

Army Forum Website: www.vojensko.cz

Image 1: http://www.vojensko.cz/hajenka-r-1988-90?image=10

Image 2: http://www.vojensko.cz/hajenka-r-1989-90?image=4

Image 3: http://www.vojensko.cz/hajenka-r-1988-90?image=3

Image 4: http://www.vojensko.cz/hajenka-r-1974?image=13

Image 5: http://www.vojensko.cz/hajenka-r-1989-90?image=5

Image 6: http://www.vojensko.cz/hajenka-r-1986-88?image=26

Image 7: http://www.vojensko.cz/hajenka-r-1982-84?image=16

BBC News 2008 news.bbc.co.uk/2/hi/Europe/7626439.stm [Accessed 2011-12-05]

BBC News 2004 http://news.bbc.co.uk/2/hi/europe/3486721.stm [Accessed 2013-06-04]

ICOMOS [1964] (1996) The Venice Charter: International Charter for the Conservation and Restoration of Monuments and Sites [online], http://www.international.icomos.org/venicecharter2004/index.html [Accessed 2013-11-19]

McWilliams, A. 2012. 'Walkover survey', Contemporary and Historical Archaeology in Theory email discussion list. Online posting: https://www.jiscmail.ac.uk/cgi-bin/webadmin?A2=ind1205&L=CONTEMP-HIST-ARCH&P=R82&1=CONTEMP-HIST-ARCH&9=A&J=on&d=No+Match%3BMatch%3BMatches&z=4 [Accessed 2013-11-19]

NMR Thesaurus: http://thesaurus.english-heritage.org.uk/thesaurus.asp?thes_no=566 [Accessed 2012-05-14]

Podyji National Park website: www.nppodyji.cz/ [Accessed 2013-11-19]

Stiftung Haus der Geschichte der Bundesrepublik Deutschland website 2012 http://www.hdg.de/fileadmin/static/english/berlin/traenenpalast-am-bahnhof-friedrichstr/ [Accessed 2012-08-28]

The Kim Foundation:
http://www.kimfoundation.com/modules/contentpage/index.php?file=intro.htm
[Accessed 2012-07-31].

UNESCO 2003 *Convention for the Safeguarding of Intangible Cultural Heritage* Paris 17 October.
http://unesdoc.unesco.org/images/0013/001325/132540e.pdf [Accessed 2013-05-27]

Vranov Castle website: www.zamek-vranov.cz [Accessed 2013-11-19]

Wellershoff, M. 1999. Musik der Freiheit. In: *Spiegel Online*:
http://www.spiegel.de/kultur/kino/sonnenallee-musik-der-freiheit-a-45232.html
[Accessed 2013-08-15].

Film

Schindler's List 1993. Universal Pictures and Amblin Entertainment, USA. Directed by Steven Spielberg.

Sonnenallee 1999. Ö-Film, Sat.1 and Boje Buck Produktion, Germany. Directed by Leander Haußmann.

The Looking Glass War 1969. Frankovich Productions for Columbia Pictures Corporation, UK. Directed by Frank Pierson.

Il mio confine, moja meja 2002. Sede Regionale Rail Per Il Friuli Venezia Guilia - Programma in Lingua Slovenia/ Kinoatelje. Directed by Velušček and Medved

Personal communication

A series of interviews as well as email correspondence with historians, locals and others carried out during fieldwork were used in compiling this thesis. Recorded interviews and emails are held by the author.

Archives

The following archives were visited:

The Military Archives, Brno, Czech Republic.

National Archives, Kew Garden, UK

Goriški Musej Archive, Solkan, Slovenia.

The Archivio storico - Biblioteca provincial, Gorizia, Italy.

Södertörn Doctoral Dissertations

1. Jolanta Aidukaite, *The Emergence of the Post-Socialist Welfare State: The case of the Baltic States: Estonia, Latvia and Lithuania*, 2004
2. Xavier Fraudet, *Politique étrangère française en mer Baltique (1871–1914): de l'exclusion à l'affirmation*, 2005
3. Piotr Wawrzeniuk, *Confessional Civilising in Ukraine: The Bishop Iosyf Shumliansky and the Introduction of Reforms in the Diocese of Lviv 1668–1708*, 2005
4. Andrej Kotljarchuk, *In the Shadows of Poland and Russia: The Grand Duchy of Lithuania and Sweden in the European Crisis of the mid-17th Century*, 2006
5. Håkan Blomqvist, *Nation, ras och civilisation i svensk arbetarrörelse före nazismen*, 2006
6. Karin S Lindelöf, *Om vi nu ska bli som Europa: Könsskapande och normalitet bland unga kvinnor i transitionens Polen*, 2006
7. Andrew Stickley. *On Interpersonal Violence in Russia in the Present and the Past: A Sociological Study*, 2006
8. Arne Ek, *Att konstruera en uppslutning kring den enda vägen: Om folkrörelsers modernisering i skuggan av det Östeuropeiska systemskiftet*, 2006
9. Agnes Ers, *I mänsklighetens namn: En etnologisk studie av ett svenskt biståndsprojekt i Rumänien*, 2006
10. Johnny Rodin, *Rethinking Russian Federalism: The Politics of Intergovernmental Relations and Federal Reforms at the Turn of the Millennium*, 2006
11. Kristian Petrov, *Tillbaka till framtiden: Modernitet, postmodernitet och generationsidentitet i Gorbačevs glasnost' och perestrojka*, 2006
12. Sophie Söderholm Werkö, *Patient patients?: Achieving Patient Empowerment through Active Participation, Increased Knowledge and Organisation*, 2008
13. Peter Bötker, *Leviatan i arkipelagen: Staten, förvaltningen och samhället. Fallet Estland*, 2007

14. Matilda Dahl, *States under scrutiny: International organizations, transformation and the construction of progress*, 2007
15. Margrethe B. Søvik, *Support, resistance and pragmatism: An examination of motivation in language policy in Kharkiv, Ukraine*, 2007
16. Yulia Gradskova, *Soviet People with female Bodies: Performing beauty and maternity in Soviet Russia in the mid 1930–1960s*, 2007
17. Renata Ingbrant, *From Her Point of View: Woman's Anti-World in the Poetry of Anna Świrszczyńska*, 2007
18. Johan Eellend, *Cultivating the Rural Citizen: Modernity, Agrarianism and Citizenship in Late Tsarist Estonia*, 2007
19. Petra Garberding, *Musik och politik i skuggan av nazismen: Kurt Atterberg och de svensk-tyska musikrelationerna*, 2007
20. Aleksei Semenenko, *Hamlet the Sign: Russian Translations of Hamlet and Literary Canon Formation*, 2007
21. Vytautas Petronis, *Constructing Lithuania: Ethnic Mapping in the Tsarist Russia, ca. 1800–1914*, 2007
22. Akvile Motiejunaite, *Female employment, gender roles, and attitudes: the Baltic countries in a broader context*, 2008
23. Tove Lindén, *Explaining Civil Society Core Activism in Post-Soviet Latvia*, 2008
24. Pelle Åberg, *Translating Popular Education: Civil Society Cooperation between Sweden and Estonia*, 2008
25. Anders Nordström, *The Interactive Dynamics of Regulation: Exploring the Council of Europe's monitoring of Ukraine*, 2008
26. Fredrik Doeser, *In Search of Security After the Collapse of the Soviet Union: Foreign Policy Change in Denmark, Finland and Sweden, 1988–1993*, 2008
27. Zhanna Kravchenko. *Family (versus) Policy: Combining Work and Care in Russia and Sweden*, 2008
28. Rein Jüriado, *Learning within and between public-private partnerships*, 2008
29. Elin Boalt, *Ecology and evolution of tolerance in two cruciferous species*, 2008
30. Lars Forsberg, *Genetic Aspects of Sexual Selection and Mate Choice in Salmonids*, 2008
31. Eglė Rindzevičiūtė, *Constructing Soviet Cultural Policy: Cybernetics and Governance in Lithuania after World War II*, 2008
32. Joakim Philipson, *The Purpose of Evolution: 'struggle for existence' in the Russian-Jewish press 1860–1900*, 2008

33. Sofie Bedford, *Islamic activism in Azerbaijan: Repression and mobilization in a post-Soviet context*, 2009
34. Tommy Larsson Segerlind, *Team Entrepreneurship: A process analysis of the venture team and the venture team roles in relation to the innovation process*, 2009
35. Jenny Svensson, *The Regulation of Rule-Following: Imitation and Soft Regulation in the European Union*, 2009
36. Stefan Hallgren, *Brain Aromatase in the guppy, Poecilia reticulate: Distribution, control and role in behavior*, 2009
37. Karin Ellencrona, *Functional characterization of interactions between the flavivirus NS5 protein and PDZ proteins of the mammalian host*, 2009
38. Makiko Kanematsu, *Saga och verklighet: Barnboksproduktion i det postsovjetiska Lettland*, 2009
39. Daniel Lindvall, *The Limits of the European Vision in Bosnia and Herzegovina: An Analysis of the Police Reform Negotiations*, 2009
40. Charlotta Hillerdal, *People in Between – Ethnicity and Material Identity: A New Approach to Deconstructed Concepts*, 2009
41. Jonna Bornemark, *Kunskapens gräns – gränsens vetande*, 2009
42. Adolphine G. Kateka, *Co-Management Challenges in the Lake Victoria Fisheries: A Context Approach*, 2010
43. René León Rosales, *Vid framtidens hitersta gräns: Om pojkar och elevpositioner i en multietnisk skola*, 2010
44. Simon Larsson, *Intelligensaristokrater och arkivmartyrer: Normerna för vetenskaplig skicklighet i svensk historieforskning 1900–1945*, 2010
45. Håkan Lättman, *Studies on spatial and temporal distributions of epiphytic lichens*, 2010
46. Alia Jaensson, *Pheromonal mediated behaviour and endocrine response in salmonids: The impact of cypermethrin, copper, and glyphosate*, 2010
47. Michael Wigerius, *Roles of mammalian Scribble in polarity signaling, virus offense and cell-fate determination*, 2010
48. Anna Hedtjärn Wester, *Män i kostym: Prinsar, konstnärer och tegelbärare vid sekelskiftet 1900*, 2010
49. Magnus Linnarsson, *Postgång på växlande villkor: Det svenska postväsendets organisation under stormaktstiden*, 2010

50. Barbara Kunz, *Kind words, cruise missiles and everything in between: A neoclassical realist study of the use of power resources in U.S. policies towards Poland, Ukraine and Belarus 1989–2008*, 2010

51. Anders Bartonek, *Philosophie im Konjunktiv: Nichtidentität als Ort der Möglichkeit des Utopischen in der negativen Dialektik Theodor W. Adornos*, 2010

52. Carl Cederberg, *Resaying the Human: Levinas Beyond Humanism and Antihumanism*, 2010

53. Johanna Ringarp, *Professionens problematik: Lärarkårens kommunalisering och välfärdsstatens förvandling*, 2011

54. Sofi Gerber, *Öst är Väst men Väst är bäst: Östtysk identitetsformering i det förenade Tyskland*, 2011

55. Susanna Sjödin Lindenskoug, *Manlighetens bortre gräns: Tidelagsrättegångar i Livland åren 1685–1709*, 2011

56. Dominika Polanska, *The emergence of enclaves of wealth and poverty: A sociological study of residential differentiation in post-communist Poland*, 2011

57. Christina Douglas, *Kärlek per korrespondens: Två förlovade par under andra hälften av 1800-talet*, 2011

58. Fred Saunders, *The Politics of People – Not just Mangroves and Monkeys: A study of the theory and practice of community-based management of natural resources in Zanzibar*, 2011

59. Anna Rosengren, *Åldrandet och språket: En språkhistorisk analys av hög ålder och åldrande i Sverige cirka 1875–1975*, 2011

60. Emelie Lilliefeldt, *European Party Politics and Gender: Configuring Gender-Balanced Parliamentary Presence*, 2011

61. Ola Svenonius, *Sensitising Urban Transport Security: Surveillance and Policing in Berlin, Stockholm, and Warsaw*, 2011

62. Andreas Johansson, *Dissenting Democrats: Nation and Democracy in the Republic of Moldova*, 2011

63. Wessam Melik, *Molecular characterization of the Tick-borne encephalitis virus: Environments and replication*, 2012

64. Steffen Werther, *SS-Vision und Grenzland-Realität: Vom Umgang dänischer und „volksdeutscher" Nationalsozialisten in Sønderjylland mit der „großgermanischen" Ideologie der SS*, 2012

65. Peter Jakobsson, *Öppenhetsindustrin*, 2012

66. Kristin Ilves, *Seaward Landward: Investigations on the archaeological source value of the landing site category in the Baltic Sea region*, 2012

67. Anne Kaun, *Civic Experiences and Public Connection: Media and Young People in Estonia*, 2012

68. Anna Tessmann, *On the Good Faith: A Fourfold Discursive Construction of Zoroastrianism in Contemporary Russia*, 2012

69. Jonas Lindström, *Drömmen om den nya staden: stadsförnyelse i det postsovjetisk Riga*, 2012

70. Maria Wolrath Söderberg, *Topos som meningsskapare: retorikens topiska perspektiv på tänkande och lärande genom argumentation*, 2012

71. Linus Andersson, *Alternativ television: former av kritik i konstnärlig TV-produktion*, 2012

72. Håkan Lättman, *Studies on spatial and temporal distributions of epiphytic lichens*, 2012

73. Fredrik Stiernstedt, *Mediearbete i mediehuset: produktion i förändring på MTG-radio*, 2013

74. Jessica Moberg, *Piety, Intimacy and Mobility: A Case Study of Charismatic Christianity in Present-day Stockholm*, 2013

75. Elisabeth Hemby, *Historiemåleri och bilder av vardag: Tatjana Nazarenkos konstnärskap i 1970-talets Sovjet*, 2013

76. Tanya Jukkala, *Suicide in Russia: A macro-sociological study*, 2013

77. Maria Nyman, *Resandets gränser: svenska resenärers skildringar av Ryssland under 1700-talet*, 2013

78. Beate Feldmann Eellend, *Visionära planer och vardagliga praktiker: Postmilitära landskap i Östersjöområdet*, 2013

79. Emma Lind, *Genetic response to pollution in sticklebacks: natural selection in the wild*, 2013

80. Anne Ross Solberg, *The Mahdi Wears Armani: An Analysis of the Harun Yahya Enterprise*, 2013

81. Nikolay Zakharov, *Attaining Whiteness: A Sociological Study of Race and Racialization in Russia*, 2013

82. Anna Kharkina, *From Kinship to Global Brand: The Discourse on Culture in Nordic Cooperation after World War II*, 2013

83. Florence Fröhlig, *Painful legacy of World War II: Nazi forced enlistment: Alsatian/Mosellan Prisoners of War and the Soviet Prison Camp of Tambov*, 2013

84. Oskar Henriksson, *Genetic connectivity of fish in the Western Indian Ocean*, 2013

85. Hans Geir Aasmundsen, *Pentecostalism, Globalisation and Society in Contemporary Argentina*, 2013

86. Anna McWilliams, *An Archaeology of the Iron Curtain: Material and Metaphor*, 2013

Stockholm Studies in Archaeology

Series editor: Anders Andrén

1. KYHLBERG, Ola. 1980. Vikt och värde. Arkeologiska studier i värdemätning, betalningsmedel och metrologi. I. Helgö. II. Birka. (Diss.)

2. AMBROSIANI, Kristina. 1981. Viking Age Combs, Comb Making and Comb Makers, in the Light of the Finds from Birka and Ribe. (Diss.)

3. SÄRLVIK, Ingegärd. 1982. Paths Towards a Stratified Society. A Study of Economic, Cultural and Social Formations in South-West Sweden during the Roman Iron Age and the Migration Period. (Diss.)

4. BLIDMO, Roger. 1982. Helgö, Husgrupp 3. En lokalkorologisk metodstudie. Helgöstudier 2. (Diss.)

5. CARLSSON, Anders. 1983. Djurhuvudformiga spännen och gotländsk vikingatid. Text och katalog. (Diss.)

6. DURING, Ebba. 1986. The Fauna of Alvastra. An Osteological Analysis of Animal Bones from a Neolithic Pile Dwelling. (Diss.)

7. BERTILSSON, Ulf. 1987. The Rock Carvings of Northern Bohuslän. Spatial Structures and Social Symbols. (Diss.)

8. CARLSSON, Anders. 1988. Vikingatida ringspännen från Gotland. Text och katalog.

9. BURSTRÖM, Mats. 1991. Arkeologisk samhällsavgränsning. En studie av vikingatida samhällsterritorier i Smålands inland. (Diss.)

10. VARENIUS, Björn. 1992. Det nordiska skeppet. Teknologi och samhällsstrategi i vikingatid och medeltid. (Diss.)

11. JAKOBSSON, Mikael. 1992. Krigarideologi och vikingatida svärdstypologi. (Diss.)

12. RINGSTEDT, Nils. 1992. Household economy and archaeology. Some aspects on theory and applications. (Diss.)

13. Withdrawn.

14. JOHANSEN, Birgitta. 1997. Ormalur. Aspekter av tillvaro och landskap. (Diss.)

15. ZACHRISSON, Torun. 1998. Gård, gräns, gravfält. Sammanhang kring ädelmetalldepåer och runstenar från vikingatid och tidigmedeltid i Uppland och Gästrikland. (Diss.)

16. CASSEL, Kerstin. 1998. Från grav till gård. Romersk järnålder på Gotland. (Diss.)

17. CARLSSON, Anders. 1998. Tolkande arkeologi och svensk forntidshistoria. Stenåldern.

18. GÖRANSSON, Eva-Marie. 1999. Bilder av kvinnor och kvinnlighet. Genus och kroppsspråk under övergången till kristendomen. (Diss.)

19. BOLIN, Hans. 1999. Kulturlandskapets korsvägar. Mellersta Norrland under de två sista årtusendena f. Kr. (Diss.)

20. STRASSBURG, Jimmy. 2000. Shamanic Shadows. One hundred Generations of Undead Subversion in Southern Scandinavia, 7,000–4,000 BC. (Diss.)

21. STORÅ, Jan 2001. Reading Bones. Stone Age Hunters and Seals in the Baltic. (Diss.)

22. CARLSSON, Anders. 2001. Tolkande arkeologi och svensk forntidshistoria. Bronsåldern.

23. HAUPTMAN WAHLGREN, Katherine. 2002. Bilder av betydelse. Hällristningar och bronsålderslandskap i nordöstra Östergötland. (Diss.)

24. ADAMS, Jonathan. 2003. Ships, Innovation and Social Change. Aspects of Carvel Shipbuilding In Northern Europe 1450–1850. (Diss.)

25. HED JAKOBSSON, Anna. 2003. Smältdeglars härskare och Jerusalems tillskyndare. Berättelser om vikingatid och tidig medeltid. (Diss.)

26. GILL, Alexander. 2003. Stenålder i Mälardalen. (Diss.)

27. WALL, Åsa. 2003. De hägnade bergens landskap. Om den äldre järnåldern på Södertörn. (Diss.)

28. STENBÄCK, Niklas. 2003. Människorna vid havet. Platser och keramik på ålandsöarna perioden 3500–2000 f. Kr. (Diss.)

29. LINDGREN, Christina. 2004. Människor och kvarts. Sociala och teknologiska strategier under mesolitikum i östra Mellansverige. (Diss.)

30. LAGERSTEDT, Anna. 2004. Det norrländska rummet. Vardagsliv och socialt samspel i medeltidens bondesamhälle. (Diss.)

31. von HEIJNE, Cecilia. 2004. Särpräglat. Vikingatida och tidigmedeltida myntfynd från Danmark, Skåne, Blekinge och Halland (ca 800-1130). (Diss.)

32. FERNSTÅL, Lotta. 2004. Delar av en grav och glimtar av en tid. Om yngre romersk järnålder, Tuna i Badelunda i Västmanland och personen i grav X. (Diss.)

33. THEDÉEN, Susanne. 2004. Gränser i livet – gränser i landskapet. Generationsrelationer och rituella praktiker i södermanländska bronsålderslandskap. (Diss.)

34. STENSKÖLD, Eva. 2004. Att berätta en senneolitisk historia. Sten och metall i södra Sverige 2350–1700 f. Kr. (Diss.)

35. REGNER, Elisabet. 2005. Den reformerade världen. Monastisk och materiell kultur i Alvastra kloster från medeltid till modern tid. (Diss.)

36. MONIÉ NORDIN, Jonas. 2005. När makten blev synlig. Senmedeltid i södra Dalarna. (Diss.)

37. FELDT, Björn. 2005. Synliga och osynliga gränser. Förändringar i gravritualen under yngre bronsålder – förromersk järnålder i Södermanland. (Diss.)

38. RUNER, Johan. 2006. Från hav till land eller Kristus och odalen. En studie av Sverige under äldre medeltid med utgångspunkt från de romanska kyrkorna. (Diss.)

39. STENQVIST MILLDE, Ylva. 2007. Vägar inom räckhåll. Spåren efter resande i det förindustriella bondesamhället. (Diss.)

40. BACK DANIELSSON, Ing-Marie. 2007. Masking Moments. The Transitions of Bodies and Beings in Late Iron Age Scandinavia. (Diss.)

41. SELLING, Susanne. 2007. Livets scener och dödens platser. Om bronsålder i södra Bohuslän utifrån en gravläggning i Faxehögen, Kareby socken. (Diss.)

42. ARNBERG, Anna. 2007. Där människor, handling och tid möts. En studie av det förromerska landskapet på Gotland. (Diss.)

43. BERGERBRANT, Sophie. 2007. Bronze Age Identities: Costume, Conflict and Contact in Northern Europe 1600–1300 BC. (Diss.)

44. FRANSSON, Ulf, SVEDIN, Marie, BERGERBRANT, Sophie och ANDROSCHUK, Fedir (red.). 2007. Cultural interaction between east and west. Archaeology, artefacts and human contacts in northern Europe.

45. MYRBERG, Nanouschka. 2008. Ett eget värde. Gotlands tidigaste myntning, ca 1140-1220. (Diss.)

46. BRATT, PETER. 2008. Makt uttryckt i jord och sten. Stora högar och maktstrukturer i Mälardalen under järnåldern. (Diss.)

47. BACK DANIELSSON, Ing-Marie, GUSTIN, Ingrid, LARSSON, Annika, MYRBERG, Nanouschka och THEDÉEN, Susanne (red.). 2009. Döda personers sällskap. Gravmaterialens identiteter och kulturella uttryck. (On the Threshold. Burial Archaeology in the Twenty-first Century).

48. REGNER, Elisabet, von HEIJNE, Cecilia, KITZLER ÅHFELDT, Laila och KJELLSTRÖM, Anna (red.). 2009. From Ephesos to Dalecarlia: Reflections on Body, Space and Time in Medieval and Early Modern Europe.

49. LINDEBERG, Marta 2009. Järn i jorden. Spadformiga ämnesjärn i Mellannorrland. (Diss.)

50. JONSSON, Kristina. 2009. Practices for the Living and the Dead. Medieval and Post-Reformation Burials in Scandinavia. (Diss.)

51. von HACKWITZ, Kim. 2009. Längs med Hjälmarens stränder och förbi. Relationen mellan den gropkeramiska kulturen och båtyxekulturen. (Diss.)

52. MONIKANDER, Anne. 2010. Våld och vatten. Våtmarkskult vid Skedemosse under järnåldern. (Diss.)

53. FAHLANDER, Fredrik och KJELLSTRÖM, Anna (red.). 2010. Making Sense of Things. Archaeologies of Sensory Perception.

54. FAHLANDER, Fredrik (red.). 2011. Spåren av de små. Arkeologiska perspektiv på barn och barndom.

55. SJÖSTRAND, Ylva. 2011. Med älgen i huvudrollen. Om fångstgropar, hällbilder och skärvstensvallar i mellersta Norrland. (Diss.)

56. BURSTRÖM, Nanouschka M. och FAHLANDER, Fredrik (red.). 2012. Matters of scale. Processes and courses of events in archaeology and cultural history.

57. BACK DANIELSSON, Ing-Marie, FAHLANDER, Fredrik och SJÖSTRAND, Ylva (red.). 2012. Encountering Imagery: Materialities, Perceptions, Relations.

58. BACK DANIELSSON, Ing-Marie and THEDÉEN, Susanne (eds.). 2012. To Tender Gender. The Pasts and Futures of Gender Research in Archaeology.

59. MCWILLIAMS, Anna. 2013. An Archaeology of the Iron Curtain: Material and Metaphor.

www.ingramcontent.com/pod-product-compliance
Lightning Source LLC
Chambersburg PA
CBHW070841160426
43192CB00012B/2261